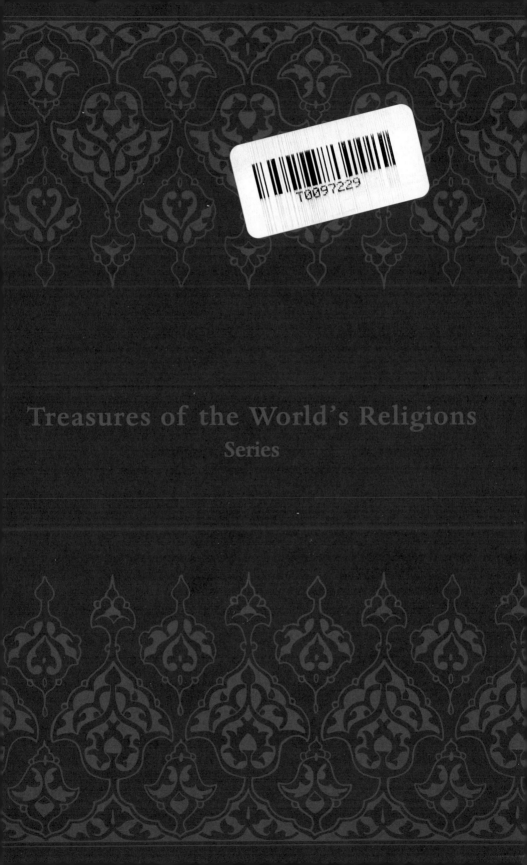

Treasures of the World's Religions
Series

About the Author and this Book

"Increasingly as a composer, I want to 'hear' God, and tend to be wary of yet another book on mysticism in any Tradition. However, James Cutsinger in *Not of This World* allows the masters of the Christian Tradition to speak on their own terms, thus permitting us to hear God through their unique perspective."

—**Sir John Tavener**, composer and author

"There are many anthologies of Christian mysticism, but few that range so widely as this: from the first century to the twentieth, and embracing equally Western Christianity—both Catholic and Protestant—and the Christian East, even the Far East."

—**Andrew Louth**, University of Durham, author of *Origins of the Christian Mystical Tradition: From Plato to Denys*

"*Not of This World* offers proof that genuine spirituality is a common and fundamental aspect of genuine Christianity. The book is complemented by an introduction which is itself worthy of being included within the textual content of the book and an excellent bibliography that provides the reader with deeper wells to fathom. One can only express one's gratitude to the compiler of this collection, which is a powerful antidote to the superficiality of most modern expressions of Christianity."

—**Rama Coomaraswamy**, author of *The Invocation of the Name of Jesus: As Practiced in the Western Church*

"Written in a clear and comprehensive style, this book is an excellent introduction to the saints and sages of the Christian tradition."

—**Sister Ilia Delio**, *O.S.F.*, Washington Theological Union, author of *Simply Bonaventure: An Introduction to His Life, Thought, and Writings*

"At a time when the Christian tradition is under siege by the profane ideologies of modernity, and when Christian institutions themselves are torn by doubt and division, this anthology serves as an urgent reminder of that quintessential wisdom which cannot be compromised by the vicissitudes of time. From the days when the Master Himself walked the shores of Galilee down to our own time, the Christian mystics have been living exemplars of a transformative and sapiential spirituality wherein both love and knowledge perform their mysterious alchemy on the soul. Professor Cutsinger is to be warmly commended for his judicious selection of mystical writings and for an arrangement which enhances their perennial themes. Here, in a single volume, may be found many Christian refractions of that ever-present Light which irradiates all integral traditions."

—**Kenneth Oldmeadow**, La Trobe University and author of *Traditionalism: Religion in the Light of the Perennial Philosophy*

"*Not of This World* presents us with keys to discerning the mystery through a unique kaleidoscope of brilliant colors—all of them so delightful and wonderful, yet all of them ultimately symbolical and indicative of a reality beyond this world. This is not a book to be read lightly. The invitation is to approach with a profound sense of respect, with the same veneration with which one is able to recognize the very traces of God in places known and unknown."

—**John Chryssavgis**, former dean of Holy Cross Greek Orthodox School of Theology and author of *Ascent to Heaven* and *In the Heart of the Desert*

World Wisdom
The Library of Perennial Philosophy

The Library of Perennial Philosophy is dedicated to the exposition of the timeless Truth underlying the diverse religions. This Truth, often referred to as the *Sophia Perennis*—or Perennial Wisdom—finds its expression in the revealed Scriptures as well as the writings of the great sages and the artistic creations of the traditional worlds.

The Perennial Philosophy provides the intellectual principles capable of explaining both the formal contradictions and the underlying unity of the great religions.

Ranging from the writings of the great sages who have expressed the *Sophia Perennis* in the past to the perennialist authors of our time, each series of our Library has a different focus. As a whole, they express the inner unanimity, transforming radiance, and irreplaceable values of the great spiritual traditions.

Not of This World appears as one of our selections in Treasures of the World's Religions series.

Treasures of the World's Religions
Series

This series of anthologies presents scriptures and the writings of the great spiritual authorities of the past on fundamental themes. Some titles are devoted to a single spiritual tradition, while others have a unifying topic that touches upon traditions from both the East and West, such as prayer and virtue. Some titles have a companion volume within The Perennial Philosophy series.

Cover Photograph: Courtyard of the Chapel of the
Burning Bush, St Catherine's Monastery, Mt Sinai

Not of This World

A Treasury of Christian Mysticism

Compiled and edited by

James S. Cutsinger

World Wisdom

Not of This World
A Treasury of Christian Mysticism
© 2003 World Wisdom, Inc.

Library of Congress Cataloging-in-Publication Data

Not of this world : a treasury of Christian mysticism / compiled and
edited by James S. Cutsinger.
    p. cm. – (Treasures of the world's religions)
Includes bibliographical references and index.
  ISBN 0-941532-41-0 (pbk. : alk. paper)
  1. Mysticism–Christianity. I. Cutsinger, James S., 1953- II. Series.

BV5082.3.N68 2003
248.2'2–dc21

                                                          2003000583

Printed on acid-free paper in Canada

For information address World Wisdom, Inc.
P.O. Box 2682, Bloomington, Indiana 47402-2682

www.worldwisdom.com

For Monica, Brigid, Felicity, and Aidan –

with prayers for their journey

CONTENTS

Introduction   xiii

PURIFICATION

I. Severity

1. Breaking the Chains	*Jakob Boehme*	5
2. The Ladder of Graces	*Theophanis the Monk*	10
3. Transposition	*Unseen Warfare*	12
4. Death	*St Thomas à Kempis*	16
5. Pure Fire	*Hugh of St Victor*	19
6. What More Must I Do?	*The Desert Fathers*	21
7. The Ceremony of Substitution	*Charles Williams*	23
8. My Desire Has Been Crucified	*St Ignatios of Antioch*	26

II. Simplicity

9. Drawn by the Flames	*St Thérèse of Lisieux*	31
10. Descending with the Breath	*Nikiphoros the Athonite*	33
11. So Many Names	*Jean-Pierre de Caussade*	35
12. What Dreams May Come	*St Diadochos of Photiki*	38
13. I Sleep but My Heart Waketh	*St Bernard of Clairvaux*	41
14. Nakedness and Sacrifice	*Jean Borella*	44
15. The Tao	*Hieromonk Damascene*	47
16. Go Not but Stay	*St Francis of Sales*	51

III. Purity

17. The Center of the Soul   *William Law*   57
18. True Prayer   *Evagrios the Solitary*   60
19. The Tabernacle of the Covenant   *Richard of St Victor*   63
20. Rank upon Rank   *St Clement of Alexandria*   67
21. Ignorance Is Bliss   *Nicholas of Cusa*   70
22. Opening the Tomb   *St Maximos the Confessor*   72
23. The Virginal Paradise   *St Louis Marie de Montfort*   77
24. Clothed in Christ   *St Symeon the New Theologian*   79

ILLUMINATION

IV. Clarity

25. Two Ways   *St Thomas Aquinas*   87
26. Dispelling Darkness   *Boethius*   89
27. Leading Strings   *François Fénelon*   92
28. More than Ourselves   *Sir Thomas Browne*   95
29. No Fixed Abode   *Pico della Mirandola*   98
30. Today   *St Patrick of Ireland*   101
31. The Teacher   *St Gregory of Sinai*   104
32. True Imagination   *George MacDonald*   106

V. Luminosity

33. Nothing Amiss   *Julian of Norwich*   113
34. Sweet Delight in God's Beauty   *Jonathan Edwards*   115
35. Thinking the Unthinkable   *St Anselm*   119
36. Prayer of the Heart   *The Way of a Pilgrim*   122
37. The Religion of Light   *Jingjing*   126
38. In the Eyes of a Child   *Thomas Traherne*   128
39. Saving Loveliness   *St Nonnus*   132
40. Uncreated Light   *St Seraphim of Sarov*   134

VI. Transparency

41. Filling Every Place   *Jeremy Taylor*   141
42. Virtues and Powers   *Paracelsus*   144
43. A Single Unified Science   *Philip Sherrard*   146
44. Practicing Presence   *Brother Lawrence*   149
45. Hidden and Glorified   *Samuel Taylor Coleridge*   152
46. As through a Mirror   *St Bonaventure*   154
47. Recognition   *The Gospel of Thomas*   158
48. Two Facades   *C. S. Lewis*   162

UNION

VII. Unity

49. A Higher School   *Henry Suso*   171
50. Flight to Greater Things   *St Gregory of Nyssa*   173
51. No Other Way   *Theologia Germanica*   177
52. God's Own Breath   *John Smith*   181
53. The Very Marrow of the Bones   *St Teresa of Avila*   185
54. Christmas in the Soul   *John Tauler*   189
55. High Fantasy Lost Power   *Dante*   194
56. Motionless Circling   *Nikitas Stithatos*   197

VIII. Unicity

57. A Reply to Active Persons   *The Cloud of Unknowing*   203
58. Closing to a Bud Again   *Lilian Staveley*   206
59. The Joyful Instant   *St Augustine*   210
60. One and the Same Mind   *Origen*   213
61. Awareness and Return   *Swami Abhishiktananda*   216
62. Waylessness   *John of Ruysbroeck*   219
63. Hidden Beauty   *St Dionysios the Areopagite*   223
64. Essence Is Simple   *St Nikolai Velimirovich*   226

IX. Identity

65. The Flight of the Eagle   *John Scotus Eriugena*   233
66. More God than a Soul   *St John of the Cross*   237
67. Unencumbered   *Marguerite Porete*   240
68. Other Suns   *St Gregory Palamas*   243
69. No Self to Forgive   *Bernadette Roberts*   247
70. To Be Quit of God   *Meister Eckhart*   249
71. Ascent to Tabor   *Hierotheos Vlachos*   255
72. Be Thyself the Book   *Angelus Silesius*   259

Sources of Readings and Recommendations
for Further Study   265

Index   275

You are going, not indeed in search of the *New* World, like Columbus and his adventurers, nor yet an *Other* World that is to come, but in search of the Other World that *now* is, and ever has been, though undreamt of by the many, and by the greater part even of the Few.

Samuel Taylor Coleridge

Introduction

"My kingdom is not of this world" (John 18:36). Guided by these words of their Master, Christian mystics have never been at home in this world. Far from being escapists, however, the best of them have always kept a firm hold on the important word *this*. God's kingdom is certainly not of *this* world—the fallen world of corruption, competition, and death. But beneath the surface of *this*, the Gospel teaches that there is also a *that*: a world "so loved" (John 3:16) by God that He has entered it fully in order to make it one with Himself. The true mystic confirms this teaching, assuring us that we can partake of that oneness even in the midst of our present life. Somewhere on the other side of what seems—right in front of us, if we would only look—there exists something more: an "Other World that *now* is", infused with Divine presence and power, and shimmering through our most cherished moments of beauty and love.

Beginning in the early years of the Church, the journey of those who were in search of that world, and who were prepared to dedicate themselves fully to this most fruitful of quests, was divided into three major stages: Purification, Illumination, and Union. This treasury of Christian mystical writings has been designed with that same basic pattern in mind.

First of all, the chains which bind us to the world of appearances must be broken. This is the goal of the first part of the journey—a goal that is reached by climbing the steps of severity, simplicity, and purity. Our selfish solicitude and fearful desire for control have resulted in a kind of imprisonment, and we are locked inside our own fantasies, indifferent to the God who exists beyond them. We must therefore be strict with ourselves, eliminating what is excessive and wasteful, and cleansing the doors of our perception. Purification is necessary because the Divine is transcendent.

Once we have begun to break free from our bonds and have achieved a certain degree of self-mastery, we shall begin to see the world as it truly is, the world as God made and is making it. This is the gift that is offered in the second stage of the search— a gift that is opened up to us gradually through an increasing clarity, luminosity, and transparency. We awaken to the truth and goodness that are around us and in us, and we begin to discern in every texture and color, every tiny motion and seeming insignificance, the resplendent plenitude of the God who exists within them. Illumination is possible because the Divine is immanent.

Finally—by a miraculous combination of God's grace and our efforts—we are permitted to enter the "Other World" and to begin living in it. This is the promise of the third and last stage of the path—a promise that is fully realized as we penetrate to an ever more irreducible oneness with God through the steps of unity, unicity, and identity. Union is inevitable—though not automatic, and never without repentance, perseverance, and faith—because the Divine is transcendent even in the midst of its immanence, and immanent in its very transcendence. To see God truly is to see that there is nothing but Him, and that He Himself is the seer. Comprehending "with all the saints what is the breadth and length and depth and height", we come to be filled, like Christ, with "all the fullness of God" (Eph. 3:18, 19; Col. 1:19).

The reader is invited to be a part of this journey. Taking the lead and giving their encouragement will be some of the wisest and most eloquent writers in the history of Christian spirituality, ranging from the second to the twentieth centuries and representing the Catholic, Eastern Orthodox, and Protestant perspectives. Students of mysticism will recognize many familiar names, including Clement of Alexandria, Augustine, Gregory of Nyssa, Symeon the New Theologian, Bernard of Clairvaux, Bonaventure, Meister Eckhart, Teresa of Avila, and Jakob Boehme. But included as well are selections by authors who are not usually considered mystics as such, but whose writings contain nonetheless some remarkably perspicacious and moving passages concerning our path back to God, among them Ignatios of Antioch, Boethius, Thomas Aquinas, Pico della Mirandola, Thomas Browne, Louis Marie de Montfort, Jonathan Edwards, Thérèse of Lisieux, and C. S. Lewis.

As the reader will discover, variety is a keynote of this collection. Some of the selections are didactic and others anecdotal; some are complex and demanding, others simple and childlike; some come from the writings of canonized saints, others from authors who were suspected, if not actually accused and condemned, of heresy; some are concerned with describing the fruits of realization or transfiguration in God, others are more focused on the necessary means to this end. One will find practical instructions on how to enter more deeply into contemplative prayer, descriptions of the metaphysical structure of the universe, discussions of the different spiritual types of men and of their varying degrees of advancement, and esoteric interpretations of doctrines, symbols, and verses of Scripture. A few surprises have been inserted as well—readings from somewhat unusual or out of the way sources—including an inscription from a Tang Dynasty stele and an interview with a contemporary Athonite hermit.

Readers will also be treated to a certain amount of variety in the placement of specific selections. If one wished, a collection of jewels could be distributed among a number of different boxes, strictly on the basis of color or size. As it happens, however, their full effect on the eye—when the lid of a treasure chest is first opened—comes at least in part from their medley or mixture, the red of this ruby being all the more radiant because of its proximity to the green of that emerald. The present treasury of mystical gems is intended to have a similar kaleidoscopic impact, with selections from widely different periods of time and by authors from varying denominational homes and backgrounds placed side by side for the sake of their mutual accentuation and illumination. Many of the readings are so rich in meaning and implication that they could not in any case be confined to a single part of the book, and we make no claim to have positioned them in the only way possible, preferring instead to allow for anticipations and recapitulations as one moves through the stages and steps. From the very moment we set foot on the path, submitting ourselves to the severity of purification, it is important to have a clear picture of our ultimate incorporation in God and to understand that death is but a prelude to resurrection. But it is equally important that the rigor of the early part of the quest remain in full view as we near the end of our travels, for the spiritual life is never a merely passive affair, but is based throughout its full extent upon virtuous effort and a willing extinction of the ego.

Underlying these different modes of variety, there is a common theme and a definite thrust to this book. In choosing the readings, our aim has not been to produce a comprehensive survey, or even a representative sampling, of the entire field of Christian spiritual literature, nor have we been concerned about selecting passages that are necessarily indicative of their authors' work as a whole. The plan instead is to follow a specific thread of Christian mystical teaching—one in which the accent is placed on the acquisition of *gnosis* or knowledge and in which *theosis* or deification is presented as the explicit goal of the journey. Readers who are interested in a full exhibition of the varieties of Christian religious experience, or who would like to go more deeply into the teachings of a few major mystical writers or to trace the historical connections between different schools of thought and spiritual traditions, will need to consult other anthologies. Here our purpose is much more focused and personal: to provide support to those who are themselves searching for a direct knowledge of God and who wish to learn by what means, and how far, they may journey in this present life toward becoming "partakers of the Divine nature" (2 Pet. 1:4).

It is widely supposed—by seekers whose contemplative journeys have taken them East, as well as by many practicing Christians—that Christianity is strictly a *bhakti-mârga*, to use the language of Hinduism: that is, a purely devotional path, in which love of the personal God is man's primary obligation and highest goal in life. Christians are often deeply suspicious, therefore, of those who lay claim to a spiritual or metaphysical knowledge, considering them guilty of intellectual pride and confusing their teachings with the sectarian Gnosticism of the first Christian centuries. What they forget, however, is that even so diligent an early hunter of heresy as St Irenaeus of Lyons entitled his most important work: "A Refutation and Overthrow of All Knowledge *Falsely So-Called*", and that St Clement of Alexandria is not the only respected authority to have spoken in defense of a specifically Christian *gnosis*. "This is eternal life," says Christ, "that they *know* Thee the only true God" (John 17:3).

One very important purpose of the present collection is to underscore this Dominical maxim—and to call the bluff on all anti-intellectualism masquerading as piety—by presenting readings, written in many cases by saints but also coming from other indisputably orthodox sources, in which the attainment of an intellective or noetic certainty is an essential part of man's reaching his destined perfection. The distinctive warmth and joy of genuine Christian love have certainly not been neglected in the pages which follow. But it is love insofar as it leads *through* devotion to a single-minded concentration on God that we have chosen to accentuate, and not that devotion itself—still less the cloying sentimentalism and lugubrious brooding which characterize much devotional and even "mystical" literature, and which are often rooted in a jealous attachment to sensible consolations and familiar styles of religious belief and behavior.

This book also differs from other similar anthologies in the stress that it places on deification. Many Christians today, especially those in the western churches, seem to be under the mistaken impression that there is an unbridgeable and eternal divide between the Divine Creator and His human creature. As a result, the only mysticism which they are prepared to accept, and then often reluctantly, is a mysticism of beholding and vision. In this life—they believe—only the rarest few are permitted a glimpse of their Lord, and even in these very exceptional cases the experience amounts to a fleeting state and not a permanent station. Even in heaven, the felicity of the faithful is said to come solely from their proximity to a God who remains "other" and "object". Ironically, this well-intentioned abridgement of our journey's true length was very firmly, if implicitly, rejected by the early Church in its condemnation of the Nestorian and Monophysite heresies. Man is not divided from God, for human nature has been hypostatically or substantially united with Deity, while nonetheless retaining its own distinctive energies and will.

This is a difficult and subtle point, which we cannot fully explain in this context. Suffice it to say, however, that the Son of God did not become "a" man, as one too often hears. He became man, with the result that our human nature as such has been infused, in and through Him, with the very nature of God. The powers and privileges exhibited by the incarnate Word did not belong to Him alone, but are open to all of us, in keeping with what the Council of Ephesus (431 A.D.) called a *communicatio idiomatum* or "communication of properties" between the Divine and the human. Were it otherwise, we would not be invited—nor could we be commanded—to "grow up into Him in all things", to acquire "the knowledge of the Son of God", and to strive to reach the level of the "perfect man", in this way attaining "unto the measure of the stature of the fullness of Christ". This and nothing less, say the Scriptures, is the "perfecting of the saints" (Eph. 4:12, 13).

Ultimate Union must therefore include nothing less than a step of identity, and this is why we have given ample space to selections which speak about God, not only as other and object, but as the true inward subject of man's own deepest self. From one point of view, the Christian exoterists of whom we were just speaking are right: God *is* our sovereign Creator and Lord, and such He will remain for all eternity, the unitive or "advaitic" doctrine of certain mystics notwithstanding. The individual man or woman cannot *become* God, although they can, and should, pray to be granted the everlasting joy of the beatific vision. Heavenly joy, however, is not the only promise of the Gospel. Even though outwardly we are always other than God, there exists inside of us, in the "inward man" (Rom. 7:22), something intrinsically Divine, with which—thanks to Christ's timeless work of atonement—every person may come at last to be completely identified, down to the very cells of his physical body. There is in the soul, says Meister Eckhart, something "uncreated and uncreatable", and for this reason, adds St Gregory Palamas, those who have reached the very end of the journey "become thereby uncreated, unoriginate, supra-temporal, and indescribable". This is the final privilege and promise of entering the "Other World that *now* is".

Of course, the fact that God has opened Himself to us so fully and that our ultimate destination is so high and exalted does not at all mean that we have arrived there already, or that we are absolved of responsibility for the struggle and striving required of those who mean to become what they are. Christian *gnosis* is no excuse for presumption or pride. As we have said, Union is inevitable, but it is not automatic—which is precisely why this greatest of quests is one upon which everyone must eventually *choose* to embark. "If it be now, 'tis not to come; if it be not to come, it will be now; if it be not now, yet it will come. The readiness is all."

We have explained that this book has three basic Parts because the spiritual journey is traditionally divided into three distinct Stages. Christians of earlier centuries would have seen other meanings in the numerical arrangement of the readings which follow, and it may be of interest, before turning to the selections themselves, to state these meanings explicitly for the modern reader, whose sense of symbolic patterns is much less precise and keen than that of his ancestors.

There are three major Parts to this treasury because it is a journey of three Days from the Good Friday of our death to *this* world to the Easter of our resurrection in God. Each Part is in turn divided into three smaller Sections because the journey would not be possible without the three Persons of the Holy Trinity. Each Person is present in our every advancement, but each is also responsible for His own proper work, for we are purified *through* the Son, illumined *by* the Holy Spirit, and unified *in* the Father. The icons which are found on the first page of each Part reflect this same symbolism. In the Crucifixion, at the beginning of Part One, there is a single Figure, in whom Purification is embodied. Part Two is entered through the Virgin of the Sign, which contains two Figures of

Illumination. And Part Three begins with the three Figures of the Holy Trinity, in and through whom is Union.

There are nine different Sections in the collection, corresponding to the nine total Steps of the Stages, because there are nine distinct Ranks among the Celestial Hierarchies or "Trinal Triplicities"—Seraphim, Cherubim, Thrones, Dominions, Principalities, Powers, Virtues, Archangels, Angels—and without their continual care and guidance, we could not but lose our way as we undertake to enter *that* world in which these Blessed Spirits dwell. As St Dionysios the Areopagite says, "It is by the mediation of hierarchically superior Beings that inferior beings are uplifted toward the Divine."

Each of the nine Sections contains eight different Readings because the mystical week of our movement toward God consists of eight Days, the Eighth Day of the Resurrection transcending linear time as we know it, and because as we travel our aim is to become worthy of the eight Blessings promised by Christ in the Sermon on the Mount (Matt. 5:3-10). According to the medieval theologian Gerhoh of Reichersberg, "Eight, as the first perfect cube (2 x 2 x 2), imprints us in body and soul with the security of Eternal Beatitude."

There are thus twenty-four Readings in each of the three Parts of the book, and this reminds us that the Four and Twenty Elders, who correspond in their turn to the Twelve Patriarchs of the Old Covenant and the Twelve Apostles of the New, sit together "clothed in white raiment" and with "crowns of gold" on their heads (Rev. 4:4), in token of their participation in the God before whose Throne they rejoice.

Finally, there are seventy-two Readings in the book as a whole because there are seventy-two Hours in the three Days of our journey; because seventy-two is the number of precious Jewels—four rows of three that "shall be square" and then "doubled" ($4 \times 3^2 \times 2$)—which are to be placed on our breastplate as we prepare to enter the Temple (Ex. 28:16); and because, in the original Hebrew of Exodus 14:19-21, there are seventy-two Letters in each of the three Verses, which together mystically describe our liberation from the world of seeming and our illumination and incorporation in God:

Introduction

"And the Angel of God, which went before the camp of Israel, removed and went behind them, and the Pillar of Cloud went from before their face, and stood behind them.

"And it came between the camp of the Egyptians and the camp of Israel, and it was a Cloud and a Darkness to them, but it gave Light by night to the other, so that the one came not near the other all the night.

"And Moses stretched out his hand over the Sea, and the Lord caused the Sea to go back by a strong East Wind all that night, and made the sea dry Land, and the Waters were divided."

A few further words about our manner of presentation are perhaps in order. For the sake of consistency and intelligibility, a number of the readings have been slightly modified: contemporary usage has been our chief guide in capitalization and spelling and in the use of punctuation—though an effort has been made as well to preserve at least something of the stylistic tone of the original materials—and we have allowed ourselves the occasional silent ellipsis when the sense of a passage might be otherwise obscured or complicated by a tangent to its primary meaning or by the introduction of foreign or technical terms already defined in the text. The Sources of Readings at the end of the book provide all the necessary bibliographical information for those who are interested in studying the selections in their originally published form and context.

We very gratefully acknowledge our debt to a number of friends, family members, and students for their valuable assistance in preparing this book. Special thanks go to Leah Cutsinger, Michael Allen, Wade Kolb, Joshua Robinson, Carl Still, Walter Purvis, and Father Mark Mancuso. The editor also wishes to thank his pastor, Father Daniel Munn, for permission to use the icons which have been placed at the beginning of each part of the book, and which come from the narthex, apse, and ceiling of the parish church of St Ignatios of Antioch in Augusta, Georgia.

James S. Cutsinger
The Dormition of the Mother of God, 2002

xxi

Purification

I

Severity

He humbled Himself and
became obedient unto death,
even the death of the cross.

Philippians 2:8

1

Breaking the Chains

Jakob Boehme

The disciple said to his master, "Sir, how may I come to the supersensual life, so that I may see God and may hear God speak?"

The master answered and said, "Son, when you can throw yourself into That in which no creature dwells, though it be but for a moment, then you shall hear what God says."

"Is That in which no creature dwells near at hand, or is it far off?"

"It is in you, my son. If you can for awhile but cease from all your own thinking and willing, you shall hear the unspeakable words of God."

"How can I hear Him speak when I stand still from thinking and willing?"

The master said, "When you stand still from the thinking of self and the willing of self, when both your intellect and will are quiet and passive to the impressions of the Eternal Word and Spirit, and when your soul is winged up and above that which is temporal, the outward senses and the imagination being locked up by holy abstraction, then the eternal hearing, seeing, and speaking will be revealed in you. Thus God hears and sees through you, being now the organ of His Spirit, and so God

---

Jakob Boehme (1575-1624), known as the "Teutonic Theosopher", was a simple German Lutheran, who practiced the trade of shoemaking throughout much of his life. His mystical insights, often couched in Hermetic and alchemical language, were written down in such treatises as *Aurora*, *The Way to Christ*, and *The Signature of All Things*. This reading is taken from his *Dialogue of the Supersensual Life*.

speaks in you, and whispers to your spirit, and your spirit hears His voice. Blessed are you therefore if you can stand still from self-thinking and self-willing, and can stop the wheel of your imagination and senses; for thus you may arrive at length to see the great salvation of God, being made capable of all manner of Divine sensations and heavenly communications. For it is nothing indeed but your own hearing and willing that hinder you, so that you cannot see and hear God."

"But with what shall I hear and see God since He is above nature and creature?"

"Son, when you are quiet and silent, then are you as God was before nature and creature; you are what God was then; you are that with which He made your nature and creature. Then you hear and see even with that with which God Himself saw and heard in you before ever your own willing or your own seeing began."

"What now hinders or keeps me back so that I cannot come to that with which God is to be seen and heard?"

The master replied, "Nothing truly but your own willing, hearing, and seeing do keep you back from it, and hinder you from coming to this supersensual state. And it is because you strive so against That out of which you yourself are descended and derived that you thus break yourself off, with your own willing, from God's willing, and with your own seeing from God's seeing. For in your own seeing you see in your own willing only, and with your own understanding you understand but in and according to your own willing, which thus stands divided from the Divine will. Your willing moreover stops your hearing and makes you deaf towards God through your own thinking upon terrestrial things and your attending to that which is outside of you; and so it brings you into a ground where you are laid hold of and captivated in nature. And having brought you hither, it overshadows you with what you have willed; it binds you with your own chains, and it keeps you in your own dark prison which you have made for yourself, so that you cannot go thence or come to that state which is supernatural and super-sensual."

The disciple asked, "But being that I am in nature, and thus bound as with my own chains and by my own natural will: pray be so kind, sir, as to tell me how I may come through nature into the supersensual and supernatural ground without destroying nature."

The master answered and said, "Be not discouraged. If you forsake the world, then you will come into That out of which the world is made; and if you lose your life, then your life is in That for whose sake you forsake it. Your life is in God, from whence it came into the body; and as your own power comes to be faint and weak and dying, the power of God will then work in you and through you.

"Nevertheless, as God has created man in and for the natural life, to rule over all creatures on earth and to be a lord over all things in this world, it seems not unreasonable that man should therefore possess this world and the things therein for his own.

"If you rule over all creatures but outwardly, there cannot be much in that. But if you have a mind to possess all things and to be a lord indeed over all things in this world, there is quite another method to be used."

The disciple asked, "Pray, how is that? And what method must I use whereby to arrive at this sovereignty?"

The master replied, "You must learn to distinguish well between the thing and that which is only an image thereof, between the sovereignty which is substantial and in the inward ground or nature and that which is imaginary and in an outward form or semblance, between that which is properly angelical and that which is no more than bestial. If you rule now over the creatures externally only and not from the right internal ground of your renewed nature, then your will and ruling is verily in a bestial kind or manner, and yours at best is but a sort of imaginary and transitory government, being void of what is substantial and permanent, which alone you are to desire and press after. Thus by your outwardly lording it over the creatures, it is most easy for you to lose the substance and the reality, while you have nothing remaining but the image or shadow only of your first and original lordship, in which you are

7

made capable to be again invested if you are wise and take your investiture from the supreme Lord in the right course and manner. Whereas by your willing and ruling thus after a bestial manner, you bring also your desire into a bestial essence, by which means you become infected and captivated, acquiring thereby a bestial nature and condition of life. But if you put off the bestial and ferine nature, and if you leave the imaginary life and quit the low imaged condition of it, then are you come into the super-imaginariness and into the intellectual life, which is a state of living above images, figures, and shadows: and so you shall rule over all creatures, being re-united with your original nature in that very Ground or Source out of which they were and are created; and henceforth nothing on earth can hurt you. For you are like all things; and nothing is unlike you."

"O loving master, pray teach me how I may come the shortest way to be like unto all things."

"With all my heart. Do but think on the words of our Lord Jesus Christ, when He said, 'Except ye be converted, and become as little children, ye shall not enter into the kingdom of heaven' (Matt. 18:3). There is no shorter way than this; neither can a better way be found. Jesus says to you that unless you turn and become as a child, hanging upon Him for all things, you shall not see the kingdom of God. Do this, and nothing shall hurt you, for you will be at friendship with all the things that are, as you depend upon the Author and Fountain of them and become like Him by such dependence and by the union of your will with His will. But mark what I have further to say and be not startled at it, though it may seem hard for you at first to conceive. If you wish to be like all things, you must forsake all things; you must turn your desire away from them all and not desire or hanker after any of them; you must not extend your will to possess them for your own or as your own. For as soon as ever you take something into your desire and receive it into yourself for your own, then this very something—of whatsoever nature it is—is the same with yourself; and this works with you in your will, and you are thence bound to protect it and to take care of it, even as of your own being. But if you receive nothing into your desire, then you are free from all things and rule over all things at once as a prince of God. For you have received nothing for your own and are nothing to all things, and all things are as nothing to you. You are as a child, who understands not what a thing is, and though perhaps you do understand it, yet you understand it without mixing with it and without its sensibly affecting or touching your perception, even in that manner wherein God rules and sees all things, He comprehending all and yet nothing comprehending Him."

The disciple was exceedingly ravished with what his master had so wonderfully and surprisingly declared, and returned his most humble and hearty thanks for that light which he had been an instrument of conveying to him. But being desirous to hear further concerning these high matters and to know somewhat more particularly, he requested him that he would give him leave to wait on him the next day again, and that he would then be pleased to show him how and where he might find what was so much beyond all price and value, and where the seat and abode of it might be in human nature, with the entire process of the discovery and bringing it forth to light. The master said to him, "This then we shall discourse about at our next conference, as God shall reveal the same to us by His Spirit, which is a searcher of all things. And if you remember well what I answered you today, you shall soon come thereby to understand that hidden mystical wisdom of God which none of the wise men of the world know, and where the mine thereof is to be found in you shall be given you from above to discern. Be silent therefore in your spirit and watch unto prayer that when we meet again tomorrow in the love of Christ, your mind may be disposed for finding that noble pearl which to the world appears nothing, but which to the children of wisdom is all things."

2

The Ladder of Graces

Theophanis the Monk

The first step is that of purest prayer.
From this there comes a warmth of heart,
And then a strange, a holy energy,
Then tears wrung from the heart, God-given.
Then peace from thoughts of every kind.
From this arises purging of the intellect,
And next the vision of heavenly mysteries.
Unheard-of light is born from this ineffably,
And thence, beyond all telling, the heart's illumination.
Last comes—a step that has no limit
Though compassed in a single line—
Perfection that is endless.

The ladder's lowest step
Prescribes pure prayer alone.
But prayer has many forms:
My discourse would be long
Were I now to speak of them:
And, friend, know that always
Experience teaches one, not words.

Theophanis the Monk is known to us only through this poem, which appears
without any introductory date or explanation in the Greek *Philokalia*, under
the title "The Ladder of Divine Graces which Experience Has Made Known to
Those Inspired by God". Compiled in the eighteenth century by St Nikodimos
of the Holy Mountain and St Makarios of Corinth, the *Philokalia* is a collection
of ascetical and mystical writings by spiritual masters of the Eastern Christian
tradition who lived from the fourth to the fifteenth centuries.

A ladder rising wondrously to heaven's vault:
Ten steps that strangely vivify the soul.
Ten steps that herald the soul's life.
A saint inspired by God has said:
Do not deceive yourself with idle hopes
That in the world to come you will find life
If you have not tried to find it in this present world.
Ten steps: a wisdom born of God.
Ten steps: fruit of all the books.
Ten steps that point towards perfection.
Ten steps that lead one up to heaven.
Ten steps through which a man knows God.

The ladder may seem short indeed,
But if your heart can inwardly experience it
You will find a wealth the world cannot contain,
A god-like fountain flowing with unheard-of life.
This ten-graced ladder is the best of masters,
Clearly teaching each to know its stages.
If when you behold it
You think you stand securely on it,
Ask yourself on which step you stand,
So that we, the indolent, may also profit.
My friend, if you want to learn about all this,
Detach yourself from everything,
From what is senseless, from what seems intelligent.
Without detachment nothing can be learnt.
Experience alone can teach these things, not talk.

3

Transposition

Unseen Warfare

Our heart constantly craves and seeks comforts and pleasures. It should find them in the inner order of things by keeping and bearing in itself Him in whose image man has been created, who is the very source of every comfort. But when in our downfall we fell away from God, preferring ourselves, we lost also our foothold in ourselves and fell into the flesh; thereby we went outside ourselves and began to seek for joys and comforts there. Our senses became our guides and intermediaries in this. Through them the soul goes outside and tastes the things experienced by each sense. It then delights in the things which delight the senses, and out of all these together it builds the circle of comforts and pleasures whose enjoyment it considers as its primary good. So the order of things has become inverted: instead of God within, the heart seeks for pleasures without and is content with them.

Those who have listened to the voice of God—"Repent!"— do repent and lay down for themselves the law of re-establishing the original order of life, that is, of returning from without to within, and from within to God, in order to live in Him and by

---

Unseen Warfare—in its original form a Counter-Reformation classic of the spiritual life—was written by Lorenzo Scupoli (1529-1610), a Roman Catholic priest of the Theatine Order. Translated into Greek by St Nikodimos of the Holy Mountain (1748-1809), an Orthodox monk and one of the compilers of the *Philokalia*, it was later revised and again translated, this time into Russian, by St Theophan the Recluse (1815-94), formerly the Orthodox Bishop of Tambov and in later life an anchorite of the Vychensky monastery. The work may thus be said to represent the combined wisdom of the Eastern and Western churches.

Him, and to have this as their first good, bearing within themselves the source of every comfort. Although the first step in re-establishing this order is strong desire and firm resolve, it is not achieved at once. A man who has taken this resolve is faced with a long work of struggling with his former habits of pleasing, pampering, and pandering to himself until they fall away and are replaced by others in keeping with his new order of life. And here is the great importance of the control and use of the outer senses.

Each sense has its own range of subjects, pleasant and unpleasant. The soul delights in pleasant things and, becoming accustomed to them, acquires a lust for them. In this way each sense introduces into the soul several lusts or tendencies and passionate attachments. They all hide in the soul and keep silent when there are no causes to stimulate them. Sometimes they are stimulated by thoughts about the objects of these lusts, but the main and strongest cause of their excitement is when these objects are directly present and experienced by the senses. In this case, lust for them arises uncontrollably, and in a man who has not yet resolved to resist, it "bringeth forth sin: and sin, when it is finished, bringeth forth death" (James 1:15). Then the words of the prophet are fulfilled in this man: "Death is come up into our windows" (Jer. 9:21), that is, into the senses, which are the windows of the soul for communication with the outer world. In a man who has let it enter, it rouses a struggle, not without danger of downfall. Therefore a man should make himself an immutable law to control and use his senses in such a way that no sensory lusts become excited, but only those impressions come in which stifle them and excite opposite feelings.

You see in what danger your senses can place you. So pay attention to yourself and learn to forestall it. Try in every way to prevent your senses from wandering hither and thither as they choose, and do not turn them only on sensory pleasures, but on the contrary direct them towards what is good, or useful, or necessary. If till now your senses sometimes broke out and rushed to sensory pleasures, from now on try to the utmost to curb them and turn them back from these enticements. Control them well, so that wherever they were previously enslaved by vain and harmful delights, they should now receive profitable impressions from every creature and every thing and introduce these into the soul. Giving birth to spiritual thoughts in the soul, such impressions will collect the soul within itself and, soaring on wings of mental contemplation, will raise it to the vision and praise of God, as the blessed Augustine says: "As many creatures as are in the world converse with righteous men, and although their language is dumb and wordless, it is nonetheless wholly effective and, for such men, easily heard and understood. From this they conceive blessed and pious thoughts and are incited to an ardent love of God."

You too can do it in the following way. When to your outer senses there is presented some physical object—which they either see, or hear, or smell, or taste, or touch—separate in your mind what is sensory and material in the object from that part which comes from the creative Divine Spirit; think how impossible it is for its being and all it contains to come from itself, but that all in it is the work of God, whose invisible power gives it its being, its good qualities, beauty, and wise structure, this power to act on others and this capacity to receive influences from them, and everything good there is in it. Then transfer such thoughts to all other visible things, and rejoice in your heart that the one God is the origin and cause of such varied, such great and marvelous, perfections, manifested in His creatures—that He contains in Himself all possible perfections, and that these perfections, seen in His creatures, are none other than a weak reflection and shadow of the boundless perfections of God. Exercise your mind in such thoughts at the sight of every creature, and you will get accustomed to looking at visible things without your attention dwelling solely on their external aspect, but penetrating within them to their Divine content, to their unseen and hidden Beauty, thus revealed to the mind. If you do this, the external side of things, attractive to your own sensory side, will escape your attention and feeling, leaving no trace, and only their inner content will impress itself on your mind, evoking and feeding its spiritual contemplations and inciting you to praise the Lord.

If you keep to this practice, then through your five senses you will be able to learn knowledge of God by always raising your mind from creature to Creator. Then the being and structure of everything created will be for you a book of theology, and while living in this sensory world, you will share in the knowledge belonging to the world beyond the world. For indeed the whole world and all nature is nothing but a certain organ in which, beneath what is seen, there is invisibly present the Architect and Artist Himself, the Maker of all things, either acting and manifesting His art visibly or revealing His invisible and immaterial actions and perfections in the visible and the material, discernible to the sight of intelligent creatures. Therefore the wise Solomon says on the one hand: "By the greatness and beauty of the creatures the Maker of them is proportionably seen" (Wisd. of Sol. 13:5), and on the other the blessed Paul testifies that: "The invisible things of Him are clearly seen from the creation of the world, being understood by the things that are made, even His eternal power and Godhead" (Rom. 1:20). In the world of God all the creatures of God, wisely fashioned, are ranged on one side, while on the other are ranged men, endowed with the power of reason, to the end that with this power of reason they may contemplate the creatures and, seeing infinite wisdom in their creation and organization, may rise to the knowledge and contemplation of the hypostatic Word that is before time, the Word by whom "all things were made" (John 1:3). Thus from actions we naturally see Him who acts; so we have but to judge rightly and soundly, and finding faith in what He has created, we shall see in the creation its Creator, God.

4

Death

St Thomas à Kempis

Very soon the end of your life will be at hand: consider, therefore, the state of your soul. Today a man is here; tomorrow he is gone. And when he is out of sight, he is soon out of mind. How dull and hard is the heart of man, which thinks only of the present and does not provide against the future! You should order your every deed and thought as though today were the day of your death. Had you a good conscience, death would hold no terrors for you; even so, it were better to avoid sin than to escape death. If you are not ready to die today, will tomorrow find you prepared? Tomorrow is uncertain; and how can you be sure of tomorrow?

Would to God that we might spend a single day really well! Many recount the years since their conversion, but their lives show little sign of improvement. If it is dreadful to die, it is perhaps more dangerous to live long. Blessed is the man who keeps the hour of his death always in mind and daily prepares himself to die. If you have ever seen anyone die, remember that you, too, must travel the same road. Each morning remember that you may not live until evening; and in the evening, do not presume to promise yourself another day. Be ready at all times, and so live that death may never find you unprepared. Many die suddenly and unexpectedly, for at the hour that we do not know

---

St Thomas à Kempis (*c.* 1380-1471) was educated by the Brethren of the Common Life and later entered a monastic house of the Augustinian canons at Agnietenberg in the Netherlands. His *Imitation of Christ*, the source of this selection, is a much-loved classic of Christian devotional literature.

the Son of Man will come. When your last hour strikes, you will begin to think very differently of your past life and grieve deeply that you have been so careless and remiss.

Happy and wise is he who endeavors to be during his life as he wishes to be found at his death. For these things will afford us sure hope of a happy death: perfect contempt of the world, fervent desire to grow in holiness, love of discipline, the practice of penance, ready obedience, self-denial, the bearing of every trial for the love of Christ. While you enjoy health, you can do much good, but when sickness comes, little can be done. Few are made better by sickness, and those who make frequent pilgrimages seldom acquire holiness by so doing.

Do not rely on friends and neighbors, and do not delay the salvation of your soul to some future date, for men will forget you sooner than you think. It is better to make timely provision and to acquire merit in this life than to depend on the help of others. And if you have no care for your own soul, who will have care for you in time to come? The present time is most precious; now is the accepted time, now is the day of salvation. It is sad that you do not employ your time better when you may win eternal life hereafter. The time will come when you will long for one day or one hour in which to amend, and who knows whether it will be granted?

Dear soul, from what peril and fear you could free yourself if you lived in holy fear, mindful of your death. Apply yourself so to live now that at the hour of death you may be glad and unafraid. Learn now to die to the world that you may begin to live with Christ. Learn now to despise all earthly things that you may go freely with Christ. Discipline your body now by penance that you may enjoy a sure hope of salvation.

Foolish man, how can you promise yourself a long life when you are not certain of a single day? How many have deceived themselves in this way and been snatched unexpectedly from life! You have often heard how this man was slain by the sword, another drowned, how another fell from a high place and broke his neck, how another died at table, how another met his end in play. One perishes by fire, another by the sword, another from

17

disease, another at the hands of robbers. Death is the end of all men, and the life of man passes away suddenly as a shadow.

Who will remember you when you are dead? Who will pray for you? Act now, dear soul; do all you can, for you know neither the hour of your death, nor your state after death. While you have time, gather the riches of everlasting life. Think only of your salvation and care only for the things of God. Make friends now, by honoring the saints of God and by following their example, that when this life is over, they may welcome you to your eternal home. Keep yourself a stranger and pilgrim upon earth, to whom the affairs of this world are of no concern. Keep your heart free and lifted up to God, for here you have no abiding city. Daily direct your prayers and longings to Heaven that at your death your soul may merit to pass joyfully into the presence of God.

5

Pure Fire

Hugh of St Victor

Three are the modes of cognition belonging to the rational soul: cogitation, meditation, contemplation. It is cogitation when the mind is touched with the ideas of things, and the thing itself is by its image presented suddenly, either entering the mind through sense or rising from memory. Meditation is the assiduous and sagacious revision of cogitation, and strives to explain the involved, and penetrate the hidden. Contemplation is the mind's perspicacious and free attention, diffused everywhere throughout the range of whatever may be explored. There is this difference between meditation and contemplation: meditation relates always to things hidden from our intelligence; contemplation relates to things made manifest, according to either their nature or our capacity. Meditation always is occupied with some one matter to be investigated; contemplation spreads abroad for the comprehending of many things, even the universe. Thus meditation is a certain inquisitive power of the mind, sagaciously striving to look into the obscure and unravel the perplexed. Contemplation is that acumen of intelligence which, keeping all things open to view, comprehends all with clear vision. Thus contemplation has what meditation seeks.

Hugh of St Victor (*c.* 1096-1141) was an Augustinian canon, probably of Saxon background, whose writings include meditations on Scripture, treatises on grammar and geometry, and a commentary on the *Celestial Hierarchies* of St Dionysios the Areopagite (see p. 223). The present reading is taken from the first of his nineteen sermons on Ecclesiastes.

There are two kinds of contemplation: the first is for beginners, and considers creatures; the kind that comes later belongs to the perfect, and contemplates the Creator. In the Proverbs, Solomon proceeds as through meditation. In Ecclesiastes, he ascends to the first grade of contemplation. In the Song of Songs, he transports himself to the final grade. In meditation there is a wrestling of ignorance with knowledge; and the light of truth gleams as in a fog of error. So fire is kindled with difficulty on a heap of green wood; but then, fanned with stronger breath, the flame burns higher, and we see volumes of smoke rolling up, with flame flashing through. Little by little the damp is exhausted, and the leaping fire dispels the smoke. Then the flame, darting through the heap of crackling wood, springs from branch to branch, and with lambent grasp catches upon every twig; nor does it rest until it penetrates everywhere and draws into itself all that it finds that is not flame. At length the whole combustible material is purged of its own nature and passes into the similitude and property of fire; then the din is hushed, and the voracious fire, having subdued all and brought all into its own likeness, composes itself to a high peace and silence, finding nothing more that is alien or opposed to itself. First there was fire with flame and smoke; then fire with flame, without smoke; and at last pure fire with neither flame nor smoke.

6

What More Must I Do?

The Desert Fathers

The abbot Sisois, sitting in his cell, always had his door closed. But it was told of him how in the day of his death, when the Fathers were sitting round him, his face shone like the sun, and he said to them, "Look, the abbot Anthony comes." And after a little while, he said again to them, "Look, the company of the prophets comes." And again his face shone brighter, and he said, "Look, the company of the apostles comes." And his face shone with a double glory, and he seemed as though he spoke with others.

And the old men entreated him, saying, "With whom are you speaking, Father?" And he said to them, "Behold, the angels came to take me, and I asked that I might be left a little while to repent." The old men said to him, "You have no need of repentance, Father." But he said to them, "I do not know that I have even begun to repent." And they all knew that he was made perfect. And again of a sudden his face was as the sun, and they all were in dread. And he said to them, "Look, the Lord comes, saying, 'Bring me my chosen from the desert.'" And straightway he gave up the ghost. And there came as it might be lightning, and all the place was filled with sweetness.

The Desert Fathers were Christian ascetics and hermits of the third, fourth, and fifth centuries who withdrew to the wilderness in Egypt, Syria, Palestine, and Arabia in order to lead lives of rigorous discipline and contemplative prayer. *The Sayings of the Desert Fathers*, from which the present sampling comes, include stories about some of the most famous of these figures, including the foremost of their number, St Anthony the Great (*c.* 251-356), as well as a record of their often pungent apothegms.

The abbot Allois said, "Unless a man shall say in his heart, 'I alone and God are in this world,' he shall not find quiet." He said again, "If a man willed it, in one day up till evening he might come to the measure of Divinity."

They told of the abbot Arsenios that on Saturday evening with the Sabbath drawing on, he would leave the sun behind him and stretching out his hands towards heaven, would pray until with the morning of the Sabbath the rising sun shone upon his face: and so he would abide.

There came to the abbot Joseph the abbot Lot, and said to him, "Father, according to my strength I keep a modest rule of prayer and fasting and meditation and quiet, and according to my strength I purge my imagination: what more must I do?" The old man, rising, held up his hands against the sky, and his fingers became like ten torches of fire, and he said, "If you wish, you can be made wholly a flame."

A brother went to the cell of the abbot Arsenios in Scete, and looked through the window, and saw the old man as it were one flame: now, the brother was worthy to look upon such things. And after he had knocked, the old man came out and saw the brother as one amazed, and said to him, "Have you been knocking here for long? Have you seen anything?" And he answered, "No." And he talked with him, and sent him away.

At one time Zachary went to his abbot Silvanos and found him in an ecstasy, and his hands were stretched out to heaven. And when he saw him thus, he closed the door and went away; and coming back about the sixth hour, and the ninth, he found him even so: but toward the tenth hour he knocked, and coming in found him lying quiet and said to him, "What ailed you today, Father?" And he said, "I was ill today, my son." But the young man held his feet saying, "I shall not let you go until you tell me what you have seen." The old man answered him: "I was caught up into heaven, and I saw the glory of God. And I stood there until now, and now am I sent away."

7

The Ceremony of Substitution

Charles Williams

Easter is not only a consequence of the cross; it is also almost an accident of it. It followed the cross, but also it began in the cross. I say "in" rather than "on", for by the time it began Christ had become, as it were, the very profoundest cross to Himself. That certainly He had always been prophetically, but now the exploration of His prophecies was complete. The cross was He, and He the cross. His will had maintained, or rather His will in His Father's will had maintained, a state of affairs among men of which physical crucifixion was at once a part and a perfect symbol. This state of things He inexorably proposed to Himself to endure; say, rather, that from the beginning He had been Himself at bottom both the endurance and the thing endured. This had been true everywhere in all men; it was now true of Himself apart from all men; it was local and particular. The physical body which was His own means of union with matter, and was in consequence the very cause, center, and origin of all human creation, was exposed to the complete contradiction of itself.

It would be perhaps too ingenious a fancy, which in these things above all is to be avoided, to say that actual crucifixion is a more exact symbol of His suffering than any other means of death. It is, however, with peculiar explicitness in the physical

Charles Williams (1886-1945), an Anglican poet and writer of Christian fantasy, was a member of the Oxford Inklings and a close friend of C. S. Lewis and J. R. R. Tolkien. T. S. Eliot said of his stories that "Williams is telling us about a world of experience known to him: he does not merely persuade us to believe in something; he communicates this experience that he has had."

category what His other agony was in the spiritual—so, for a moment, to differentiate them. He was stretched, He was bled, He was nailed, He was thrust into, but not a bone of Him was broken. The dead wood drenched with the blood, and the dead body shedding blood, have an awful likeness; the frame is doubly saved. It was the cross which sustained Him, but He also sustained the cross. He had, through the years, exactly preserved the growth of the thorn and of the wood, and had endued with energy the making of the nails and the sharpening of the spear; through the centuries He had maintained vegetable and mineral in the earth for this. His providence overwatched it to no other end, as it over-watches so many instruments and intentions of cruelty then and now. The cross therefore is the express image of His will; it depends in its visible shape and strength wholly on Him.

In the moment of the final so-near-to-identity of Himself and His wooden image, He spoke. He said: "It is finished" (John 19:30). It is at that moment that Easter began. It is not yet Easter; the Deposition has not yet taken place. He speaks while yet He can—while He is not yet as speechless as the wood—and He announces the culmination of that experience. Life has known absolutely all its own contradiction. He survives; He perfectly survives. His victory is not afterwards, but then. His actual death becomes almost a part of His resurrection, almost what Patmore called the death of the Divine Mother: a "ceremony". Not so, for the ceremony was itself a work and a discovery, but then proper ceremonies are so; they achieve, as this does. The joy of His self-renewed knowledge perfectly exists, and His resurrection is—in His Father and Origin—at His own decision and by His own will. It is the will of His unalterable joy which, having absorbed, exists.

This moment of consummation is therefore related to man's inevitable demand that all things should be justified in the moment that they happen. We must perhaps, joyously or reluctantly, consent to leave the knowledge of that justification till afterwards, but we must be willing to believe that it is now. Or better, that the result is neither here nor there, neither now nor then, and yet both here and there, both now and then.

There has indeed been much admiration, much gratitude, much love, that God should be made like us, but then there is at least equal satisfaction that it is an Unlike us who is so made. It is an alien Power which is caught and suspended in our very midst. "Blessed be God," said John Donne, "that He is God only and divinely like Himself." It is that other kind of existence which here penetrates our hearts, and is at all points credibly justified by our justice. The supreme error of earthly justice was the supreme assertion of the possibility of justice. In His mortal life He never pretended, in making all His impossible and yet natural demands, that He judged as we do. The parable of the laborers, the reply to James and John, are alien from our equality; and so is the incredible comment on Judas: "It were good for that man if he had not been born" (Mark 14:21). And who caused him to be born? Who maintained his life up to and in that awful less than good? It is in the gospels that the really terrifying attacks on the gospel lie.

He was not like us, and yet He became us. What happened there the church itself has never seen, except that in the last reaches of that living death to which we are exposed He substituted Himself for us. He submitted in our stead to the full results of the Law which is He. We may believe He was generous if we know that He was just. By that central substitution, which was the thing added by the cross to the Incarnation, He became everywhere the center of, and everywhere He energized and reaffirmed, all our substitutions and exchanges. He took what remained after the Fall of the torn web of humanity in all times and places, and not so much by a miracle of healing as by a growth within it made it whole. Supernaturally he renewed our proper nature. It is finished; we too do but play out the necessary ceremony.

8

My Desire Has Been Crucified

St Ignatios of Antioch

ary's virginity and Her giving birth escaped the notice of the prince of this world, as did the Lord's death—those three secrets crying to be told, but wrought in God's silence. How then were they revealed to the ages? A star shone in heaven brighter than all the stars. Its light was indescribable, and its novelty caused amazement. The rest of the stars, along with the sun and the moon, formed a ring around it; yet it outshone them all, and there was bewilderment whence this unique novelty had arisen. As a result all magic lost its power and all witchcraft ceased. Ignorance was done away with, and the ancient kingdom of evil was utterly destroyed, for God was revealing Himself as a man, to bring newness of eternal life.

It is a grand thing for my life to set on the world, and for me to be on my way to God, so that I may rise in His presence. It is not that I want merely to be called a Christian, but actually to *be* one. Yes, if I prove to be one, then I can have the name. I shall be a convincing Christian only when the world sees me no more. Nothing you can see has real value. Our God Jesus Christ, indeed, has revealed Himself more clearly by returning to the Father. The greatness of Christianity lies in its being hated by the world, not in its being convincing to it.

St Ignatios (*c.* 35 - *c.* 107)—who followed St Peter as bishop of the ancient see of Antioch—was taken under guard to be martyred in Rome. During this final journey of his life, he corresponded with a number of the churches he had visited. The "Desire" of which he speaks in this passage is at once the energy of his *eros* and its Divine object.

I am corresponding with all the churches and bidding them all realize that I am voluntarily dying for God—if, that is, you do not interfere. I plead with you, do not do me an unseasonable kindness. Let me be fodder for wild beasts; that is how I can get to God. I am God's wheat, and I am being ground by the teeth of wild beasts to make a pure loaf for Christ. I would rather that you fawn on the beasts so that they may be my tomb and no scrap of my body be left. Thus, when I have fallen asleep, I shall be a burden to no one. Then I shall be a real disciple of Jesus Christ when the world sees my body no more. Pray Christ for me that by these means I may become God's sacrifice.

Sympathize with me, my brothers! Do not stand in the way of my coming to life; do not wish death on me. Do not give back to the world one who wants to be God's; do not trick him with material things. Let me get into the clear light, and manhood will be mine. Let me imitate the Passion of my God. If anyone has Him in him, let him appreciate what I am longing for, and sympathize with me, realizing what I am going through. For though alive, it is with a passion for death that I am writing to you. My Desire has been crucified, and there burns in me no passion for material things. There is living water in me, which speaks and says inside me, "Come to the Father." I take no delight in corruptible food or in the dainties of this life. What I want is God's bread, which is the flesh of Christ, who came from David's line; and for drink I want His blood: an immortal love feast indeed.

I do not want to live any more on a human plane.

II

Simplicity

Whosoever shall not receive
the kingdom of God as a little
child shall not enter therein.

Mark 10:15

9

Drawn by the Flames

St Thérèse of Lisieux

After Holy Communion one day, our Lord made me understand the significance of these words in the Song of Songs: "Draw me: we will run after You because of the savor of Your good ointments" (Song of Sol. 1:3, 4). There is no need to say, "In drawing me, draw also the souls I love." The simple words "Draw me" are enough. When a soul has been captivated by the intoxicating perfume of Your ointments, she cannot run alone. Every soul she loves is drawn after her—a natural consequence of her being drawn to You. As a river sweeps along it carries with it all it meets down to the depths of the sea, and so, my Jesus, the soul which plunges into the boundless ocean of Your love carries with it all its treasures. You know that my treasures are those souls which You have linked with mine.

Jesus said: "No man can come to Me except the Father who has sent Me draw him" (John 6:44). Later He teaches us that we have only to knock and it will be opened, to seek and we shall find, to hold out our hand humbly to receive. He adds: "If you ask the Father anything in My Name, He will give it to you" (John 11:22, 14:14). And that no doubt is why the Holy Spirit, long before the birth of Jesus, dictated this prophetic prayer: "Draw me: we will run." When we ask to be drawn, we are wanting to be closely united with the object which has won our heart.

St Thérèse of Lisieux (1873-97)—canonized as St Teresa of the Child Jesus and popularly known as "The Little Flower"—was a Carmelite nun who was drawn to the life of perfection as a very young child. This selection comes from her spiritual autobiography, *The Story of a Soul*, written at the command of her superiors shortly before her death at age 24.

31

If fire and iron could reason, and if the iron said to the fire, "Draw me", that would prove its wish to be so identified with the fire as to share its very substance. Well, that is just what my prayer is. I ask Jesus to draw me into the flames of His love and to unite me so closely to Him that He lives and acts in me. I feel that the more the fire of love encompasses my heart, the more I shall say, "Draw me", and the more will those souls who are near to mine "run swiftly in the sweet savor of the Beloved". Yes, they will run and we shall run together, for souls on fire cannot stay still, even though, like Mary, they may sit at the feet of Jesus, listening to His gentle yet exciting words. They seem to give Him nothing, and yet they give much more than Martha, who is anxious "about many things" (Luke 10:41). Jesus does not of course blame Martha's work, but only her worrying about it.

This lesson has been understood by all the saints, perhaps especially by those who have illumined the world with the teaching of the Gospels. Was it not in prayer that St Paul, St Augustine, St Thomas Aquinas, St John of the Cross, St Teresa, and so many other friends of God found that wonderful knowledge which has enraptured the greatest intellects? Archimedes said: "Give me a fulcrum, and with a lever I will move the world." What he could not get, the saints have been given. The Almighty has given them a fulcrum: Himself alone. For a lever, they have that prayer which burns with the fire of love. Thus they have moved the world, and it is with this lever that those still battling in the world move it and will go on moving it till the end of time.

10

Descending with the Breath

Nikiphoros the Athonite

You know that what we breathe is air. When we exhale it, it is for the heart's sake, for the heart is the source of life and warmth for the body. The heart draws towards itself the air inhaled when breathing, so that by discharging some of its heat when the air is exhaled it may maintain an even temperature. The cause of this process, or rather its agent, is the lungs. The Creator has made these capable of expanding and contracting like bellows, so that they can easily draw in and expel their contents. Thus by taking in coolness and expelling heat through breathing, the heart performs unobstructed the function for which it was created, that of maintaining life.

Seat yourself, then, concentrate your intellect, and lead it into the respiratory passage through which your breath passes into your heart. Put pressure on your intellect and compel it to descend with your inhaled breath into your heart. Once it has entered there, what follows will be neither dismal nor glum. Just as a man, after being far away from home, on his return is overjoyed at being with his wife and children again, so the intellect,

---

Nikiphoros the Athonite (*fl.* second half of the thirteenth century), an Orthodox monk of the Holy Mountain, was among the first to write about the psychosomatic method of concentration—similar in certain respects to the yogic practice of *prânâyâma*—which has come to be associated with Hesychast spirituality. "Intellect", a translation of the Greek term *nous*, is the name which the eastern fathers give to the highest faculty in man, one which—in contrast to the "discursive faculty" or *dianoia*—is able to apprehend Divine truth by means of direct spiritual perception. The reading is taken from "On Watchfulness and the Guarding of the Heart".

once it is united with the soul, is filled with indescribable delight. Therefore, train your intellect not to leave your heart quickly, for at first it is strongly disinclined to remain constrained and circumscribed in this way. But once it becomes accustomed to remaining there, it can no longer bear to be outside the heart. For the kingdom of heaven is within us (*cf.* Luke 17:21); and when the intellect concentrates its attention in the heart and through pure prayer searches there for the kingdom of heaven, all external things become abominable and hateful to it. If after your first attempts you enter through your intellect into the abode of the heart in the way that I have explained, give thanks and glory to God and exult in Him. Continually persevere in this practice, and it will teach you what you do not know.

Moreover, when your intellect is firmly established in your heart, it must not remain there silent and idle; it should constantly repeat and meditate on the prayer, "Lord Jesus Christ, Son of God, have mercy on me", and should never stop doing this. For this prayer protects the intellect from distraction, renders it impregnable to diabolic attacks, and every day increases its love and desire for God. If, however, in spite of all your efforts you are not able to enter the realms of the heart in the way I have enjoined, do what I now tell you, and with God's help you will find what you seek.

You know that everyone's discursive faculty is centered in his breast; for when our lips are silent we speak and deliberate and formulate prayers, psalms, and other things in our breast. Banish, then, all thoughts from this faculty—you can do this if you want to—and in their place put the prayer, "Lord Jesus Christ, Son of God, have mercy on me", and compel it to repeat this prayer ceaselessly. If you continue to do this for some time, it will assuredly open for you the entrance to your heart in the way we have explained, and as we ourselves know from experience.

Then, along with the attentiveness you have so wished for, the whole choir of the virtues—love, joy, peace, and the others (*cf.* Gal. 5:22)—will come to you. Through the virtues all your petitions will be answered in Christ Jesus our Lord, to whom with the Father and the Holy Spirit be glory, power, honor, and worship now and always and throughout the ages. Amen.

11

So Many Names

Jean-Pierre de Caussade

very moment we live through is like an ambassador who declares the will of God, and our hearts always utter their acceptance. Our souls steadily advance, never halting, but sweeping along with every wind. Every current, every technique, thrusts us onward in our voyage to the Infinite. Everything works to this end and, without exception, helps us toward holiness. We can find all that is necessary in the present moment. We need not worry about whether to pray or be silent, whether to withdraw into retreat or mix with people, to read or write, to meditate or make our minds a receptive blank, to shun or seek out books on spirituality. Nor do poverty or riches, sickness or health, life or death matter in the least. What does matter is what each moment produces by the will of God. We must strip ourselves naked, renounce all desire for created things, and retain nothing of ourselves or for ourselves, so that we can be wholly submissive to God's will and so delight Him. Our only satisfaction must be to live in the present moment as if there were nothing to expect beyond it.

If what happens to a soul abandoned to God is all that is necessary for it, it is clear that it can lack nothing and that it should never complain, for this would show that it lacked faith and was living by the light of its reason and the evidence of its senses.

Jean-Pierre de Caussade (1675-1751) was a noted Jesuit preacher and spiritual director. Among those in his charge was a group of nuns at the Visitation convent in Nancy, who preserved his letters and their notes from his talks, assembling them after his death as the book *Abandonment to Divine Providence.*

Neither reason nor the senses are ever satisfied, for they never see the sufficiency of grace. To hallow the name of God is, according to the Scriptures, to recognize His holiness and to love and adore it in all the things which proceed like words from the mouth of God. For what God creates at each moment is a Divine thought which is expressed by a thing, and so all these things are so many names and words through which He makes known His wishes. God's will is single and individual, with an unknown and inexpressible name, but it is infinitely diverse in its effects, which are as many as the names it assumes. To hallow God's name is to know, to worship, and to love the ineffable being who bears it. It is also to know, to worship, and to love His adorable will every moment and all that it does, regarding all that happens as so many veils, shadows, and names beneath which this eternal and most holy will is always active. It is holy in all it does, holy in all it says, holy in every manifestation, and holy in all the names it bears.

It is thus that Job blessed the name of God. This holy man blessed the utter desolation which fell upon him, for it displayed the will of God. His ruin he regarded as one of God's names, and in blessing it he was declaring that, no matter how terrible its manifestations, it was always holy under whatever name or form it appeared. And David never ceased to bless it. It is by this continual recognition of the will of God, as displayed and revealed in all things, that God reigns in us, that His will is done on earth as in heaven, and that He nourishes us continually.

The full and complete meaning of self-abandonment to His will is embraced in the matchless prayer given to us by Jesus Christ. By the command of God and the church, we recite it several times a day, but apart from this, if we love to suffer and obey His adorable will, we shall utter it constantly in the depths of our hearts. What we can utter through our mouths—which takes time—our hearts can speak instantly; and it is in this manner that simple people are called to bless God from the depths of their souls. Yet they complain bitterly that they cannot praise Him as much as they desire, for God gives to them so much that they feel they cannot cope with such riches. A secret working of the Divine wisdom is to pour treasure into the heart whilst impoverishing the senses, so that the one overflows whilst the other is drained and emptied.

The events of every moment are stamped with the will of God. How holy is His name! How right it is to bless it and to treat it as something which sanctifies all it touches. Can we see anything which carries this name without showing it with infinite love? It is a Divine warmth from heaven and gives us a ceaseless increase of grace. It is the kingdom of heaven which penetrates the soul. It is the bread of angels which is eaten on earth as well as in heaven. There is nothing trivial about our passing moments, as they enclose the whole kingdom of holiness and the food on which angels feed.

O Lord, may You rule my heart, nourish it, purify it, make it holy, and let it triumph over all its enemies. Most precious moment! How small it is to my bodily eyes, but how great to the eyes of my faith! How can I think of it as nothing when it is thought of so highly by my heavenly Father? All that comes from Him is most excellent and bears the imprint of its origin.

12

What Dreams May Come

St Diadochos of Photiki

Sometimes the soul is kindled into love for God and, free from all fantasy and image, moves untroubled by doubt towards Him; and it draws, as it were, the body with it into the depths of that ineffable love. This may occur when the person is awake or else beginning to fall asleep under the influence of God's grace. The soul is aware of nothing except what it is moving towards. When we experience things in this manner, we can be sure that it is the energy of the Holy Spirit within us. For when the soul is completely permeated with that ineffable sweetness, at that moment it can think of nothing else, since it rejoices with uninterrupted joy. But if at that moment the intellect conceives any doubt or unclean thought, and if this continues in spite of the fact that the intellect calls on the holy name—not now simply out of love for God, but in order to repel the evil one—then it should realize that the sweetness it experiences is an illusion of grace, coming from the deceiver with a counterfeit joy.

Let no one who hears us speak of the perceptive faculty of the intellect imagine that by this we mean that the glory of God appears to man visibly. We do indeed affirm that the soul, when

---

St Diadochos (d. before 486) was Bishop of Photiki in Epirus (North Greece). His century of chapters "On Spiritual Knowledge and Discrimination", from which this passage is taken, was described by St Nikodimos of the Holy Mountain, one of the compilers of the *Philokalia*, as revealing "the deepest secrets of the virtue of prayer". For a balanced perspective on the subject of dreams, see also the selection "More than Ourselves" (p. 95).

pure, perceives God's grace, tasting it in some ineffable manner; but no invisible reality appears to it in a visible form, since now "we walk by faith, not by sight", as St Paul says (2 Cor. 5:7). If light or some fiery form should be seen by one pursuing the spiritual way, he should not on any account accept such a vision: it is an obvious deceit of the enemy. Many indeed have had this experience and, in their ignorance, have turned aside from the way of truth. We ourselves know, however, that so long as we dwell in this corruptible body, "we are absent from the Lord" (2 Cor. 5:6)—that is to say, we know that we cannot see visibly either God Himself or any of His celestial wonders.

The dreams which appear to the soul through God's love are unerring criteria of its health. Such dreams do not change from one shape to another; they do not shock our inward sense, resound with laughter, or suddenly become threatening. But with great gentleness they approach the soul and fill it with spiritual gladness. As a result, even after the body has woken up, the soul longs to recapture the joy given to it by the dream. Demonic fantasies, however, are just the opposite: they do not keep the same shape or maintain a constant form for long. For what the demons do not possess as their chosen mode of life, but merely assume because of their inherent deceitfulness, is not able to satisfy them for very long. They shout and menace, often transforming themselves into soldiers and sometimes deafening the soul with their cries. But the intellect, when pure, recognizes them for what they are and awakes the body from its dreams. Sometimes it even feels joy at having been able to see through their tricks; indeed it often challenges them during the dream itself and thus provokes them to great anger. There are, however, times when even good dreams do not bring joy to the soul, but produce in it a sweet sadness and tears unaccompanied by grief. But this happens only to those who are far advanced in humility.

We have now explained the distinction between good and bad dreams, as we ourselves heard it from those with experience. In our quest for purity, however, the safest rule is never to trust anything that appears to us in our dreams. For dreams are generally nothing more than images reflecting our wandering thoughts, or else they are the mockery of demons. And if ever God in His goodness were to send us some vision and we were to refuse it, our beloved Lord Jesus would not be angry with us, for He would know we were acting in this way because of the tricks of the demons. Although the distinction between types of dreams established above is precise, it sometimes happens that when the soul has been sullied by an unperceived beguilement—something from which no one, it seems to me, is exempt—it loses its sense of accurate discrimination and mistakes bad dreams for good. As an illustration of what I mean, take the case of the servant whose master, returning at night after a long absence abroad, calls to him from outside his house. The servant categorically refuses to open the door to him, for he is afraid of being deceived by some similarity of voice, and so of betraying to someone else the goods his master has entrusted to him. Not only is his master in no way angry with him when day comes; but on the contrary he even praises him highly, because in his concern not to lose any of his master's goods he even suspected the sound of his master's voice to be a trick.

You should not doubt that the intellect, when it begins to be strongly energized by the Divine light, becomes so completely translucent that it sees its own light vividly. This takes place when the power of the soul gains control over the passions. But when St Paul says that "Satan himself is transformed into an angel of light" (2 Cor. 11:14), he definitely teaches us that everything which appears to the intellect, whether as light or as fire, if it has a shape, is the product of the evil artifice of the enemy. So we should not embark on the ascetic life in the hope of seeing visions clothed with form or shape; for if we do, Satan will find it easy to lead our soul astray. Our one purpose must be to reach the point when we perceive the love of God fully and consciously in our heart—that is, "with all your heart, and with all your soul, and with all your mind" (Luke 10:27). For the man who is energized by the grace of God to this point has already left this world, though still present in it.

13

I Sleep but My Heart Waketh

St Bernard of Clairvaux

ℑ charge you, daughters of Jerusalem, by the gazelles and hinds of the fields, not to stir my beloved or rouse her until she pleases" (Song of Sol. 2:7).

Let me explain if I can what this sleep is which the Bridegroom wishes His beloved to enjoy, from which He will not allow her to be wakened under any circumstances, except at her good pleasure; for if someone should read the apostle's words: "It is full time now for you to wake from sleep" (Rom. 13:11), or read how God was asked by the prophet to enlighten his eyes lest he sleep the sleep of death (*cf.* Ps. 13:3), he might be troubled by the ambiguity of the words and be entirely unable to form any worthy sentiments about the sleep of the bride that is here described. Nor does it resemble that sleep of Lazarus which the Lord mentions in the Gospel: "Our friend Lazarus has fallen asleep, but I go to wake him out of sleep" (John 11:11). He said this about the death of his body, though the disciples were thinking of sleep. This sleep of the bride, however, is not the tranquil repose of the body that for a time sweetly lulls the fleshly senses, nor that dreaded sleep whose custom is to take life away completely. Farther still is it removed from that deathly sleep by which a man perseveres irrevocably in sin and

---

St Bernard of Clairvaux (1090-1153), a Cistercian monk and prolific writer on the mystical life, was one of the most influential and widely respected men of his age. Like numerous other Christian contemplatives, he regarded the Song of Songs as a mystical allegory describing the relationship between the soul and God, and he preached nearly one hundred exegetical sermons on this single book. Here he explains the spiritual meaning of sleep.

so dies. It is a slumber which is vital and watchful, which enlightens the heart, drives away death, and communicates eternal life. For it is a genuine sleep that yet does not stupefy the mind but transports it. And—I say it without hesitation—it is a death, for the apostle Paul in praising people still living in the flesh spoke thus: "For you have died, and your life is hid with Christ in God" (Col. 3:3).

It is not absurd for me to call the bride's ecstasy a death, then, but one that snatches away not life but life's snares, so that one can say: "We have escaped as a bird from the snare of the fowlers" (Ps. 124:7). In this life we move about surrounded by traps, but these cause no fear when the soul is drawn out of itself by a thought that is both powerful and holy, provided that it so separates itself and flies away from the mind that it transcends the normal manner and habit of thinking; for a net is spread in vain before the eyes of winged creatures. Why dread wantonness where there is no awareness of life? For since the ecstatic soul is cut off from awareness of life, though not from life itself, it must of necessity be cut off from the temptations of life. "O that I had wings like a dove! I would fly away and be at rest" (Ps. 55:6). How often I long to be the victim of this death that I may escape the snares of death, that I may not feel the deadening blandishments of a sensual life, that I may be steeled against desire, against the surge of cupidity, against the goads of anger and impatience, against the anguish of worry and the miseries of care. Let me die the death of the just, that no injustice may ensnare or wickedness seduce me. How good the death that does not take away life but makes it better; good in that the body does not perish but the soul is exalted. Men alone experience this. But, if I may say so, let me die the death of angels that, transcending the memory of things present, I may cast off the desire not only for things corporeal and inferior but even their images, that I may enjoy pure conversation with those who bear the likeness of purity.

This kind of ecstasy, in my opinion, is alone or principally called contemplation. Not to be gripped during life by material desires is a mark of human virtue, but to gaze without the use of bodily likenesses is the sign of angelic purity. Each, however, is a

Divine gift, each is a going out of oneself, each a transcending of self, but in one a man goes much farther than in the other. Happy the man who can say: "See, I have escaped far away and found a refuge in the wilderness" (Ps. 55:7). He was not satisfied with going out if he could not go far away, so that he could be at rest. You have so over-leaped the pleasures of the flesh that you are no longer responsive to its concupiscence even in the least, nor gripped by its allure. You have advanced, you have placed yourself apart, but you have not yet put yourself at a distance, unless you succeed in flying with purity of mind beyond the material images that press in from every side. Until that point promise yourself no rest. You err if you expect to find before then a place of rest, the privacy of solitude, unclouded light, the abode of peace. But show me the man who has attained to this, and I shall promptly declare him to be at rest. Rightly may he say: "Return, O my soul, to your rest, for the Lord has dealt bountifully with you" (Ps. 116:7). For this place is truly a solitude where one dwells in the light, precisely what the prophet calls "a shade by day from the heat, a refuge and a shelter from rain and tempest" (Isa. 4:6), or as holy David said: "He hid me in his shelter in the day of trouble; he concealed me under the cover of his tent" (Ps. 27:5).

Consider therefore that the bride has retired to this solitude. There, overcome by the loveliness of the place, she sweetly sleeps within the arms of her Bridegroom, in ecstasy of spirit.

14

Nakedness and Sacrifice

Jean Borella

 allen man, by the coagulation of the ego, is bewitched by himself. Having lost God, all that remains is his own imperfection. To renounce this imperfection, which constitutes his whole reality, is to renounce all that remains to him of himself. Unable to rest within himself and to find joy in his own ego, however, he disguises this shameful passion for himself in the form of punishment, and by that justifies the passion. Such is the nearly invincible illusion of remorse. Since I know, judge, and accuse myself in my own unbearable imperfection, to my own eyes I am justified in my desire for it. Original sin (the fall of the "I" into the psyche), usurping the function of the guardian angel, appoints us guardians of ourselves. The basis of the ego is remorse for the ontological fault. Remorse is even, in a certain way, a poor imitation of a perfection that has become inaccessible through an amorous returning to one's own imperfection. As guardian of myself, far from protecting and guiding myself like the angelic guardian, I appoint myself as tormentor to punish and justify myself for not being more beautiful than my desire. Man spends his life in this way: his past is remorse, his present vile, his future an illusion. In remorse he takes for his desire's end the imperfection that was at the beginning; in vile-

---

Jean Borella (1930-) is a Catholic theologian and Professor Emeritus of Ancient and Medieval Philosophy at the University of Nancy. Deeply influenced by the traditionalist school of Frithjof Schuon and René Guénon, he is the author of a number of books on Christian esoterism, including *Ésotérisme guénonien et mystère chrétien* and *The Secret of the Christian Way*, from which this passage has been chosen.

ness he abandons himself and consents to its ugliness; in illusion he hopes, ineradicably, to surprise in himself the blossoming of an impossible perfection—as if I might, by chance, become what I will never be.

There is a moment in love when a man and woman must stand naked before each other. Without doubt the nakedness is clothed by desire and also, later, by habit. But this nakedness is part of love's destiny. To love, to commit oneself to the destiny of love, is to accept one day this encounter with nakedness. Now to stand naked is also to be stood naked, to offer oneself such as one is, in objectivity, and therefore somehow to renounce oneself. We never know in advance whether our nakedness will be saved and clothed again with the grace of desire. In nakedness there is necessarily a moment of sacrifice and *vice versa*: nakedness, in one mode or another, is an integral part of sacrifice.

It cannot happen otherwise for the love of self. In a certain manner, we need to be exposed to ourselves, to renounce our imperfection, that is, to accept it as such. Fallen man no longer has any other "property" than his decadence. He also refuses to be separated from it and watches over it jealously, free to accuse and condemn himself indefinitely so as to justify this jealous vigil. This is remorse, and this its illusion. I do not deny the difficulty of my analysis, but it stems from what man spontaneously thinks about with regard to the ego. All too easily the renunciation of one's own imperfections seems to imply a prideful desire for an inaccessible perfection, or seems to be the effect of a too scrupulous conscience. In reality, by virtue of the ego's illusory subjectivity, to renounce one's imperfection and to see oneself objectively, such as one is, are the two faces of one and the same conversion. Humility is objectivity first. It should not be humiliation, even and above all when it is ourselves whom we humiliate. So we need to stand naked in ourselves, to strip ourselves of egoic garments, to accept no longer watching over ourselves, to lose sight of ourselves. Doubtless, we cannot leave and turn our back on ourselves so as finally to face the sun without shivering and dying, because then we would no longer be there to cover ourselves.

The symbolism of the respective positions of the Virgin and Christ, both in His holy Infancy and in the Crucifixion, in this regard seems to be of the utmost importance. In many respects the Virgin represents the human psyche and Christ the Intellect, and therefore the true "I". The Virgin, the denuded and liberated soul, humility-made-creature, is always situated in Christian art behind the child Jesus, who never looks at Her. Only at the Crucifixion does Christ turn toward His Mother in the nakedness of His sacrifice. This means that the egoic illusion is the nakedness and the crucifixion of God within us; within us at every moment a God dies naked upon the cross of our ego. And yet it is at every moment and within ourselves that we must welcome Him, clothe Him, feed Him, and quench His thirst, just as He has commanded in the words of the Last Judgment. In Mary, the human soul contemplates upon the cross both the ultimate consequence of its sin, which is nothing less than the death of God, and the chief image of its destiny, which is nothing less than its own death. This is why the sacrifice of Christ prefigures and renders inevitable our own sacrifice, so that, according to a certain perspective, the story of Jesus retraces the human story in reverse order. What is at the beginning of Christ's life, the birth of the Word in the pure Marian substance, is at the end of our spiritual destiny in the grace of filial adoption *(theosis* or "deification"). What is at the term of His humanity, in His death upon the cross, is our birth to the truth of our nothingness. The birth of the Word is death for the ego; Christ's death upon the cross is our birth to the Spirit. From the viewpoint of temporal flow, this reversal shows that the end of our spiritual destiny is really an origin and that spirituality is therefore a return to the beginning, a veritable re-ascent of time back to its non-temporal source.

15

The Tao

Hieromonk Damascene

"The Valley and the Spirit do not die," said the Ancient Sage.
"They form what is called the Mystic Mother,
From whose gate comes the Origin of heaven and earth."
And "this gate shall be shut", said the Ancient Prophet.
"It shall not be opened, and no one shall pass through it;
For the Lord shall enter by it."

The Mind spoke, and through His Word
Answered the earth's elemental moan.
Above that roaring cry
He answered with a still, small voice:
I will come. Will you receive me, then?
But no man heard that voice.
Only a small young woman,
Who had lived, unknown, in silence and purity
in the Great Temple,
Was given to hear it.
And in a still, small voice She gave voice to the whole earth.
She answered for all those beings and created forms
who could not speak,
She answered for all the people who could not hear.

Hieromonk Damascene [Christensen] (1961-) is a priest-monk of the Russian Orthodox Church. The "Ancient Sage" in this selection is Lao Tzu, author of the Chinese sacred text the *Tao Te Ching*; the two references to the "Ancient Prophet" correspond respectively to the prophets Ezekiel and Daniel.

And to the question of the Uncreated Mind,
She answered: Yes, I will receive You.
Be it unto me according to Your Word.

In Her the Way had found the lowest place
in the entire earth—
The nadir of the Valley,
The supreme humility, lowliness—
And there He came and made His abode.
He took flesh of Her whom He loved above all others
who dwelled on the earth,
Who was meek and humble like Himself.
And lowering Himself, emptying Himself, in His love,
to the lowest place,
He became a tiny child within Her, the Mystic Mother.

Because of Her profound and intangible humility,
Her gate, opened by no man,
Through which no one had passed,
Became the gate from which came
the Origin of heaven and earth.
Because She had returned to the state of the uncarved
block, the pristine simplicity,
She became the "mountain unhewn by the hand of man"
Whom the Ancient Prophet had foretold.
And the Spirit, the Breath of Heaven,
Rested upon Her, the Valley of humility, as He had upon the
first-formed world.

"Water", said the Ancient Sage, "greatly benefits all things
But does not compete with them.
It dwells in lowly places that all disdain,
and so it is like the Way."
The Way came down and emptied Himself in a lowly cave:
Not amidst human dwellings,
but in the home of lowly animals.
Born on a lowly bed, dirty straw strewn on the ground.

Happy, prosperous people slept in soft beds in the nearby
inn.
But while other infants wept that night, He was silent.
And the sheep bleated like rippling water.

All the way down
To where you no longer calculate and think,
And care not what others think.
All, all the way down
To where you have nothing to lose,
Nowhere to go, nowhere to hide.
This is the point of emptiness.

"Emptiness penetrates the impenetrable,"
said the Ancient Sage.
"The softest things in the world overcome the hardest.
Through this I know the benefit of acting without desire."

Acting without desire,
You will see a flash of the beauty you had forgotten
From when you were a little child.

A little child does not calculate.
Humble, he has not yet formed the desires
which break the original unity and harmony.
Soft and yielding like water, his mind is therefore boundless.
Spontaneous, he accepts without thought the Course
that all things follow.

Therefore the Ancient Sage, follower of the Way, said:
"One who possesses abundant virtue resembles an infant
child.
This is the consummation of harmony."
And the Way, when He took flesh, said:
"Whoever shall humble himself as this little child,
The same is the greatest in the kingdom of heaven."

Again the Ancient Sage said:

"Controlling the breath to make it gentle,
One can be as a little child.
Then, when desires arise,
One can put them to death with the Way:
The Way of nameless Simplicity."

Descending with the mind into the secret place of the heart,
And gently checking the breath,
Followers of the Way now call upon the Name of Him
who had once been nameless.
And the Way, who took flesh,
Puts to death all the passions of their flesh—
All pride, ambition, rancor, and resentment—
Purifying their hearts,
Re-creating them in His image,
The image of a pure and innocent child,
The image of the nameless Simplicity.

16

Go Not but Stay

St Francis of Sales

We may well believe that the most sacred Virgin, our Lady, received so much pleasure in carrying Her little Jesus in Her arms that delight beguiled weariness, or at least made it agreeable. For if a branch of agnus castus can solace and unweary travelers, what solace did not the glorious Mother receive in carrying the immaculate Lamb of God? And though She permitted Him now and then to run on foot by Her, She holding Him by the hand, yet this was not because She would not rather have had Him hanging about Her neck and on Her breast, but it was to teach Him to form His steps and walk alone.

We ourselves, as little children of the heavenly Father, may walk with Him in two ways. For we may in the first place walk with the steps of our own will which we conform to His, holding always with the hand of our obedience the hand of His Divine intention, and following it wherever it leads—which is what God requires from us by the significance of His will; for since He wills me to do what He ordains, He wills me to have the will to do it. God has signified that He wills me to keep holy the day of rest; since He wills me to do it, He wills then that I will do it, and for this end I should have a will of my own by which I follow His, conforming myself and corresponding to His. But we may on other occasions walk with our Savior without any will of our

---

St Francis of Sales (1567-1622), Bishop of Geneva from 1602, was a leading figure in the Counter-Reformation. Proclaimed a Doctor of the Church by Pope Pius IX, he was a noted preacher and the founder of the Visitation Order. His most important spiritual writings are *Introduction to the Devout Life* and *Treatise on the Love of God*.

own, letting ourselves simply be carried at His Divine good-pleasure, as a little child in its mother's arms, by a certain kind of consent which may be termed union, or rather unity, of our heart with God's. And this is the way that we are to endeavor to comport ourselves in God's will of good-pleasure since the effects of this will of good-pleasure proceed purely from His Providence, and we do not effect them, but they happen to us. True it is we may will them to come according to God's will, and this willing is excellent; yet we may also receive the events of heaven's good-pleasure by a most simple tranquility of our will, which, willing nothing whatever, simply acquiesces in all that God would have done in us, on us, or by us.

If one had asked the sweet Jesus, when He was carried in His Mother's arms, whither He was going, might He not with good reason have answered, "I go not; it is My Mother that goes for Me." And if one had said to Him, "But at least do you not go with Your Mother?", might He not reasonably have replied, "No, I do not go, or if I go whither My Mother carries Me, I do not Myself walk with Her nor by My own steps, but by My Mother's, by Her and in Her." But if one had persisted with Him, saying, "But at least, O most dear Divine Child, You really will to let Yourself be carried by Your sweet Mother?", "No, verily," might He have said, "I will nothing of all this, but as My entirely good Mother walks for Me, so She wills for Me; I leave Her the care as well to go as to will to go for Me where She likes best; and as I go not but by Her steps, so I will not but by Her will. And from the instant I find Myself in Her arms, I give no attention either to willing or not willing, turning all other cares over to My Mother, save only the care to be on Her bosom, to suck Her sacred breasts, and keep myself close-clasped to Her most beloved neck, that I may most lovingly kiss Her with all the kisses of My mouth. And be it known to you that while I am amidst the delights of these holy caresses which surpass all sweetness, I consider My Mother as a tree of life and Myself on Her as its fruit; and I am of Her own heart in Her breast or Her soul in the midst of Her heart, so that as Her going serves both Her and Me without My troubling Myself to take a single step, so Her will serves us both without My producing any act of My will about going or coming. Nor do I ever take notice whether She goes fast or slow, hither or thither, nor do I inquire whither She means to go, contenting Myself with this, that go whither She please I go still locked in Her arms, close-laid to Her beloved breasts where I feed as amongst the lilies."

Go then soul, O most amiable dear little babe, or rather go not but stay, thus holily fastened to your sweet Mother's breasts. Go always in Her and never be without Her whilst you remain a child.

III

Purity

Blessed are the pure in heart,
for they shall see God.

Matthew 5:8

The Center of the Soul

William Law

The greatest part of mankind—nay, of Christians—may be said to be asleep, and that particular way of life which takes up each man's mind, thoughts, and actions may be very well called his particular dream.

This degree of vanity is equally visible in every form and order of life. The learned and the ignorant, the rich and the poor, are all in the same state of slumber, only passing away a short life in a different kind of dream. But why so? It is because man has an eternity within him, is born into this world, not for the sake of living here, not for anything this world can give him, but only to have time and place to become either an eternal partaker of a Divine life with God or to have a hellish eternity among fallen angels. And therefore, every man who has not his eye, his heart, and his hands continually governed by this twofold eternity may be justly said to be fast asleep—to have no awakened sensibility of himself. And a life devoted to the interests and enjoyments of this world, spent and wasted in the slavery of earthly desires, may be truly called a dream, as having all the shortness, vanity, and delusion of a dream; only with this great difference, that when a dream is over nothing is lost but fictions and fancies; but when the dream of life is ended only by

William Law (1686-1761) was an Anglican non-juror and spiritual writer who was much influenced by St Thomas à Kempis (see p. 16), John of Ruysbroeck (p. 219), John Tauler (p. 189), and—in later years—Jakob Boehme (p. 5), and who in turn contributed to the theological formation of such major figures as John Wesley, George Whitefield, and Samuel Johnson. This reading is drawn from Law's *Spirit of Prayer*.

death, all that eternity is lost, for which we were brought into being.

There is no misery in this world, nothing that makes either the life or death of man to be full of calamity, but this blindness and insensibility of his state, into which he so willingly—nay, obstinately—plunges himself. Everything that has the nature of evil and distress in it takes its rise from hence. Do but suppose a man to know himself that he comes into this world on no other errand but to rise out of the vanity of time into the riches of eternity; do but suppose him to govern his inward thoughts and outward actions by this view of himself, and then to him every day has lost all its evil; prosperity and adversity have no difference, because he receives and uses them both in the same spirit; life and death are equally welcome, because they are equally parts of his way to eternity. For poor and miserable as this life is, we have all of us free access to all that is great and good and happy, and carry within ourselves a key to all the treasures that heaven has to bestow upon us. We starve in the midst of plenty, groan under infirmities, with the remedy in our own hand; live and die without knowing and feeling anything of the one only Good, whilst we have it in our power to know and enjoy it in as great a reality as we know and feel the power of this world over us; for heaven is as near to our souls as this world is to our bodies; and we are created, we are redeemed, to have our conversation in it.

Consider the treasure thou hast within thee: the Savior of the world, the eternal Word of God, lies hid in thee, as a spark of the Divine nature which is to overcome sin and death and hell within thee, and generate the life of heaven again in thy soul. Turn to thy heart, and thy heart will find its Savior, its God within itself. Thou seest, hearest, and feelest nothing of God because thou seekest for Him abroad with thy outward eyes; thou seekest for Him in books, in controversies, in the church, and outward exercises, but there thou wilt not find Him till thou hast first found Him in thy heart. Seek for Him in thy heart, and thou wilt never seek in vain, for there He dwells—there is the seat of His Light and Holy Spirit.

This turning to the Light and Spirit of God within thee is thy only true turning unto God; there is no other way of finding Him but in that place where He dwells in thee. For though God be everywhere present, yet He is only present to thee in the deepest and most central part of thy soul. Thy natural senses cannot possess God or unite thee to Him; nay, thy inward faculties of understanding, will, and memory can only reach after God, but cannot be the place of His habitation in thee. But there is a root or depth in thee from whence all these faculties come forth, as lines from a center or as branches from the body of the tree. This depth is called the center, the *fund* or bottom of the soul. This depth is the unity, the eternity—I had almost said the infinity—of thy soul; for it is so infinite that nothing can satisfy it or give it any rest but the infinity of God. In this depth of the soul the Holy Trinity brought forth its own living image in the first created man, bearing in himself a living representation of Father, Son, and Holy Ghost, and this was his dwelling in God and God in him. This was the kingdom of God within him, and made Paradise without him. But the day that Adam did eat of the forbidden earthly tree, in that day he absolutely died to this kingdom of God within him. This depth or center of his soul, having lost its God, was shut up in death and darkness and became a prisoner in an earthly animal that only excelled its brethren, the beasts, in an upright form and serpentine subtlety. Thus ended the fall of man. But from that moment that the God of mercy inspoke into Adam the Bruiser of the Serpent, from that moment all the riches and treasures of the Divine nature came again into man, as a seed of salvation sown into the center of the soul, and only lies hidden there in every man till he desires to rise from his fallen state and to be born again from above.

Awake, then, thou that sleepest, and Christ, who from all eternity has been espoused to thy soul, shall give thee light. Begin to search and dig in thine own field for this pearl of eternity that lies hidden in it; it cannot cost thee too much, nor canst thou buy it too dear, for it is all; and when thou hast found it thou wilt know that all which thou hast sold or given away for it is as mere a nothing as a bubble upon the water.

18

True Prayer

Evagrios the Solitary

When you pray, keep your memory under close custody. Do not let it suggest your own fancies to you, but rather have it convey the awareness of your reaching out to God. Remember this—the memory has a powerful proclivity for causing detriment to the spirit at the time of prayer.

Whether you pray along with the brethren or alone, strive to make your prayer more than a mere habit. Make it a true inner experience.

We seek after virtues for the sake of attaining to the inner meaning of created things. We pursue these latter, that is, the inner meaning of what is created, for the sake of attaining to the Lord who has created them. It is in the state of prayer that He is accustomed to manifest Himself.

The state of prayer can be aptly described as a habitual state of imperturbable calm or *apatheia*. It snatches to the heights of intelligible reality the spirit which loves wisdom and which is truly spiritualized by the most intense love.

Evagrios the Solitary (346-99), also known as Evagrius Ponticus, spent much of his life among the Desert Fathers of Egypt (see p. 21), whose rigorous asceticism and complete detachment from worldly affairs he much admired. Although he was later condemned for certain speculative views derived from the teaching of Origen (p. 213), his practical teachings on the life of prayer were of decisive influence on subsequent spiritual authorities, notably his disciple St John Cassian, who transmitted his master's method to the Latin West. These aphorisms come from his *Chapters on Prayer*. The Greek term *apatheia* means "dispassion".

The man who strives after true prayer not only must learn to master anger and his lust, but must free himself from every thought that is colored by passion.

One who has become free of disturbing passion does not necessarily truly pray. It is quite possible for a man to have none but the purest thoughts and yet be so distracted mulling over them that he remains far removed from God.

Even when the spirit does avoid getting involved with these simple thoughts of things, it does not by that fact alone attain to the place of prayer. It may get involved in the contemplation of objects and waste time in considering their inner nature. For even though these concepts are simple, considerations of real things that they are, they do impress a certain form on the spirit and draw one far away from God.

Even if the spirit should rise above the contemplation of corporeal nature, still it does not as yet see the perfect place of God. For it might well be engaged in the contemplation of intelligible things and partake of their multiplicity.

A man who worships "in spirit and truth" (John 4:24) no longer honors the Creator because of His works, but praises Him because of Himself.

If you are a theologian, you truly pray. If you truly pray, you are a theologian.

When, because of your ardent longing for God, your spirit withdraws little by little from the flesh and turns away from every thought that derives from sensibility or memory or temperament and is filled with reverence and joy at the same time, then you can be sure that you are drawing near that country whose name is prayer.

Whereas others derive their reasonings and ideas and principles from the changing states of the body, yet God does the contrary. He descends upon the spirit itself and infuses His knowledge into it as He pleases. Calm peace He brings to the body's disturbed state through the spirit.

If you long to pray, then avoid all that is opposed to prayer. Then when God draws near He has only to go along with you.

When you are praying do not fancy the Divinity like some image formed within yourself. Avoid also allowing your spirit to be impressed with the seal of some particular shape, but rather, free from all matter, draw near the immaterial Being, and you will attain understanding.

You will not be able to pray purely if you are all involved with material affairs and agitated with unremitting concerns. For prayer is the rejection of concepts.

Knowledge! The great possession of man. It is a fellow-worker with prayer, acting to awaken the power of thought to contemplate the Divine knowledge.

Just as bread is nourishment for the body and virtue for the soul, so is spiritual prayer nourishment for the intelligence.

By true prayer a monk becomes another angel, for he ardently longs to see the face of the Father in heaven.

Do not by any means strive to fashion some image or visualize some form at the time of prayer.

Do not cherish the desire to see sensibly angels or powers or even Christ, lest you be led completely out of your wits, and taking a wolf for your shepherd, come to adore the demons who are your enemies.

Let me repeat this saying of mine that I have expressed on some other occasions: happy is the spirit that attains to perfect formlessness at the time of prayer.

Happy is the spirit that becomes free of all matter and is stripped of all at the time of prayer.

Happy is the spirit that attains to complete unconsciousness of all sensible experience at the time of prayer.

Happy is the man who considers all men as god—after God.

Let the virtues that deal with the body be a pledge of the virtues of the soul, and those of the soul a pledge of those dealing with the spirit, and these latter a pledge of immaterial knowledge.

Do you wish to pray? Then banish the things of this world. Have heaven for your homeland and live there constantly—not in mere word but in actions that imitate the angels and in a more godlike knowledge.

When attention seeks prayer it finds it. For if there is anything that marches in the train of attention it is prayer; and so it must be cultivated.

19

The Tabernacle of the Covenant

Richard of St Victor

By the tabernacle of the covenant
we understand the state of perfection.

Where perfection of the soul is,
there also is the habitation of God.

The more the mind approaches perfection,
the more closely it is joined in a covenant with God.

However, the tabernacle itself
ought to have an atrium round about it.

By atrium we understand discipline of the body;
by tabernacle we understand discipline of the mind.

Where exterior discipline is lacking,
interior discipline certainly cannot be observed.

But on the other hand, without discipline of the mind,
discipline of the body is certainly not beneficial.

Richard of St Victor (d. 1173) came as a young man to the Abbey of St Victor in Paris, where he was made prior in 1162. Noted for an important treatise on the Trinity, he also devoted much of his work to an anagogical or mystical exegesis of Scripture, as in his *Mystical Ark*, where he interprets the esoteric significance of the "pattern of the tabernacle, and the pattern of all the instruments thereof", as described in Exodus 25.

An atrium lies uncovered under the open sky;
discipline of the body is open for all to see.

Those things which are in the tabernacle
are not open to the outside.

No one knows what belongs to the inner person
except the spirit that is in him.

The nature of the inner person is divided
into a rational and an intellectual nature.

The rational is understood by the exterior tabernacle,
but the intellectual is understood by the interior tabernacle.

We call the rational sense
that by which we discern the things of our self;

In this place we call the intellectual sense that by which
we are raised up to the speculation of Divine things.

A person goes out from the tabernacle into the atrium
through the exercise of work.

A person enters into the first tabernacle
when he returns to himself.

A person enters into the second tabernacle
when he goes beyond himself.

When going beyond himself,
surely a person is elevated to God.

A person remains in the first tabernacle
by consideration of himself;
in the second, by contemplation of God.

Behold, concerning the atrium, the first tabernacle
and the second: these places had five things
for sanctification.

The atrium had only one thing,
so also the second tabernacle.
The first tabernacle had the remaining three.

In the atrium of the tabernacle was
the altar of burnt offering.

In the first tabernacle were
the candelabrum, the table, and the altar of incense.

In the interior tabernacle was
the Ark of the Covenant.

The exterior altar is affliction of the body;
the interior altar is contrition of the mind.

The candelabrum is the grace of discretion;
the table is the teaching of sacred reading.

By the Ark of the Covenant
we understand the grace of contemplation.

On the exterior altar the bodies of animals were burned up;
by affliction of the body carnal longings are annihilated.

On the interior altar aromatic smoke was offered
to the Lord; by contrition of heart the flame
of celestial longings is kindled.

A candelabrum is a holder for lights;
discretion is the lamp of the inner person.

On the table bread is placed;
by it those who are hungry may be refreshed.

Purity

However, sacred reading certainly is
the refreshment of the soul.

An ark is a secret place for gold and silver;
the grace of contemplation lays hold of the treasury
of celestial Wisdom.

20

Rank upon Rank

St Clement of Alexandria

eing the power of the Father, the Son of God easily prevails over whomsoever He will, not leaving even the smallest atom of His government uncared for: else the universe of His creation would have been no longer good. And I think the greatest power is shown where there is an inspection of all the parts, proceeding with minute accuracy even to the smallest, while all gaze on the supreme Administrator of the universe, as He pilots all in safety according to the Father's will, rank being subordinated to rank under different leaders, till in the end the great High Priest is reached. For on one original principle, which works in accordance with the Father's will, depend the first and second and third gradations; and then at the extreme end of the invisible world, there is the blessed ordinance of angels; and so, even down to ourselves, ranks below ranks are appointed, all saving and being saved by the initiation and through the instrumentality of the One. Just as the remotest particle of iron is drawn by the influence of the magnet extending through a long series of iron rings, so also through the attraction of the Holy Spirit, the virtuous are adapted to the highest rank, and the others in their order even to the last rank: but they that are wicked from weakness, having fallen into an

---

St Clement of Alexandria (*c.* 150 - *c.* 215) was head of the famous Catechetical School of that city, the first Christian university. Taking to heart the Gospel teaching: "This is eternal life, that they know Thee the only true God, and Jesus Christ whom Thou hast sent" (John 17:3), he regarded knowledge or *gnosis*, based upon faith and virtue, as the distinguishing mark of final union with God. This selection comes from his treatise *On Spiritual Perfection.*

evil habit owing to unrighteous greed, neither keep hold themselves nor are held by another, but collapse and fall to the ground, being entangled in their passions. For this is the law from the beginning, that he who would have virtue must choose it.

It was for this reason that both the commandments according to the law and the commandments previous to the law given to those who were not yet under law—for law is not enacted for a just man—ordained that he who chose should obtain eternal life and a blessed reward, and on the other hand permitted him who delighted in wickedness to consort with what he chose. Again they ordained that the soul that at any time improved as regards the knowledge of virtue and increase in righteousness should obtain an improved position in the universe, pressing onwards at every step to a passionless state, until it comes to a perfect man, a pre-eminence at once of knowledge and of inheritance. These saving revolutions are each severally portioned off, according to the order of change and by variety of time and place and honor and knowledge and inheritance and service, up to the transcendent orbit which is next to the Lord, which is occupied in eternal contemplation. And that which is lovely has power to draw to contemplation of itself everyone who through love of knowledge has applied himself wholly to contemplation.

Accordingly He made all things to be helpful for virtue, insofar as might be without hindering the freedom of man's choice, and showed them to be so, in order that He who is indeed the only Almighty might, even to those who can see only darkly, be in some way revealed as a good God, a Savior from age to age through the instrumentality of His Son, and in all ways absolutely guiltless of evil. For by the Lord of the universe all things are ordered both generally and particularly with a view to the safety of the whole. It is the work then of saving righteousness always to promote the improvement of each according to the possibilities of the case. For the lesser things also are managed with a view to the safety and continuance of the superior in accordance with their own characters. Whatever is possessed of virtue changes to better habitations, the cause of the change being that independent choice of knowledge with which the soul was gifted to begin with; but those who are more hardened are constrained to repent by necessary chastisements, inflicted either through the agency of the attendant angels or through various preliminary judgments or through the great and final judgment, by the goodness of the great Judge whose eye is ever upon us.

As to the rest I keep silent, giving glory to God: only I say that the gnostic souls are so carried away by the magnificence of the vision that they cannot confine themselves within the lines of the constitution by which each holy degree is assigned and in accordance with which the blessed abodes of the gods have been marked out and allotted; but being counted as holy among the holy, and translated absolutely and entirely to another sphere, they keep on always moving to higher and yet higher regions, until they no longer greet the Divine vision in or by means of mirrors, but feast forever on the uncloying, never-ending sight, radiant in its transparent clearness, while throughout the endless ages they taste a never-wearying delight, and thus continue all alike honored with an identity of pre-eminence. This is the apprehensive vision of the pure in heart. This, therefore, is the life-work of the perfected gnostic: namely, to hold communion with God through the great High Priest, being made like the Lord as far as may be, by means of all his service towards God, a service which extends to the salvation of men by his solicitous goodness towards us and also by public worship and by teaching and active kindness. And in being thus assimilated to God, the gnostic is making and fashioning himself and also forming those who hear him, while, so far as may be, he assimilates to That which is by nature free from passion that which has been subdued by training to a passionless state.

21

Ignorance Is Bliss

Nicholas of Cusa

Fire is ever aglow, and so likewise is that yearning love which is directed toward You, O God, who are the form of all that is desirable and that truth which in every desire is desired.

Because I have begun to taste of Your honeysweet giving, Your sweetness beyond understanding—which pleases me all the more as it appears to me more and more limitless—I perceive that the reason You are unknown to all creatures is that they may have in this Divine ignorance a greater rest, just as in a treasure beyond reckoning and inexhaustible. For he who finds a treasure that he knows to be utterly beyond reckoning and unlimited is moved by a far greater joy than he who finds one that may be counted and that is limited. Hence the Divine ignorance of Your greatness is the most desirable nourishment for my intellect.

O Fount of riches, You will to be held in my possession and yet to abide incomprehensible and infinite, for You are the treasury of delights of which no man can desire an end. How should desire covet not-being? For whether the will covets being or not-being, desire itself cannot rest, but is carried along into infinity. You descend, O Lord, that You may be comprehended,

---

Nicholas of Cusa (1401-64) was a German theologian, philosopher, and cardinal of the Roman Catholic Church. In his *Vision of God*, he presents the Supreme Reality as a *coincidentia oppositorum* or "coincidence of opposites", which can be fittingly approached only by the person who deliberately cultivates a state of *ignorantia docta* or "learned ignorance". Like Socrates, he knew that the greatest knowledge consists in recognizing that one really knows nothing.

and yet You continue to be beyond reckoning and infinite; and unless You did continue as infinite, You would not be the end of desire. Therefore, You are infinite that You may be the end of all desire.

Desire does not turn itself toward what can be greater or more desirable. But all on this side of infinity may be greater. The end of desire is therefore infinite. Thus You are truly Infinity, O God, for which alone I yearn in every desire, but to the knowledge of which I cannot approach more nearly than that I know it to be infinite. Therefore, the more I understand that You are not to be understood, the more I attain You, because the more I attain the end of my desire. Accordingly I reject as delusion any idea occurring to me which seeks to show You as comprehensible. My yearning, bright with You, leads me unto You; it spurns all that is finite and comprehensible, for in these it cannot rest, being led by You to You. You are beginning without beginning and end without end. Therefore, my desire is led by the eternal beginning, from whom it comes to be desire, unto the end without end, and He is infinite. If then I, a poor little man, could not be content with You, my God, if I knew You to be comprehensible, it is because I am led by You to You, who are incomprehensible and infinite.

I behold You, my God, in a kind of mental trance, for if sight is not satisfied with seeing, nor the ear with hearing, then much less is the intellect with understanding. Accordingly, that which satisfies the intellect, or which is its end, is not that which it understands; neither can that satisfy it which it does not at all understand, but that alone which it understands by not under-standing. For the intelligible which it knows does not satisfy it, nor the intelligible of which it is utterly ignorant, but only the intelligible which it knows to be so intelligible that it can never be fully understood—it is this alone which can satisfy it. Even so a man's insatiable hunger cannot be appeased by partaking of scanty food or by food that is out of his reach, but only by food that is within his reach, and which, though it be continuously partaken of, can never be utterly consumed, since it is such that by eating it is not diminished.

22

Opening the Tomb

St Maximos the Confessor

The Lord's tomb stands equally either for this world or for the heart of each faithful Christian. The linen clothes are the inner essences of sensible things together with their qualities of goodness. The napkin is the simple and homogeneous knowledge of intelligible realities together with the vision of God insofar as it is granted. Through these things the Logos is initially recognized, for without them any higher apprehension of what He is would be altogether beyond our capacity.

Those who bury the Lord with honor will also see Him raised with glory, but He is not seen by anyone else. For He can no longer be apprehended by His enemies, as He does not wear those outer coverings through which He seemed to let Himself be captured by those who sought Him, and in which He endured suffering for the salvation of all. He who buries the Lord with honor is revered by all who love God. For he has not allowed the Lord's body, nailed to the cross, to be left exposed to the blasphemy of unbelievers, but has befittingly delivered Him from derision and insult. Those who sealed the tomb and

---

St Maximos the Confessor (580-662) was one of the greatest and most prolific of Orthodox ascetical and mystical writers. A monk and later abbot of the monastery of Philippikos near Constantinople, he played a leading role in opposing the heresy of monotheletism, which contends that Christ did not possess a human will and which thus subverts, in the view of St Maximos, the full reality of man's deification in Christ. Because of his outspoken views on this matter, he was arrested, tortured, and sent into exile—hence his epithet "the Confessor"—only to have his teaching confirmed posthumously by the Sixth Ecumenical Council. This passage comes from his "First Century on Theology and the Incarnate Dispensation of the Son of God".

set soldiers to watch (Matt. 27:66) are hateful because of their scheming. When the Logos had risen, they slandered Him, saying that His body had been stolen away. In the same way that they bribed the false disciple with silver to betray the Lord—by false disciple I mean a pretense of holiness for the sake of display—so they bribed the soldiers to make a false accusation against the risen Savior.

Whoever possesses spiritual knowledge knows the significance of what has been said, for he is not ignorant of how and in how many ways the Lord is crucified, buried, and rises again. Such a person makes corpses, as it were, of the impassioned thoughts which have been insinuated by the demons into his heart, and which through the temptations they suggest cut in pieces the qualities of moral beauty as if they were garments (Matt. 27:35); and he breaks like seals the impressions stamped deeply into his soul by the sins of prepossession.

Whenever a lover of riches who feigns virtue by an outward show of devotion finds he has procured the material possessions he desires, he repudiates the way of life that made people think he was a disciple of the Logos. When you see arrogant men not able to endure praise being given to others better than they, and contriving to suppress the truth by denying it with countless insinuations and baseless slanders, you must understand that the Lord is again crucified by these men and buried and guarded with soldiers and seals. But the Logos rises afresh and puts them to confusion. The more the Logos is attacked, the more clearly He reveals Himself as steeled in dispassion through His sufferings. The Logos is stronger than all else: not only is He called truth, but He is truth.

The mystery of the incarnation of the Logos is the key to all the arcane symbolism and typology in the Scripture, and in addition gives us knowledge of created things, both visible and intelligible. He who apprehends the mystery of the cross and the burial apprehends the inward essences of created things, while he who is initiated into the inexpressible power of the resurrection apprehends the purpose for which God first established everything. All visible realities need the cross, that is, the state in which they are cut off from things acting upon them through the senses. All intelligible realities need burial, that is, the total quiescence of the things which act upon them through the intellect. When all relationship with such things is severed, and their natural activity and stimulus is cut off, then the Logos, who exists alone in Himself, appears as if raised from the dead. He encompasses all that comes from Him, but nothing enjoys kinship with Him by virtue of natural relationship. For the salvation of the saved is by grace and not by nature (Eph. 2:5).

Ages, times, and places belong to the category of relationship, and consequently no object necessarily associated with these things can be other than relative. But God transcends the category of relationship, for nothing else whatsoever is necessarily associated with Him. Therefore if the inheritance of the saints is God Himself, he who is found worthy of this grace will be beyond all ages, times, and places: he will have God Himself as his place, in accordance with the text, "Be to me a God who is a defender and a fortified place of my salvation" (Ps. 71:3). The consummation bears no resemblance whatsoever to the intermediary state, for otherwise it would not be a consummation. The intermediary state consists of everything that is sequent to the origin but falls short of the consummation. But if all ages, times, and places, together with all that is necessarily associated with them, are sequent to God—since He is an unoriginate Origin—and also fall far short of God—since He is an infinite Consummation—then clearly they belong to the intermediary state. The consummation of those who are saved is God; in this supreme consummation no trace of the intermediary state will be observed in those who have been saved.

The whole world, limited as it is by its own inner principles, is called both the place and age of those dwelling in it. There are modes of contemplation natural to it which are able to engender in created beings a partial understanding of the wisdom of God that governs all things. So long as they make use of these modes to gain understanding, they cannot have more than a mediate and partial apprehension. But when what is perfect appears, what is partial is superseded: all mirrors and indistinct images pass away when truth is encountered face to face (1 Cor. 13:10-12). When he who is saved is perfected in

God, he will transcend all worlds, ages, and places in which hitherto he has been trained as a child.

So long as we only see the Logos of God as embodied multifariously in symbols in the letter of Holy Scripture, we have not yet achieved spiritual insight into the incorporeal, simple, single, and unique Father as He exists in the incorporeal, simple, single, and unique Son, according to the saying, "He who has seen Me has seen the Father . . . and I am in the Father and the Father in Me" (John 14:9-10). We need much knowledge so that, having first penetrated the veils of the sayings which cover the Logos, we may with a naked intellect see— insofar as men can—the pure Logos as He exists in Himself, clearly showing us the Father in Himself. Hence a person who seeks God with true devotion should not be dominated by the literal text, lest he unwittingly receive not God but things appertaining to God; that is, lest he feel a dangerous affection for the words of Scripture instead of for the Logos. For the Logos eludes the intellect which supposes that it has grasped the incorporeal Logos by means of His outer garments, like the Egyptian woman who seized hold of Joseph's garments instead of Joseph himself (Gen. 39:7-13), or like the ancients who were content merely with the beauty of visible things and mistakenly worshipped the creation instead of the Creator (Rom. 1:25).

It is by means of the more lofty conceptual images that the inner principle of Holy Scripture can be stripped gradually of the complex garment of words with which it is physically draped. Then to the visionary intellect—the intellect which through the total abandonment of its natural activities is able to attain a glimpse of the simplicity that in some measure discloses this principle—it reveals itself as though in the sound of a delicate breeze. This was the case with Elijah, who was granted such a vision in the cave of Horeb (1 Kings 19:12). Horeb signifies fallow land just broken up, which is the firm possession of the virtues established through the new spirit of grace. The cave is the hidden sanctuary of wisdom within the intellect; he who enters it will mystically perceive the spiritual knowledge that is beyond perception, in which God is said to dwell. Therefore everyone who like Elijah truly seeks God will not only arrive at

Horeb—that is, not only will he through ascetic practice attain the state of virtue—but will also enter the cave at Horeb—that is, as a contemplative he will enter into that hidden sanctuary of wisdom found only by those who have attained the state of virtue.

When our intellect has shaken off its many opinions about created things, then the inner principle of truth appears clearly to it, providing it with a foundation of real knowledge and removing its former preconceptions as though removing scales from the eyes, as happened in the case of St Paul (Acts 9:18). For an understanding of Scripture that does not go beyond the literal meaning and a view of the sensible world that relies exclusively on sense-perception are indeed scales, blinding the soul's visionary faculty and preventing access to the pure Logos of truth.

23

The Virginal Paradise

St Louis Marie de Montfort

He who is deigned to come down to us who are not and turned our nothingness into God. He did this perfectly by giving and submitting Himself entirely to the young Virgin Mary without ceasing to be in time He who is from all eternity. Likewise it is through Mary that we who are nothing may become God by grace and glory. We accomplish this by giving ourselves to Her so perfectly and so completely as to remain nothing as far as self is concerned, and to be everything in Her without any fear of illusion.

There are some very sanctifying interior practices for those souls who feel called by the Holy Spirit to a high degree of perfection. They may be expressed in four words: doing everything through Mary, with Mary, in Mary, and for Mary, in order to do them more perfectly through Jesus, with Jesus, in Jesus, and for Jesus.

We must do everything *through* Mary, that is, we must obey Her always and be led in all things by Her spirit, which is the Holy Spirit of God. We should place and leave ourselves in Her virginal hands, like a tool in the hands of a craftsman or a lute in the hands of a good musician. We should cast ourselves into

---

St Louis Marie de Montfort (1673-1716) was a French priest and missionary who dedicated many of his sermons and much of his writing to promoting *True Devotion to the Blessed Virgin*, to refer to the title of the book from which this passage is taken. "Mary," he writes elsewhere in this popular work, "is entirely relative to God. Indeed, I would say that She is relative only to God, because She exists uniquely in reference to Him. She is an echo of God, speaking and repeating only *God*."

Her like a stone thrown into the sea. This is done easily and quickly by a mere thought, a slight movement of the will, or just a few words, such as: "I renounce myself and give myself to you, my dear Mother." And even if we do not experience any emotional fervor in this spiritual encounter, it is nonetheless real.

We must do everything *with* Mary, that is to say, in all our actions we must look upon Mary, although a simple human being, as the model of every virtue and perfection, fashioned by the Holy Spirit for us to imitate as far as our limited capacity allows. In every action, then, we should consider how Mary performed it or how She would perform it if She were in our place.

We must do everything *in* Mary. To understand this we must realize that the Blessed Virgin is the true earthly paradise of the new Adam and that the ancient paradise was only a symbol of Her. There are in this earthly paradise untold riches, beauties, rarities, and delights, which the new Adam, Jesus Christ, has left there. In this place the air is perfectly pure. There is no night, but only the brilliant day of the sacred humanity; the resplendent, spotless sun of the Divinity; the blazing furnace of love, melting all the base metal thrown into it and changing it into gold. We should be delighted to remain in Mary. We should rest there peacefully, rely on Her confidently, hide ourselves there with safety, and abandon ourselves unconditionally to Her, so that within Her virginal bosom we may be formed in our Lord and our Lord formed in us. For Her womb is the house of Divine secrets where Jesus and all the elect have been conceived.

Finally, we must do everything *for* Mary. Since we have given ourselves completely to Her service, it is only right that we should do everything for Her as if we were Her personal servant and slave. This does not mean that we take Her for the ultimate end of our service, for Jesus alone is our ultimate end. But we take Mary for our proximate end, our mysterious intermediary, and the easiest way of reaching Him. As a reward for these little services, we should expect nothing in return save the honor of belonging to such a lovable Queen and the joy of being united through Her to Jesus, Her Son, by a bond that is indissoluble in time and in eternity. Glory to Jesus in Mary! Glory to Mary in Jesus! Glory to God alone!

24

Clothed in Christ

St Symeon the New Theologian

Hear things that strike us dumb with awe: we become members of Christ, and Christ becomes our members. Christ is my hand and my lowly foot, and I am His own foot and hand. I move my hand, and Christ is all my hand, for God is indivisible in His Divinity. I move my foot, and behold it shines like Him.

Do not accuse me of blasphemy, but welcome these things and adore Christ, fulfilling Him in yourself. If you so wish, you will become a member of Christ, and so all of our members individually will become members of Christ and Christ our members, and all that is dishonorable in us He will make honorable by adorning it with His Divine beauty and glory. Living with God, we shall become gods, no longer seeing the shamefulness of our body at all, but made completely like Christ.

Well you recognized Christ in my hand and my foot, but in this other organ—did you not shudder or blush? God was not ashamed to become like you; are you ashamed to be like Him? "No," you reply, "I am not ashamed to be like Him, but when

---

St Symeon the New Theologian (949-1022) was the greatest of Byzantine mystical writers. In the Christian East, the title "theologian" signifies one who is able to speak about God on the basis of direct experience. Symeon is one of only three authorities who have been judged worthy of the epithet in the Orthodox Church, the other two being St John the Evangelist, author of the most esoteric of the Gospels, and St Gregory Nazianzos, one of the Cappadocian fathers and a gifted writer of contemplative poetry. The above reading is taken from the fifteenth of the *Hymns of Divine Love*, the other Symeon to whom the author refers—the "Studite" (*c.* 917-86)—was his spiritual master.

you said that He became like a shameful member, I feared that you were uttering a blasphemy." Well, you were wrong to fear, for there is nothing shameful. The hidden members of Christ, because one covers them, are for that reason more worthy of honor than the others, for they are the hidden members, invisible to all, of the One who is hidden, of the One who sows the seed in Divine union, Divine seed, made, amazingly, according to the image of God, born of Divinity itself. It is truly a marriage which takes place, ineffable and Divine: God unites Himself with each one, and each becomes one with the Master. If therefore in your body you have put on the total Christ, you will understand without blushing all that I am saying, but if you have done nothing about it, or if of the immaculate garment—I am speaking of Christ—you have put on only a small piece, it covers but one spot, and you are therefore ashamed of the remainder of your members.

When I utter these formidable words about holy members and with an enlightened mind consider all of their glory, I am filled with joy, without thinking of anything sensual. But you consider your own flesh, all soiled, and you run over your infamous actions where your mind ever crawls like a worm; that is why you project your shame on Christ and on me, saying: "Do you not blush at these shameful words, disparaging Christ by associating Him with shameful members?" But I say in my turn: "See Christ in the womb of His mother; picture to yourself the interior of this womb and Him escaping from it, and whence my God had to pass to come out of it." You will find there much more than what I have spoken about. He accepted all for our glory, so that no one would blush to imitate Him, or to say or to suffer himself what He suffered.

He became totally man, He truly totally God—He the Unique One, without division, perfect man without doubt, and the same One completely God in the totality of all His members. So there was, even now in these latter days, Symeon the saint, the pious one, the Studite. He did not blush before the members of anyone, neither to see other men naked, nor to show himself naked, for he possessed Christ completely, and he was completely Christ, and all his own members and the members of everyone else, all and each one, were always like Christ in his eyes: he remained motionless, unhurt, and impassive; he was all Christ himself, and as Christ he considered all the baptized, clothed with the whole of Christ. But you, if you are naked and your flesh touches flesh, you are in heat like a donkey or a horse. How do you dare then to speak against the saint and to blaspheme Christ, the One who united Himself with us and has given impassiveness to His holy servants? For He becomes a spouse—do you hear?—each day, and all the souls with whom the Creator unites Himself become spouses, and they in turn are united with Him in a wholly spiritual marriage. And even if He takes them dishonored, by uniting Himself with them He at once restores their integrity, and what was formerly soiled by corruption in their eyes is no longer anything but sanctity and incorruption, perfectly healed. They glorify the merciful One; they are in love with the most beautiful One. They are entirely united to His total love; or rather, by receiving His holy seed into themselves, they completely possess God, who has taken the form of man.

Does not what I say truly correspond with the Scriptures? But if you are clothed with the shamefulness of your flesh, if you have not bared your mind nor stripped your soul—if you have not succeeded in seeing the light, buried as you are in your darkness—what can I really do for you, how shall I show you the formidable mysteries? Let us therefore hasten by penance, since it is by it that all the expelled may return. There is no other way to enter into the interior or to see the mysteries which were accomplished there, and are still accomplished there even now and till the end of time in Christ, my God: to whom is due all glory, all honor, and all adoration, now and forever. Amen.

Illumination

IV

Clarity

The invisible things of God,
even His eternal power and
Godhead, are clearly seen in
the things that are made.

Romans 1:20

25

Two Ways

St Thomas Aquinas

𝕴t would seem that in the present state of life the contem-plative life can reach to the vision of the Divine Essence. For Jacob said: "I have seen God face to face, and my soul has been saved" (Gen. 32:30). Now the vision of God's face is the vision of the Divine Essence. Therefore it would seem that in the present life one may come, by means of contemplation, to see God in His Essence.

Further, Gregory says that "contemplative men withdraw within themselves in order to explore spiritual things, nor do they ever carry with them the shadows of things corporeal, or if these follow them they prudently drive them away: but being desirous of seeing the incomprehensible light, they suppress all the images of their limited comprehension, and through longing to reach what is above them, they overcome that which they are". Now man is not hindered from seeing the Divine Essence, which is the incomprehensible light, save by the necessity of turning to corporeal phantasms. Therefore it would seem

St Thomas Aquinas (*c.* 1225-74), the "Angelic Doctor", was a Dominican the-ologian and philosopher, often regarded as the most important Catholic teacher of all time. Well known for his Aristotelian premise that all human knowledge requires a basis in the physical senses and for his resulting convic-tion that the highest truths concerning God must be accepted on faith, he was nonetheless obliged by his trust in the Scriptures to admit an exception to this epistemological limit, and therefore the possibility of mystical or noetic vision, at least in the case of St Paul, who speaks of being "caught up into Paradise" and hearing "unspeakable words"—"whether in the body or out of the body, I cannot tell" (2 Cor. 12:3, 4). This selection is taken from St Thomas's *Summa Theologica.* Compare with "The Flight of the Eagle" (p. 233).

that the contemplation of the present life can extend to the vision of the incomprehensible light in its Essence.

And yet Gregory also says that "as long as we live in this mortal flesh, no one reaches such a height of contemplation as to fix the eyes of his mind on the ray itself of incomprehensible light". And Augustine says, "No one seeing God lives this mortal life in which the bodily senses have their play: and unless in some way he departs this life, whether by going altogether out of his body or by withdrawing from his carnal senses, he is not caught up into that vision."

Accordingly we must state that one may be in this life in two ways. First, with regard to act, that is, by actually making use of the bodily senses, and thus contemplation in the present life *cannot* attain to the vision of God's Essence. Secondly, one may be in this life potentially and not with regard to act, that is, when the soul is united to the mortal body as its form, and yet so as to make use neither of the bodily senses nor even of the imagination, as happens in rapture; and in this way the contemplation of the present life *can* attain to the vision of the Divine Essence. Consequently, the highest degree of contemplation in the present life is that which Paul had in rapture, whereby he was in a middle state between the present life and the life to come.

26

Dispelling Darkness

Boethius

here appeared standing over my head a Woman's form whose countenance was full of majesty, whose eyes shone as with fire and in power of insight surpassed the eyes of men, whose color was full of life, whose strength was yet intact, though She was so full of years that none would ever think Her subject to such age as ours. One could but doubt Her varying stature, for at one moment She repressed it to the common measure of a man, and at another She seemed to touch the very heavens with Her crown: and when She had raised higher Her head, it pierced even the sky and baffled the sight of those who would look upon it. Her clothing was wrought of the finest thread and was brought by subtle workmanship to an indivisible piece. This She had woven with Her own hands, as I afterwards did learn by Her own showing. Its beauty was somewhat dimmed by the dullness of long neglect, as is seen in the smoke-grimed masks of our ancestors. On the border below was inwoven the symbol Π; on that above was to be read a Θ. And between the two letters there could be marked degrees by which, as by the rungs of a ladder, ascent might be made.

Boethius (*c.* 480 - *c.* 524), canonized as St Severinus, was a philosopher, statesman, and master of the Seven Liberal Arts, including astronomy. His *Consolation of Philosophy*, from which this reading is taken, is one of the most popular and influential books in the history of Christian thought. The celestial Woman in this passage is the Lady Wisdom, whose seamless garment is marked at the bottom with the Greek letter Π for *Praxis* or Action and at the top with the letter Θ for *Theoria* or Contemplation.

For my part, my eyes were dimmed with tears, and I could not discern who this Woman was of such commanding power. I was amazed, and turning my eyes to the ground, I began in silence to await what She should do. Then She approached nearer and sat down upon the end of my couch: She looked into my face heavy with grief and cast down by sorrow to the ground, and then She spoke concerning the trouble of my mind in these words: "How blunted grows the mind when sunk below the overwhelming flood! Its own true light no longer burns within, and it would break forth to outer darkness. How often care, when fanned by earthly winds, grows to a larger and unmeasured bane. This man has been free beneath the open heaven: his habit has it been to wander into the paths of the sky: his to watch the light of the bright sun, his to inquire into the brightness of the chilly moon; he, like a conqueror, held fast-bound in its order every star that makes its wandering circle, turning its peculiar course. Deeply has he searched into the springs of nature, whence came the roaring blasts that ruffle the ocean's bosom calm: what is the spirit that makes the firmament revolve; wherefore does the evening star sink into the western wave but to rise from the radiant East; what is the cause which so tempers the season of Spring that it decks the earth with rose blossoms; whence comes it to pass that Autumn is prolific in the years of plenty and overflows with teeming vines: deeply to search these causes was his wont, and to bring forth secrets deep in nature hid. Now he lies there: extinct his reason's light, his neck in heavy chains thrust down, his countenance with grievous weight downcast, and the brute earth is all he can behold.

"But now," She said, "is the time for the physician's art rather than for complaining." Then fixing Her eyes wholly on me She said, "Are you the man who was nourished upon the milk of My learning, brought up with My food until you had won your way to the power of a manly soul? Surely I had given you such weapons as would keep you safe and your strength unconquered if you had not thrown them away. Do you know Me? Why do you keep silence? Are you dumb from shame or from dull amazement? I would it were from shame, but I see that amazement has overwhelmed you." When She saw that I was not only silent, but utterly tongue-tied and dumb, She put her hand gently upon my breast and said, "There is no danger: you are suffering from drowsiness, that disease which attacks so many minds which have been deceived. You have forgotten yourself for a moment and will quickly remember, as soon as you recognize Me. That you may do so, let me brush away from your eyes the darkening cloud of thoughts of matters perishable." So saying, She gathered Her robe into a fold and dried my swimming eyes. Then was dark night dispelled, the shadows fled away, and my eyes received returning power as before. It was just as when the heavenly bodies are enveloped by the west wind's rush and the sky stands thick with watery clouds; the sun is hidden and the stars are not yet come into the sky, and night descending from above overspreads the earth: but if the north wind smites this scene, launched forth from the Thracian cave, it unlocks the imprisoned daylight; the sun shines forth, and thus sparkling Phoebus smites with his rays our wondering eyes.

27

Leading Strings

François Fénelon

The forgetfulness of self of which we often speak does not keep souls who want wholeheartedly to seek God from being thankful for His gifts. For this reason: this forgetting does not mean never seeing anything in relation to ourselves, but only never staying shut up within ourselves, concerned with our blessings or our troubles simply from the point of view of our own possessions or welfare. It is this preoccupation with ourselves which keeps us from love pure and simple, which contracts our hearts, and which turns us from our true perfection, because it makes us seek it with pressure, trouble, and uneasiness for love of ourselves.

The vision of God which we seek often results in a new view of ourselves. It is like a man who looks at another behind whom there is a great mirror. In considering the other, he sees himself and discovers himself without intending to. Thus it is in the pure light of God that we see ourselves clearly. The presence of God, when it is pure, simple, and sustained by a true faithfulness of soul and the most strict vigilance over ourselves, is this great mirror in which we discern even the least stain on our soul. A peasant shut up in his village only partially knows his wretch-

---

François de Salignac de La Mothe Fénelon (1651-1715) was Archbishop of Cambrai and a popular spiritual director. His views concerning the soul's passivity in the hands of God and his defense of Madame Guyon's quietist teachings led to attacks on his own position. But it is very clear in this passage from *Christian Perfection* that, in his view, not all are called to a state of complete indifference, while sincere gratitude for God's blessings, however much it may stem from a certain kind of self-interest, is a necessary part of spiritual growth.

edness, but let him see rich palaces, a superb court, and he will realize all the poverty of his village. He cannot endure its hovels after a sight of so much magnificence. It is thus that we see our ugliness and worthlessness in the beauty and the infinite grandeur of God.

Show as much as you please of the vanity and nothingness of the creature by the faults of creatures. Call to notice the brevity and uncertainty of life, the fickleness of fortune, the faithlessness of friends, the illusion of great places, the bitterness which is inevitable there, the disappointment of the most beautiful hopes, the emptiness of all the good things we possess, the reality of all the evils we suffer: all this moralizing, true and reasonable as it is, only skims the heart. It does not sink in. The inner man is not changed at all. He sighs to see himself a slave to vanity, and does not get out of his slavery. But if the ray of the Divine light shines within, he sees the abyss of good which is God. He renounces himself. He gives himself up to God. He loses himself in Him. Happy loss! For then he finds himself without seeking. He has no more interest in his own affairs, and everything prospers with him, because everything turns to good for those who love God. He sees the mercy which comes into this abyss of weakness, of nothing, and of sin. He sees, and he is content with the sight.

As the entire detachment of the will is very rare in this life, there are hardly any souls who do not still regard the mercies they have received in relation to the fruits which they receive from them for their own salvation. Thus these souls, although they intend to have no self-interest, still do not cease to be very sensitive to this great interest. They are delighted to see an all-powerful hand which has snatched them from themselves, delivered them from their own desires, broken their chains when they thought they were only going deeper into bondage, and saved them, so to speak, in spite of themselves. The entirely pure and detached souls, such as are those of the saints in heaven, regard the mercies shed on others with as much love and satisfaction as they do the mercies which they themselves have received. For not considering themselves at all, they love God's good-pleasure, the riches of His grace, and the glory which He derives from the sanctification of another as much as that which He derives from their own sanctification. Everything is the same then, because the "I" is lost and annihilated; the "I" is no more myself than another. It is God alone who is all in all. It is He alone whom we love, whom we admire, and who makes all the joy of our hearts in this heavenly and disinterested love. We are enraptured by His mercies, not for love of self, but for love of Him. We thank Him for having performed His will and for having glorified Himself, as we ask Him in the "Our Father" that He carry out His will and glorify His name. In this state, it is not for ourselves that we thank Him.

But waiting for this happy state, the soul clinging still to self is touched by this remainder of reversion to self. All that there still is of this reversion stirs a lively thankfulness. This thankfulness is a love still slightly mixed and bent back toward self; whereas the thankfulness of the souls lost in God, such as those of the saints, is an immense love, a love without any coming back to self-interest, a love as transported by the mercy shown to others as by the mercy shown to their own selves—a love which admires and receives the gifts of God only for the pure interest and glory of God Himself. But as nothing is more dangerous than to go beyond the limits of our state, nothing would be more harmful to a soul who needs to be upheld by feelings of gratitude than to deprive itself of this nourishment suited to it, and to run after ideas of a higher perfection for which it is not ready. When the soul is touched by the memory of all that God has done for it, it is a sure sign that it needs this memory, even taking for granted that its joy in this memory is mixed with some self-interest in its own good fortune. We must leave this joy entirely free, because love, although partly self-centered, sanctifies the soul. And we must wait patiently until God Himself comes to purify it. It would be to anticipate Him, and to undertake what is reserved for Him alone, to want to deprive a man of all motives in which interest in self mixes with that in God. Man himself ought not to trouble his heart in the least over that, nor give up ahead of time the supports which his weakness needs. The child who walks alone before he is allowed to will soon fall. It is not for him to do away with the leading strings with which his governess supports him.

28

More than Ourselves

Sir Thomas Browne

s for the world, I count it not an inn but a hospital, and a place not to live but to die in. That world which I regard is myself; it is the microcosm of mine own frame that I cast mine eye on; for the other, I use it but like my globe, and turn it round sometimes for my recreation.

Men that look upon my outside, perusing only my condition and fortunes, do err in my altitude; for I am above Atlas's shoulders and, though I seem on earth to stand, on tiptoe in heaven. The earth is a point, not only in respect of the heavens above us, but of that heavenly and celestial part within us. That mass of flesh that circumscribes me limits not my mind: that surface that tells the heavens it hath an end cannot persuade me I have any. I take my circle to be above three hundred and sixty, and though the number of the arc do measure my body, it comprehendeth not my mind. Whilst I study to find how I am a microcosm or little world, I find myself something more than the great. There is surely a piece of Divinity in us, something that was before the elements and owes no homage unto the sun. Nature tells me I am the image of God as well as Scripture. He that understands not thus much hath not his introduction or first lesson, and is yet to begin the alphabet of man.

Sir Thomas Browne (1605-82) was a physician and Anglican spiritual writer, best known for his *Religio Medici*—"The Religion of a Doctor"—which concerns, among many other ideas, the place of man in the World, and of the world in Man. This passage may be usefully read in concert with the selection "What Dreams May Come" (p. 38).

Let me not injure the felicity of others if I say I am as happy as any. I have that in me that can convert poverty into riches, transform adversity into prosperity: I am more invulnerable than Achilles; fortune hath not one place to hit me. So that whatsoever happens, it is but what our daily prayers desire. In brief, I am content, and what should providence add more? Surely this is it we call happiness, and this do I enjoy. With this I am happy in a dream, and as content to enjoy a happiness in a fancy as others in a more apparent truth and reality. For there is surely a nearer apprehension of anything that delights us in our dreams than in our awakened senses. With this I can be a king without a crown, rich without a royalty, in heaven though on earth, enjoy my friend and embrace him at a distance; without which I cannot behold him. Without this I were unhappy; for my awakened judgment discontents me, ever whispering unto me that I am from my friend; but my friendly dreams in the night requite me, and make me think I am within his arms. I thank God for my happy dreams as I do for my good rest; for there is a satisfaction in them unto reasonable desires, and such as can be content with a fit of happiness; and surely it is not a melancholy conceit to think we are all asleep in this world and that the conceits of this life are as mere dreams to those of the next, as the phantasms of the night to the conceits of the day. There is an equal delusion in both, and the one doth but seem to be the emblem and picture of the other.

We are somewhat more than ourselves in our sleeps, and the slumber of the body seems to be but the waking of the soul. It is the ligation of sense, but the liberty of reason; our waking conceptions do not match the fancies of our sleeps. At my nativity my ascendant was the watery sign of Scorpius: I was born in the planetary hour of Saturn, and I think I have a piece of that leaden planet in me. I am no way facetious, nor disposed for the mirth and galliardise of company, yet in one dream I can compose a whole comedy, behold the action, apprehend the jests, and laugh myself awake at the conceits thereof. Were my memory as faithful as my reason is then fruitful I would never study but in my dreams, and this time also would I choose for my devotions; but our grosser memories have then so little hold of our abstracted understandings that they forget the story, and can only relate to our awakened souls a confused and broken tale of what hath passed. Aristotle, who hath written a singular tract of sleep, hath not methinks thoroughly defined it, nor yet Galen, though he seem to have corrected it; for those noctam-buloes and nightwalkers, though in their sleep, do yet enjoy the action of their senses.

We must therefore say that there is something in us that is not in the jurisdiction of Morpheus, and that these abstracted and ecstatic souls do walk about in their own corpse as spirits with the bodies they assume, wherein they seem to hear, see, and feel, though indeed the organs are destitute of sense, and their natures of those faculties that should inform them. Thus it is observed that men sometimes, upon the hour of their depar-ture, do speak and reason above themselves; for then the soul, beginning to be freed from the ligaments of the body, begins to reason like herself and to discourse in a strain above mortality.

29

No Fixed Abode

Giovanni Pico della Mirandola

I have read in the records of the Arabians that Abd Allah the Saracen, when questioned as to what on this stage of the world, as it were, could be seen most worthy of wonder, replied: "There is nothing to be seen more wonderful than man." In agreement with this opinion is the saying of Hermes Trismegistus: "A great miracle, Asclepius, is man."

But when I weighed the reason for these maxims, the many grounds for the excellence of human nature reported by many men failed to satisfy me: that man is the intermediary between creatures, the intimate of the gods, the king of the lower beings; by the acuteness of his senses, by the discernment of his reason, and by the light of his intelligence the interpreter of nature; the interval between fixed eternity and fleeting time, and (as the Persians say) the bond—nay, rather the marriage song—of the world, on David's testimony but little lower than the angels. Admittedly great though these reasons be, they are not the principal grounds, that is, those which may rightfully claim for themselves the privilege of the highest admiration. For why should

---

Giovanni Pico della Mirandola (1463-94) was an Italian nobleman, linguist, poet, and Christian philosopher. Educated like most Renaissance men of letters in the classical languages and literature of the West, he also knew Hebrew, Aramaic, and Arabic, and was among the first to seek an esoteric interpretation of the Christian mysteries based upon the Kabala. He was, however, far from a syncretist: "I bear on my brow the name of Jesus Christ," he insisted. "I am neither a magician nor a Jew, nor an Ishmaelite nor a heretic. It is Jesus whom I worship, and His cross I bear upon my body." This selection comes from his famous "Oration on the Dignity of Man".

we not admire more the angels themselves and the blessed choirs of heaven?

At last it seems to me I have come to understand why man is the most fortunate of creatures and consequently worthy of all admiration and what precisely is that rank which is his lot in the universal chain of being—a rank to be envied not only by brutes but even by the stars and by minds beyond this world. It is a matter past faith and a wondrous one. Why should it not be? For it is on this very account that man is rightly called and judged a great miracle and a wonderful creature indeed.

God the Father, the supreme Architect, had already built this cosmic home we behold, the most sacred temple of His Godhead, by the laws of His mysterious wisdom. The region above the heavens He had adorned with intelligences, the heavenly spheres He had quickened with eternal souls, and the excrementary and filthy parts of the lower world He had filled with a multitude of animals of every kind. But when the work was finished, the Craftsman kept wishing that there were someone to ponder the plan of so great a work, to love its beauty, and to wonder at its vastness. Therefore, when everything was done (as Moses and Timaeus bear witness), He finally took thought concerning the creation of man. But there was not among His archetypes that from which He could fashion a new offspring, nor was there in His treasure-houses anything which He might bestow on His new son as an inheritance, nor was there in the seats of all the world a place where the latter might sit to contemplate the universe. All was now complete; all things had been assigned to the highest, the middle, and the lowest orders. But in its final creation it was not the part of the Father's power to fail as though exhausted. It was not the part of His wisdom to waver in a needful matter through poverty of counsel. It was not the part of His kindly love that he who was to praise God's Divine generosity in regard to others should be compelled to condemn it in regard to himself.

At last the Best of Artisans ordained that that creature to whom He had been able to give nothing proper to himself should have joint possession of whatever had been peculiar to each of the different kinds of being. He therefore took man as a creature of indeterminate nature and, assigning him to a place in the middle of the world, addressed him thus: "Neither a fixed abode nor a form that is thine alone nor any function peculiar to thyself have We given thee, Adam, to the end that according to thy longing and according to thy judgment thou mayest have and possess what abode, what form, and what function thou thyself shalt desire. The nature of all other beings is limited and constrained within the bounds of laws prescribed by Us. Thou, constrained by no limits, in accordance with thine own free will in whose hand We have placed thee, shalt ordain for thyself the limits of thy nature. We have set thee at the world's center that thou mayest from thence more easily observe whatever is in the world. We have made thee neither of heaven nor of earth, neither mortal nor immortal, so that with freedom of choice and with honor, as though the maker and molder of thyself, thou mayest fashion thyself in whatever shape thou shalt prefer. Thou shalt have the power to degenerate into the lower forms of life, which are brutish. Thou shalt have the power, out of thy soul's judgment, to be reborn into the higher forms, which are Divine."

O supreme generosity of God the Father, O highest and most marvelous felicity of man! To him it is granted to have whatever he chooses, to be whatever he wills. Beasts as soon as they are born bring with them from their mother's womb all they will ever possess. Spiritual beings, either from the beginning or soon thereafter, become what they are to be for ever and ever. On man when he came into life, the Father conferred the seeds of all kinds and the germs of every way of life. Whatever seeds each man cultivates will grow to maturity and bear in him their own fruit. If they be vegetative, he will be like a plant. If sensitive, he will be brutish. If rational, he will grow into a heavenly being. If intellectual, he will be an angel and the son of God. And if happy in the lot of no created thing he withdraws into the center of his own unity, then his spirit—made one with God in the solitary darkness of God, who is set above all things—shall surpass them all.

30

Today

St Patrick of Ireland

𝕴 arise today through a mighty strength,
the invocation of the Trinity,
Through belief in the threeness,
Through confession of the oneness,
Of the Creator of creation.

I arise today
Through the strength of Christ's birth with His baptism,
Through the strength of His crucifixion with His burial,
Through the strength of His resurrection
with His ascension,
Through the strength of His descent for the judgment
of doom.

I arise today
Through the strength of the love of cherubim,
In obedience of angels,
In the service of archangels,
In hope of resurrection to meet with reward,
In prayers of patriarchs,
In predictions of prophets,
In preachings of apostles,

St Patrick (*c.* 390 - *c.* 460) was a bishop of the ancient Celtic Church in Ireland.
It is said that he chanted this mystical hymn, traditionally known as "The
Deer's Cry", as a protection from evil at the time of his initial encounter with
Loegaire, the king of pre-Christian Ireland, and his Druidic counselors.

In faiths of confessors,
In innocence of holy virgins,
In deeds of righteous men.
I arise today
Through the strength of heaven:
Light of sun,
Radiance of moon,
Splendor of fire,
Speed of lightning,
Swiftness of wind,
Depth of sea,
Stability of earth,
Firmness of rock.

I arise today
Through God's strength to pilot me:
God's might to uphold me,
God's wisdom to guide me,
God's eye to look before me,
God's ear to hear me,
God's word to speak for me,
God's hand to guard me,
God's way to lie before me,
God's shield to protect me,
God's host to save me
From snares of devils,
From temptation of vices,
From every one who shall wish me ill,
Afar and anear,
Alone and in a multitude.

I summon today all these powers between me
and these evils:
Against every cruel, merciless power
that may oppose my body and soul:
Against incantations of false prophets,
Against black laws of pagandom,
Against false laws of heretics,

Against craft and idolatry,
Against spells of smiths and wizards,
Against every knowledge that corrupts man's body and soul.
Christ to shield me today
Against poison, against burning,
Against drowning, against wounding,
So that there may come to me abundance of reward.
Christ with me, Christ before me, Christ behind me,
Christ in me, Christ beneath me, Christ above me,
Christ on my right, Christ on my left,
Christ when I lie down, Christ when I sit down,
Christ when I arise,
Christ in the heart of everyone who thinks of me,
Christ in the mouth of everyone who speaks of me,
Christ in every eye that sees me,
Christ in every ear that hears me.

I arise today
Through a mighty strength, the invocation of the Trinity,
Through belief in the threeness,
Through confession of the oneness,
Of the Creator of creation.

31

The Teacher

St Gregory of Sinai

According to the wise, a true teacher is he who through his all-embracing cognitive insight comprehends created things concisely, as if they constituted a single body, establishing distinctions and connections between them according to their generic difference and identity, so as to indicate which possess similar qualities. Or he may be described as one who can truly demonstrate things apodictically. Or again, a true spiritual teacher is he who distinguishes and relates the general and universal qualities of created things—classified as five in number, but compounded in the incarnate Logos—in accordance with a particular formulation that embraces everything. But his apodictic skill is not a matter of mere verbal dexterity, like that of profane philosophers, for he is able to enlighten others through the contemplative vision of created things manifested to him by the Holy Spirit.

A true philosopher is one who perceives in created things their spiritual Cause, or who knows created things through knowing their Cause, having attained a union with God that transcends the intellect and a direct, unmediated faith. He does not simply learn about Divine things, but actually experiences

---

St Gregory of Sinai (*c.* 1265-1346) was an Eastern Orthodox anchorite and *starets* or spiritual father, who here describes the characteristics of true spiritual mastery. Following a not uncommon pattern, he lived for about twenty-five years in a secluded hermitage on Mount Athos, intent upon the solitary practice of *ascesis* and contemplative prayer, before agreeing to accept disciples in the last part of his life. This reading comes from his "On Commandments and Doctrines".

them. Or again, a true philosopher is one whose intellect is conversant equally with ascetic practice and contemplative wisdom. Thus the perfect philosopher or lover of wisdom is one whose intellect has attained—alike on the moral, natural, and theological levels—love of wisdom or, rather, love of God. That is to say, he has learnt from God the principles of ascetic practice (moral philosophy), an insight into the spiritual causes of created things (natural philosophy), and a precise contemplative understanding of doctrinal principles (theology).

Or again, a teacher initiated into things Divine is one who distinguishes principial beings from participative beings or beings that have no autonomous self-subsistent reality; he adduces the essences of principial beings from beings that exist through participating in them, and inspired by the Holy Spirit, he perceives the essences of principial beings embodied in participative beings. In other words, he interprets what is intelligible and invisible in terms of what is sensible and visible, and the visible sense-world in terms of the invisible and suprasensory world, conscious that what is visible is an image of what is invisible, and that what is invisible is the archetype of what is visible. He knows that things possessing form and figure are brought into being by what is formless and without figure, and that each manifests the other spiritually; and he clearly perceives each in the other and conveys this perception in his teaching of the truth. His knowledge of the truth, with all its sun-like radiance, is not expressed in anagogical or allegorical form; on the contrary, he elucidates the true underlying principles of both worlds with spiritual insight and power, and expounds them forcibly and vividly. In this way the visible world becomes our teacher and the invisible world is shown to be an eternal Divine dwelling-place manifestly brought into being for our sake.

32

True Imagination

George MacDonald

very fact in nature is a revelation of God, is there such as it
is because God is such as He is; and I suspect that all its
facts impress us so that we learn God unconsciously. True, we
cannot think of any one fact thus except as we find the soul of
it—its fact of God; but from the moment when first we come
into contact with the world, it is to us a revelation of God, His
things seen, by which we come to know the things unseen. How
should we imagine what we may of God without the firmament
over our heads, a visible sphere, yet a formless infinitude? What
idea could we have of God without the sky? The truth of the sky
is what it makes us feel of the God that sent it out to our eyes. If
you say the sky could not but be so and such, I grant it—with
God at the root of it. There is nothing for us to conceive in its
stead; therefore indeed it must be so. In its discovered laws, light
seems to me to be such because God is such. Its so-called laws
are the waving of His garments, waving so because He is
thinking and loving and walking inside them.

We are here in a region far above that commonly claimed
for science, open only to the heart of the child, and the childlike man and woman—a region in which the poet is among his
own things, and to which he has often to go to fetch them. For

---

George MacDonald (1824-1905), whom C. S. Lewis (see p. 162) credited with
having "baptized [his] imagination", was a Scottish poet, novelist, and
Congregationalist minister. The clarity of vision that one finds in his *Unspoken
Sermons*, from which this selection is taken, is given compelling and persuasive
form in such stories as *Lilith, Phantastes*, and *At the Back of the North Wind*.

things as they are, not as science deals with them, are the reve-lation of God to His children. I would not be misunderstood: there is no fact of science not yet incorporated in a law, no law of science that has got beyond the hypothetical and tentative, that has not in it the will of God, and therefore may not reveal God; but neither fact nor law is there for the sake of fact or law; each is but a means to an end; in the perfected end we find the intent, and there God—not in the laws themselves, save as His means.

Ask a man of mere science what is the truth of a flower: he will pull it to pieces, show you its parts, explain how they operate, how they minister each to the life of the flower; he will tell you what changes are wrought in it by scientific cultivation: where it lives originally, where it can live; the effects upon it of another climate; what part the insects bear in its varieties—and doubtless many more facts about it. Ask the poet what is the truth of the flower, and he will answer: "Why, the flower itself, the perfect flower, and what it cannot help saying to him who has ears to hear it." The truth of the flower is not the facts about it, be they correct as ideal science itself, but the shining, glowing, gladdening, patient thing throned on its stalk—the compeller of smile and tear from child and prophet. The man of science laughs at this because he is only a man of science and does not know what it means; but the poet and the child care as little for his laughter as the birds of God, as Dante calls the angels, for his treatise on aerostation. The children of God must always be mocked by the children of the world, whether in the church or out of it—children with sharp ears and eyes, but dull hearts. Those that hold love the only good in the world under-stand and smile at the world's children, and can do very well without anything they have got to tell them. In the higher state to which their love is leading them, they will speedily outstrip the men of science, for they have that which is at the root of science, that for the revealing of which God's science exists. What shall it profit a man to know all things, and lose the bliss, the consciousness of well-being, which alone can give value to his knowledge?

God's science in the flower exists for the existence of the flower in its relation to His children. If we understand, if we are at one with, if we love, the flower, we have that for which the science is there, that which alone can equip us for true search into the means and ways by which the Divine idea of the flower was wrought out to be presented to us. The idea of God is the flower; His idea is not the botany of the flower. Its botany is but a thing of ways and means—of canvas and color and brush in relation to the picture in the Painter's brain. When we see how they are loved by the ignorant and degraded, we may well believe the flowers have a place in the history of the world, as written for the archives of heaven, which we are yet a long way from understanding, and which science could not, to all eternity, understand, or enable to understand. Watch that child! He has found one of his silent and motionless brothers, with God's clothing upon it, God's thought in its face. In what a smile breaks out the Divine understanding between them! Watch his mother when he takes it home to her—no nearer understanding it than he! It is no old association that brings those tears to her eyes, powerful in that way as are flowers, and things far inferior to flowers; it is God's thought, unrecognized as such, holding communion with her. She weeps with a delight inexplicable. It is only a daisy! only a primrose! only a pheasant-eye-narcissus! only a lily of the field! only a snowdrop! only a sweet-pea! only a brave yellow crocus! But here to her is no mere fact; here is no law of nature; here is a truth of nature, the truth of a flower.

What, I ask, is the truth of water? Is it that it is formed of hydrogen and oxygen? That the chemist has now another mode of stating the fact of water will not affect my illustration. His new mode will probably be one day yet more antiquated than mine is now. Is it for the sake of the fact that hydrogen and oxygen combined form water that the precious thing exists? Is oxygen-and-hydrogen the Divine idea of water? Or has God put the two together only that man might separate and find them out? He allows His child to pull his toys to pieces; but were they made that he might pull them to pieces? He were a child not to be envied for whom his inglorious father would make toys to such an end. A school-examiner might see therein the best use of a toy, but not a father. Find for us what in the constitution of the two gases makes them fit and capable to be thus honored in forming the lovely thing, and you will give us a revelation about more than water, namely, about the God who made oxygen and hydrogen. There is no water in oxygen, no water in hydrogen: it comes bubbling fresh from the imagination of the living God, rushing from under the great white throne of the glacier. The very thought of it makes one gasp with an elemental joy no metaphysician can analyze. The water itself, that dances, and sings, and slakes the wonderful thirst—symbol and picture of that draught for which the woman of Samaria made her prayer to Jesus—this lovely thing itself, whose very wetness is a delight to every inch of the human body in its embrace—this live thing which, if I might, I would have running through my room, yea, babbling along my table—this water is its own self its own truth, and is therein a truth of God. Let him who would know the love of the Maker become sorely athirst, and drink of the brook by the way—then lift up his heart, not at that moment to the maker of oxygen and hydrogen, but to the inventor and mediator of thirst and water, that man might foresee a little of what his soul may find in God.

The truth of a thing, then, is the blossom of it, the thing it is made for, the topmost stone set on with rejoicing; truth in a man's imagination is the power to recognize this truth of a thing; and wherever, in anything that God has made, in the glory of it, be it sky or flower or human face, we see the glory of God, there a true imagination is beholding a truth of God.

V

Luminosity

And His raiment became shining,
exceeding white as snow.

Mark 9:3

33

Nothing Amiss

Julian of Norwich

𝕴 saw God in a point, that is to say, in my understanding, by which sight I saw that He is in all things. I beheld and considered, seeing and knowing in sight, with a soft dread, and thought: "What is sin?" For I saw truly that God does all things, be they ever so little. And I saw truly that nothing is done by chance or adventure, but all things by the foreseeing wisdom of God. If by chance or adventure in the sight of man, our blindness and our unforesight are the cause. For the things that are in the foreseeing wisdom of God from without beginning—which rightfully and worshipfully and continually He leads to the best of ends—as they come about fall to us suddenly, ourselves unwitting; and thus by our blindness and our unforesight we say that these are chances and adventures. But to our Lord God they are not so.

Therefore it behooves me to grant that all things that are done are well done, for our Lord God does all. For the working of creatures was not shown to me at this time, but the working of our Lord God in the creature: for He is in the mid-point of all things and does all things. And I was certain He does no sin. And here I saw verily that sin is no deed: for in all this sin was not shown. And I no longer marveled in this, but beheld our

Julian of Norwich (*c.* 1342-1420) was an English laywoman who lived in solitude as an anchoress attached to St Julian's church in Norwich, whence her name. On 8 May 1373 she experienced a series of visions or "Divine Showings" that were recorded some twenty years later in her *Revelations of Divine Love*, from which this well-known passage is taken.

Lord, what He would show. And thus, as much as it might be for the time, the rightfulness of God's working was shown to the soul. Rightfulness has two fair properties: it is right, and it is full. And so are all the works of our Lord God: they need neither the working of mercy nor grace, for they are entirely rightful, wherein nothing fails.

This vision was shown to my understanding in order that our Lord might have the soul turned truly unto the beholding of Him, and generally of all His works. For they are entirely good; and all His doings are easy and sweet, and to great ease they bring the soul that is turned from the beholding of the blind workings of man unto the fair, sweet working of our Lord God. For a man beholds some deeds well done and some deeds evil, but our Lord beholds them not so: for as all that has being in nature is of Godly making, so is all that is done properly of God's doing. For it is easy to understand that the best deed is well done: and so well as the best deed is done, so well is the least deed done, and everything in its property and in the order that our Lord has ordained it to from without beginning. For there is no doer but He. I saw full surely that He changes never His purpose in any manner of thing, nor ever shall without end. For there was nothing unknown to Him in His rightful ordinance from without beginning. And therefore everything was set in order before anything was made so that it should stand without end; and no manner of thing shall fail at that point. For He made all things in fullness of goodness, and therefore the blessed Trinity is ever full pleased in all His works.

And all this showed He full blissfully, signifying thus: "See! I am God: see! I am in all things: see! I do all things: see! I lift never My hands off My works, nor ever shall, without end: see! I lead all things to the end I ordained them to from without beginning, by the same Might, Wisdom, and Love whereby I made it. How should anything be amiss?" Thus mightily, wisely, and lovingly was the soul examined in this vision. Then saw I that it behooved me of need to assent with great reverence, enjoying in God.

34

Sweet Delight in God's Beauty

Jonathan Edwards

The first that I remember that ever I found anything of that sort of inward, sweet delight in God and Divine things that I have lived much in since was on reading those words, "Now unto the King eternal, immortal, invisible, the only wise God, be honor and glory for ever and ever. Amen" (1 Tim. 1:17). As I read the words, there came into my soul, and was as it were diffused through it, a sense of the glory of the Divine Being, a new sense, quite different from anything I ever experienced before. Never any words of Scripture seemed to me as these words did. I thought with myself how excellent a Being that was and how happy I should be if I might enjoy that God and be rapt up to God in heaven, and be as it were swallowed up in Him.

From about that time, I began to have a new kind of apprehensions and ideas of Christ and the work of redemption, and the glorious way of salvation by Him. I had an inward, sweet sense of these things that at times came into my heart, and my soul was led away in pleasant views and contemplations of them. And my mind was greatly engaged to spend my time in reading and meditating on Christ and the beauty and excellency of His person and the lovely way of salvation by free grace

---

Jonathan Edwards (1703-58), whom many regard as the greatest of American philosophers and theologians, was a Calvinist preacher and evangelist, best known perhaps for his famous sermon "Sinners in the Hands of an Angry God". But he was also a deeply contemplative man, sensitive to the beauties of virgin nature and the sanctified soul, as can be seen in this selection from his "Personal Narrative".

in Him. I found no books so delightful to me as those that treated of these subjects. Those words used to be abundantly with me: "I am the Rose of Sharon and the Lily of the valleys" (Song of Sol. 2:1). The words seemed to me sweetly to represent the loveliness and beauty of Jesus Christ. And the whole book of Canticles used to be pleasant to me, and I used to be much in reading it about that time and found, from time to time, an inward sweetness that used, as it were, to carry me away in my contemplations: in what I know not how to express otherwise than as a calm, sweet abstraction of soul from all the concerns of this world, and a kind of vision, or fixed ideas and imaginations, of being alone in the mountains or some solitary wilderness, far from all mankind, sweetly conversing with Christ and rapt and swallowed up in God. The sense I had of Divine things would often of a sudden as it were kindle up a sweet burning in my heart, an ardor of my soul that I know not how to express.

Not long after I first began to experience these things, I gave an account to my father of some things that had passed in my mind. I was pretty much affected by the discourse we had together, and when the discourse was ended, I walked abroad alone in a solitary place in my father's pasture for contemplation. And as I was walking there and looked upon the sky and clouds, there came into my mind so sweet a sense of the glorious majesty and grace of God that I know not how to express. I seemed to see them both in a sweet conjunction, majesty and meekness joined together; it was a sweet and gentle and holy majesty, and a majestic meekness: an awful sweetness, a high and great and holy gentleness.

After this my sense of Divine things gradually increased and became more and more lively and had more of that inward sweetness. The appearance of everything was altered; there seemed to be as it were a calm, sweet cast or appearance of Divine glory in almost everything. God's excellency, His wisdom, His purity and love, seemed to appear in everything: in the sun, moon, and stars; in the clouds and blue sky; in the grass, flowers, trees; in the water and all nature, which used greatly to fix my mind. I often used to sit and view the moon for a long time, and so in the daytime spent much time in viewing the clouds and sky to behold the sweet glory of God in these things, in the meantime singing forth with a low voice my contemplations of the Creator and Redeemer. And scarce anything among all the works of nature was so sweet to me as thunder and lightning: formerly nothing had been so terrible to me. I used to be a person uncommonly terrified with thunder, and it used to strike me with terror when I saw a thunderstorm rising. But now on the contrary it rejoiced me. I felt God at the first appearance of a thunderstorm and used to take the opportunity at such times to fix myself to view the clouds and see the lightnings play and hear the majestic and awful voice of God's thunder, which oftentimes was exceeding entertaining, leading me to sweet contemplations of my great and glorious God; and while I viewed I used to spend my time, as it always seemed natural to me, to sing or chant forth my meditations, to speak my thoughts in soliloquies, and speak with a singing voice.

The delights which I now felt in things of religion were of an exceeding different kind from those that I had when I was a boy. They were totally of another kind, and what I then had no more notion or idea of than one born blind has of pleasant and beautiful colors. They were of a more inward, pure, soul-animating, and refreshing nature. Those former delights never reached the heart and did not arise from any sight of the Divine excellency of the things of God, or any taste of the soul-satisfying and life-giving good there is in them. The heaven I now desired was a heaven of holiness: to be with God and to spend my eternity in Divine love and holy communion with Christ. My mind was very much taken up with contemplations on heaven and the enjoyments of those there, and living there in perfect holiness, humility, and love. And it used at that time to appear a great part of the happiness of heaven that there the saints could express their love to Christ. It appeared to me a great clog and hindrance and burden to me that what I felt within I could not express to God and give vent to as I desired. The inward ardor of my soul seemed to be hindered and pent up and could not freely flame out as it would. I used often to think how in heaven this sweet principle should freely and fully vent and express itself. Heaven appeared to me exceeding delightful as a world of love. It appeared to me that all happiness consisted in living in pure, humble, heavenly, Divine love.

I remember the thoughts I used then to have of holiness. I remember I then said sometimes to myself: I do certainly know that I love holiness such as the Gospel prescribes. It appeared to me there was nothing in it but what was ravishingly lovely. It appeared to me to be the highest beauty and amiableness above all other beauties, that it was a *Divine* beauty, far purer than anything here upon earth, and that everything else was like mire, filth, and defilement in comparison of it. Holiness, as I then wrote down some of my contemplations on it, appeared to me to be of a sweet, pleasant, charming, serene, calm nature. It seemed to me it brought an inexpressible purity, brightness, peacefulness, and ravishment to the soul, and that it made the soul like a field or garden of God with all manner of pleasant flowers that is all pleasant, delightful, and undisturbed, enjoying a sweet calm and the gently vivifying beams of the sun. The soul of a true Christian, as I then wrote my meditations, appeared like such a little white flower as we see in the spring of the year: low and humble on the ground, opening its bosom to receive the pleasant beams of the sun's glory, rejoicing as it were in a calm rapture, diffusing around a sweet fragrancy, standing peacefully and lovingly in the midst of other flowers round about, all in like manner opening their bosoms to drink in the light of the sun.

There was no part of creature-holiness that I then and at other times had so great a sense of the loveliness of as humility, brokenness of heart, and poverty of spirit, and there was nothing that I had such a spirit to long for. My heart as it were panted after this, to lie low before God and in the dust, that I might be nothing and that God might be all, that I might become as a little child.

35

Thinking the Unthinkable

St Anselm

Come now, insignificant man, fly for a moment from your affairs, escape for a little while from the tumult of your thoughts. Put aside now your weighty cares, and leave your wearisome toils. Abandon yourself for a little to God, and rest for a little in Him. Enter into the inner chamber of your soul, shut out everything save God and what can be of help in your quest for Him, and having locked the door, seek Him out. Speak now, my whole heart, speak now to God: "I seek Your countenance, O Lord, Your countenance I seek" (Ps. 27:8).

Lord, You who give understanding to faith, grant that I may understand, as much as You see fit, that You exist as we believe You to exist, and that You are what we believe You to be. We believe that You are something than which nothing greater can be thought. Or can it be that a thing of such a nature does not exist, since "the fool has said in his heart, there is no God" (Ps. 14:1, 53:1)? But surely, when this same fool hears what I am speaking about, namely, something than which nothing greater can be thought, he understands what he hears, and what he understands is in his mind, even if he does not understand that it actually exists. For it is one thing for an object to exist in the mind, and another thing to understand that an object actually

St Anselm (*c.* 1033-1109), Archbishop of Canterbury and a Doctor of the Roman Catholic Church, had long desired to find "one single argument" that would "suffice to prove that God really exists". After many labors, his now-famous proof, based upon the paradoxical capacity of the mind to see beyond its own limits, was suddenly revealed to him in the midst of the night during the office of matins.

exists. Thus, when a painter plans beforehand what he is going to execute, he has the picture in his mind, but he does not yet think that it actually exists because he has not yet executed it. However, when he has actually painted it, then he both has it in his mind and understands that it exists because he has now made it. Even the fool, then, is forced to agree that something than which nothing greater can be thought exists in the mind, since he understands this when he hears it, and whatever is understood is in the mind. And surely that than which nothing greater can be thought cannot exist in the mind alone. For if it exists solely in the mind, it can be thought to exist in reality also, which is greater. If then that than which nothing greater can be thought exists in the mind alone, this same that than which nothing greater can be thought is that than which a greater *can* be thought. But this is obviously impossible. Therefore there is absolutely no doubt that something than which a greater cannot be thought exists both in the mind and in reality.

Have you found, O my soul, what you were seeking? You were seeking God, and you found Him to be something which is the highest of all, than which a greater cannot be thought. If you have not found your God, what is this which you have found, and which you have understood with such certain truth and true certitude? But if you have found Him, why is it that you do not experience what you have found? Why, O Lord God, does my soul not experience You if it has found You? Or has it not found that which it has found to be the light and the truth? But then how did it understand this save by seeing the light and the truth? Could it understand anything at all about You save through "Your light and Your truth" (Ps. 43:3)? If it saw the light and the truth, it saw You. If it did not see You, then it did not see the light or the truth. Or is it the case that it saw both the truth and the light, and yet it did not see You because it saw You only partially and did not see You as You really are?

Lord my God, You who have formed and reformed me, tell my desiring soul what You are beside what it has seen, so that it may see clearly that which it desires. It strives so that it may see more, but it sees nothing beyond what it has seen save darkness. Why is this, Lord? Is its eye darkened by its own littleness, or is

World Wisdom

World Wisdom
P. O. Box 2682
Bloomington, IN 47402-2682
U.S.A.

World Wisdom

Send us this card, or contact us at

www.worldwisdom.com

Please Print

Book in which this card was found _____

Name _____

Address _____

City _____ Zip or Postal Code _____

State _____

Country (if outside the USA) _____

E-mail _____

Please detach bookmark before mailing card.

When the mind
becomes purified
like a mirror,
Knowledge is
revealed in it.
Care should
therefore be taken
to purify the mind.

—Sri Sankaracharya

World Wisdom

visit

www.worldwisdom.com

it dazzled by Your splendor? In truth it is both darkened in itself and dazzled by You. It is darkened by its own littleness and overwhelmed by Your immensity. It is restricted by its own limitedness and overcome by Your fullness. For how great is that light from which shines every truth that gives light to the understanding! How complete is that truth in which is everything that is true and outside of which nothing exists save nothingness and falsity! How boundless is that which in one glance sees everything that has been made, and by whom and through whom and in what manner it was made from nothing! What purity, what simplicity, what certitude and splendor are there! Truly it is more than can be understood by any creature.

Therefore, Lord, not only are You that than which a greater *cannot* be thought, but You are also something greater than *can* be thought. For since it is possible to think that there is such a one, then if You were not this same being, something greater than You could be thought—which cannot be. Truly, Lord, this is the inaccessible light in which You dwell. For there is nothing else which can penetrate through it so that it might discover You there. I do not see this light, since it is too much for me; and yet whatever I see I see through it, just as an eye that is weak sees what it sees by the light of the sun, which it cannot look at in the sun itself. My understanding is not able to attain to that light. It shines too much, and my understanding does not grasp it, nor does the eye of my soul allow itself to be turned towards it for long. It is dazzled by its splendor, overcome by its fullness, overwhelmed by its immensity, confused by its extent. O supreme and inaccessible Light, O whole and blessed Truth, how far You are from me who am so close to You! How distant You are from my sight, while I am so present to Your sight! You are wholly present everywhere, and I do not see You. In You I move, and in You I have my being, and yet I cannot come near to You. You are within me and around me, but I do not have any experience of You.

36

Prayer of the Heart

The Way of a Pilgrim

$\mathfrak{I}$ began to read the *Philokalia* very attentively from beginning to end. In a short time I read the whole book, and I realized what wisdom, holiness, and depth it contains. However, since the book contains so many varied themes and exhortations, I could not understand everything. I was unable to pull all the ideas together, particularly about interior prayer, so that I could learn the ceaseless self-activating prayer of the heart. And this is precisely what I longed for, as the Apostle Paul directs: "Be ambitious for the higher gifts" (1 Cor. 12:31), and "Never try to suppress the Spirit" (1 Thess. 5:19). I thought and thought, but was incapable of understanding this, and there was no one to explain it to me.

I will implore the Lord in prayer, I thought, and He will help me to understand it somehow. So I prayed ceaselessly for twenty-four hours, not stopping even for a little while. My thoughts quieted down, and I fell asleep. I had a dream in which I saw myself in the cell of my late elder, and he was explaining the *Philokalia* to me: "This book is full of wisdom; it is a secret treasure of illustrations of the hidden judgments of God. And although it is not readily available to everyone, it does contain

---

The Way of a Pilgrim is a nineteenth-century Russian Orthodox classic in which the author, an anonymous wayfarer in the forests of Siberia, recounts his discovery and practice of the art of unceasing prayer. The *Philokalia*, from which a number of selections in the present volume are taken, is a compilation of ascetical and mystical writings concerning the Hesychast practice of prayer of the heart. See also the reading called "Descending with the Breath" (p. 33).

instructions for all. It has profound sayings for the wise and simple ones for the simple-minded. The writings of these Fathers contain complete directions about interior prayer of the heart and can be easily understood by everyone. If, however, you desire even simpler information regarding interior prayer, then find the summarized version of Patriarch Kallistos of Constantinople in the fourth part of the book." I held the copy of the *Philokalia* in my hands and was looking for the mentioned section, but I was slow in finding it. Then the elder himself turned a few pages and said, "Here it is. I will mark it for you," and picking up a piece of charcoal from the floor, he made a mark in the margin where the passage was found. I listened attentively to all that the elder explained and tried to remember it.

It was still dark when I awoke, so I lay there and recalled the dream I had and what the elder had told me. I found myself thinking, God knows whether it was the soul of the elder which I saw or perhaps just my imagination since I think so much about the elder and the *Philokalia*. At dawn I got up with this perplexing question in my mind, and to my astonishment I saw on the stone which served as my table the copy of the *Philokalia* opened to that very page which the elder had shown me and the section marked exactly as I saw in the dream, and even the charcoal was lying beside the book. I was completely amazed, as I remembered distinctly that the book was not there the night before; it was closed and was at the head of the bed; and I was also sure that there was no mark of any kind in that section before. This incident strengthened my faith in dreams and in the holiness of my departed spiritual father. Now I began to read the *Philokalia* in the order pointed out to me, and I read it once and then a second time. The reading enkindled in my heart a desire and zeal to experience all that I read, for now I understood clearly what interior prayer is, what means are necessary to reach it, what the results of it are, how it fills the heart and soul with joy, and how to recognize whether that joy is from God or from nature, or whether it is a deception.

My first practical step was to find the place of the heart according to the directions of St Symeon the New Theologian. I closed my eyes and imagined looking into my heart; my desire was to visualize the heart in the left breast and to listen attentively to its beating. At first I was occupied like this for half an hour several times a day. At the beginning I was not aware of anything but darkness; and then slowly the heart appeared, and I noticed its movement. Then I began to say the Jesus Prayer interiorly to the rhythm of my breathing according to the directions of St Gregory of Sinai and of Kallistos and Ignatios: that is, while looking into the heart and inhaling I said, "Lord Jesus Christ," and while exhaling, "have mercy upon me." At first I did this for an hour or two, and then I increased it so that in the end I spent practically the entire day in this exercise. When doubts or heaviness or slothfulness would come upon me, I would promptly read the section of the *Philokalia* which speaks of the activity of the heart, and in this way I would renew my desire and zeal for prayer. After three weeks I began to feel pain in the heart, then a very pleasant warmth, delight, and peace. This encouraged me to even more earnest practice of the Prayer, so that all my thoughts were now directed to this, and I experienced great joy. From this time, periodically, I began to experience various feelings and perceptions in my heart and mind. Sometimes I felt a sweet burning in my heart and such ease, freedom, and consolation that I seemed to be transformed and caught up in ecstasy. Sometimes I experienced a burning love toward Jesus Christ and all of God's creation. Sometimes I shed joyful tears in thanksgiving to God for His mercy to me, a great sinner. Sometimes difficult concepts became crystal clear and new ideas came to me which of myself I could not have imagined. Sometimes the warmth of the heart overflowed throughout my being, and with tenderness I experienced God's presence within me. Sometimes I felt great joy in calling on the name of Jesus Christ, and I realized the meaning of the words, "The kingdom of God is within you" (Luke 17:21).

These and similar consolations led me to conclude that the fruits of the prayer of the heart can be experienced in three ways: in the spirit, in the emotions, and in revelations. In the spirit one can experience the sweetness of the love of God, inner peace, purity of thought, awareness of God's presence, and ecstasy; in the emotions, a pleasant warmth of the heart, a feeling of delight throughout one's being, joyful bubbling in the heart, lightness and courage, joy of life, and indifference to sickness and sorrow; and in revelations one receives enlightenment of the mind, understanding of Holy Scripture, knowledge of the speech of all creatures, renunciation of vanities, awareness of the sweetness of interior life, and confidence in the nearness of God and His love for us.

After spending almost five months in this prayerful occupation and enjoyment of the mentioned gifts, I became so accustomed to the prayer of the heart that I practiced it without ceasing, and finally I felt that the Prayer of itself, without any effort on my part, began to function both in my mind and heart; it was active both day and night without the slightest interruption, regardless of what I was doing. My soul praised God, and my heart overflowed with joy. The prayer of the heart consoled me to such a degree that I considered myself the happiest man on earth, and I wondered whether the beatific vision could bring any greater consolation. Not only was I experiencing deep interior joy, but I sensed a oneness with all of God's creation: people, animals, trees, and plants all seemed to have the name of Jesus Christ imprinted upon them. At times I felt such freedom of movement that it seemed I had no body which walked, but I was delightfully carried through the air; at other times I descended within myself and clearly saw all my organs, and was astonished at the wisdom of the composition of the human body; at still other times I felt as happy as a king, and with all these consolations I had a great desire to die and be poured out in praise and thanksgiving at the feet of Christ in the world of the spirit.

37

The Religion of Light

Jingjing

In the beginning was the natural constant, the true stillness of the Origin, and the primordial void of the Most High. The Spirit of the void emerged as the Most High Lord, moving in mysterious ways to enlighten the holy ones. He is Ye Su, my True Lord of the Void, who embodies the three subtle and wondrous bodies, and who was condemned to the cross so that the people of the four directions might be saved.

He beat up the primordial winds, and the two vapors were created. He differentiated the gray emptiness and opened up the sky and the earth. He set the sun and moon on their course, and day and night came into being. He crafted the myriad things and created the first people. He gave to them the original nature of goodness and appointed them as guardians of all creation. Their minds were empty, they were content, and their hearts were simple and innocent. Originally they had no desire, but under the influence of Satan, they abandoned their pure and simple goodness for the glitter and the gold. Falling into the trap of death and lies, they became embroiled in the three hundred and sixty-five forms of sin. In doing so, they have woven the web of retribution and have bound themselves inside it. Some believe in the material origin of things, some have sunk into chaotic ways, some think that they can receive blessings

---

Jingjing (*fl.* 781) was a priest-monk of the ancient Church of the East and the author of this brief Taoist version of the Gospel, which was found inscribed in Chinese characters on a Tang Dynasty stele, first discovered near the city of Xian in 1625.

simply by reciting prayers, and some have abandoned kindness for treachery. Despite their intelligence and their passionate pleas, they have gone nowhere. Forced into the overturning wheel of fire, they are burned and obliterated. Having lost their way for eons, they can no longer return.

Therefore my Lord Ye Su, the One emanating in three subtle bodies, hid His true power, became a human, and came on behalf of the Lord of Heaven to preach the good teachings. A Virgin gave birth to the Sacred in a dwelling in the Western Empire. The message was given to the Persians, who saw and followed the bright light to offer Him gifts. The twenty-four holy ones have given us the teachings, and Heaven has decreed that the new religion of the Three-in-One Purity that cannot be spoken of should now be proclaimed. These teachings can restore goodness to sincere believers, deliver those living within the boundaries of the eight territories, refine the dust and transform it into truth, reveal the gate of the three constants, lead us to life, and destroy death. The teachings of the Religion of Light are like the resplendent sun: they have the power to dissolve the dark realm and destroy evil forever.

The Lord set afloat the raft of salvation and compassion so that we might use it to ascend to the palace of light and be united with the Spirit. He carried out the work of deliverance, and when the task was completed, He ascended to immortality in broad daylight. He left twenty-seven books of scriptures to inspire our spirit, He revealed the workings of the Origin, and He gave to us the method of purification by water. Thus we purify our hearts and return to the simple and natural Way of the truth. This truth cannot be named, but its power surpasses all expectations. When forced to give it a name, we call it the Religion of Light. As it is with the Way, that which is sacred is not sacred unless it is highly sacred, and that which is the Way is not the Way unless it is the Great Way.

38

In the Eyes of a Child

Thomas Traherne

The noble inclination whereby man thirsteth after riches and dominion is his highest virtue when rightly guided, and carries him as in a triumphant chariot to his sovereign happiness. Men are made miserable only by abusing it. Taking a false way to satisfy it, they pursue the wind: nay, labor in the very fire, and after all reap but vanity. Whereas, as God's love, which is the fountain of all, did cost us nothing, so were all other things prepared by it to satisfy our inclinations in the best of manners, freely, without any cost of ours.

Seeing therefore all satisfactions are near at hand, by going further we do but leave them, and wearying ourselves in a long way round about, like a blind man, forsake them. They are immediately near to the very gates of our senses. It becometh the bounty of God to prepare them freely: to make them glorious, and their enjoyment easy. For because His love is free, so are His treasures. He therefore that will despise them because he hath them is marvelously irrational: the way to possess them is to esteem them. And the true way of reigning over them is to break the world all into parts, to examine them asunder; and if we find them so excellent that better could not possibly be made, and so made they could not be more ours, to rejoice in all with pleasure answerable to the merit of their Goodness. We

---

Thomas Traherne (*c.* 1636-74) was a parish priest of the Church of England and the author of four *Centuries of Meditation,* from which this selection is taken. Steeped in the traditions of Christian Platonism, he was also a writer of verse and is often included among the English Metaphysical Poets.

being then Kings over the whole world, when we restore the pieces to their proper places, being perfectly pleased with the whole composure. This shall give you a thorough grounded contentment, far beyond what troublesome wars or conquests can acquire. Is it not a sweet thing to have all covetousness and ambition satisfied, suspicion and infidelity removed, courage and joy infused? Yet is all this in the fruition of the world attained. For thereby God is seen in all His wisdom, power, goodness, and glory.

Your enjoyment of the world is never right till you so esteem it that everything in it is more your treasure than a King's exchequer full of Gold and Silver. And that exchequer yours also in its place and service. Can you take too much joy in your Father's works? He is Himself in everything. Some things are little on the outside, and rough and common, but I remember the time when the dust of the streets was as pleasing as Gold to my infant eyes, and now they are more precious to the eye of reason.

You never enjoy the world aright till the Sea itself floweth in your veins, till you are clothed with the heavens and crowned with the stars, and perceive yourself to be the sole heir of the whole world, and more than so, because men are in it who are every one sole heirs as well as you. Till you can sing and rejoice and delight in God, as misers do in gold, and Kings in scepters, you never enjoy the world. Till your spirit filleth the whole world, and the stars are your jewels; till you are as familiar with the ways of God in all Ages as with your walk and table; till you are intimately acquainted with that shady nothing out of which the world was made; till you love men so as to desire their happiness, with a thirst equal to the zeal of your own; till you delight in God for being good to all: you never enjoy the world. Till you more feel it than your private estate, and are more present in the hemisphere, considering the glories and the beauties there, than in your own house; till you remember how lately you were made, and how wonderful it was when you came into it: and more rejoice in the palace of your glory than if it had been made but to-day morning.

Will you see the infancy of this sublime and celestial greatness? Those pure and virgin apprehensions I had from the
womb, and that Divine light wherewith I was born, are the best
unto this day, wherein I can see the Universe. By the Gift of God
they attended me into the world, and by His special favor I
remember them till now. Verily they seem the greatest gifts His
wisdom could bestow, for without them all other gifts had been
dead and vain. They are unattainable by book, and therefore I
will teach them by experience. Pray for them earnestly, for they
will make you angelical, and wholly celestial. Certainly Adam in
Paradise had not more sweet and curious apprehensions of the
world than I when I was a child.

All appeared new and strange at first, inexpressibly rare and
delightful and beautiful. I was a little stranger, which at my
entrance into the world was saluted and surrounded with
innumerable joys. My knowledge was Divine. I knew by intuition
those things which since my apostasy I collected again by the
highest reason. My very ignorance was advantageous. I seemed
as one brought into the Estate of Innocence. All things were
spotless and pure and glorious: yea, and infinitely mine, and
joyful and precious. I knew not that there were any sins, or
complaints or laws. I dreamed not of poverties, contentions, or
vices. All tears and quarrels were hidden from mine eyes.
Everything was at rest, free and immortal. I knew nothing of
sickness or death or rents or exaction, either for tribute or
bread. In the absence of these I was entertained like an Angel
with the works of God in their splendor and glory and saw all in
the peace of Eden; Heaven and Earth did sing my Creator's
praises, and could not make more melody to Adam than to me.
All Time was Eternity, and a perpetual Sabbath. Is it not strange
that an infant should be heir of the whole world and see those
mysteries which the books of the learned never unfold?

The corn was orient and immortal wheat, which never
should be reaped nor was ever sown. I thought it had stood from
everlasting to everlasting. The dust and stones of the street were
as precious as gold: the gates were at first the end of the world.
The green trees, when I saw them first through one of the gates,
transported and ravished me; their sweetness and unusual

beauty made my heart to leap, and almost mad with ecstasy, they were such strange and wonderful things. The Men! O what venerable and reverend creatures did the aged seem! Immortal Cherubim! And young men glittering and sparkling Angels, and maids strange seraphic pieces of life and beauty! Boys and girls tumbling in the street, and playing, were moving jewels. I knew not that they were born or should die; but all things abided eternally as they were in their proper places. Eternity was manifest in the Light of the Day, and something infinite behind everything appeared: which talked with my expectation and moved my desire. The city seemed to stand in Eden, or to be built in Heaven. The streets were mine, the temple was mine, the people were mine, their clothes and gold and silver were mine, as much as their sparkling eyes, fair skins, and ruddy faces. The skies were mine, and so were the sun and moon and stars, and all the world was mine; and I the only spectator and enjoyer of it. I knew no churlish proprieties, nor bounds, nor divisions, but all proprieties and divisions were mine: all treasures and the possessors of them. So that with much ado I was corrupted, and made to learn the dirty devices of this world. Which now I unlearn, and become, as it were, a little child again that I may enter into the Kingdom of God.

39

Saving Loveliness

St Nonnus

Certain of the bishops besought my master Nonnus that they might have some instruction from his lips; and straightway the good bishop began to speak to the weal and health of all that heard him.

And as we sat marveling at his holy learning, suddenly she who was first of the actresses of Antioch passed by: first of the dancers was she, and riding on an ass; and with all fantastic graces did she ride, so decked that nothing could be seen upon her but gold and pearls and precious stones: the very nakedness of her feet was hidden under gold and pearls: and with her was a splendid train of young men and maidens clad in robes of price, with torques of gold about their necks. Some went before and some came after her: but of the beauty and the loveliness of her there could be no wearying for a world of men. Passing through our midst, she filled the air with the fragrance of musk and of all scents that are sweetest. And when the bishops saw her so shamelessly ride by, bare of head and shoulder and limb, in pomp so splendid, and not so much as a veil upon her head or about her shoulders, they groaned, and in silence turned away their heads as from great and grievous sin.

But the most blessed Nonnus did long and most intently regard her: and after she had passed by, still he gazed and still

---

St Nonnus (*fl.* 451) was Bishop of Edessa and a signatory at the Council of Chalcedon. The woman of the story is St Pelagia, who was converted by the bishop who had been so thankful to God for her beauty, and this selection is taken from her *Life.*

his eyes went after her. Then turning his head, he looked upon the bishops sitting round him. He asked, "Did not the sight of her great beauty delight you?" They answered him nothing. And he sank his face upon his knees, and the holy book that he held in his good hands, and his tears fell down upon his breast, and sighing heavily he said again to the bishops, "Did not the sight of her great beauty delight you?" But again they answered nothing. Then said he, "Verily, it greatly delighted me, and well pleased was I with her beauty: whom God shall set in the presence of His high and terrible seat, in judgment of ourselves and our episcopate."

40

Uncreated Light

St Seraphim of Sarov

ut how," I asked Father Seraphim, "can I know that I am in the grace of the Holy Spirit?"

"It is very simple, your Godliness," he replied. "That is why the Lord says: 'All things are simple to those who find knowledge' (Prov. 8:9). The trouble is that we do not seek this Divine knowledge which does not puff up, for it is not of this world. This knowledge which is full of love for God and for our neighbor builds up every man for his salvation. Of this knowledge the Lord said that God 'wills all men to be saved, and to come to the knowledge of the truth' (1 Tim. 2:4). And of the lack of this knowledge He said to His Apostles: 'Are ye also without understanding' (Matt. 15:16), or 'have ye not read the Scriptures' (Matt. 21:42), and 'did ye not understand this parable' (Mk. 4:13). Concerning this understanding, it is said in the Gospel: 'Then opened He their understanding' (Luke 24:45), and the Apostles also perceived whether the Spirit of God was dwelling in them or not; and being filled with understanding, they saw the presence of the Holy Spirit with them and

St Seraphim of Sarov (1759-1833), perhaps the best-known of modern Russian saints, was an Orthodox monk, ascetic, and *starets*. Living in complete seclusion for over thirty years, first as a hermit in the forest and then in the monastery at Sarov, he returned to the wilderness in 1825 but now with his door opened to visitors, and during the remaining eight years of his life received a constant stream of seekers from all over Russia. In this well-known report of a conversation with one of these pilgrims, a judge named Nicholas Alexandrovich Motovilov, the saint offers a tangible sign of what it means truly to live in God's presence.

declared positively that their work was holy and entirely pleasing to the Lord God. That explains why in their epistles they wrote: 'It seemed good to the Holy Spirit and to us' (Acts 15:28). Only on these grounds did they offer their epistles as immutable truth for the benefit of all the faithful. Thus the holy Apostles were consciously aware of the presence in themselves of the Spirit of God. And so you see, your Godliness, how simple it is."

"Nevertheless," I replied, "I do not understand how I can be certain that I am in the Spirit of God. How can I discern for myself His true manifestation in me?"

Father Seraphim replied: "I have already told you, your Godliness, that it is very simple; and I have related in detail how people come to be in the Spirit of God and how we can recognize His presence in us. So what do you want, my dear?"

"I want to understand it well," I said.

Then Father Seraphim took me very firmly by the shoulders and said: "We are both in the Spirit of God now, my dear. Why do you not look at me?"

I replied: "I cannot look, Father, because your eyes are flashing like lightning. Your face has become brighter than the sun, and my eyes ache with pain."

Father Seraphim said: "Do not be alarmed, your Godliness! Now you yourself have become as bright as I am. You are now in the fullness of the Spirit of God yourself; otherwise you would not be able to see me as I am."

Then bending his head towards me, he whispered softly in my ear: "Thank the Lord God for His unutterable mercy to us! You saw that I did not even cross myself; and only in my heart I prayed mentally to the Lord God and said within myself: 'Lord, grant him to see clearly with his bodily eyes that descent of Thy Spirit which Thou grantest to Thy servants when Thou art pleased to appear in the light of Thy magnificent glory.' And you see, my dear, the Lord instantly fulfilled the humble prayer of poor Seraphim. How then shall we not thank Him for this unspeakable gift to us both? Even to the greatest hermits, my dear, the Lord God does not always show His mercy in this way. This grace of God, like a loving mother, has been pleased to comfort your contrite heart at the intercession of the Mother of

God Herself. But why, my dear, do you not look me in the eyes? Just look, and do not be afraid! The Lord is with us!"

After these words I glanced at his face, and there came over me an even greater reverent awe. Imagine in the center of the sun, in the dazzling light of its midday rays, the face of a man talking to you. You see the movement of his lips and the changing expression of his eyes, you hear his voice, you feel someone holding your shoulders; yet you do not see his hands, you do not even see yourself or his figure, but only a blinding light spreading far around for several yards and illumining with its glaring sheen both the snow blanket which covered the forest glade and the snowflakes which besprinkled me and the great Elder. You can imagine the state I was in!

"How do you feel now?" Father Seraphim asked me.

"Extraordinarily well," I said.

"But in what way? How exactly do you feel well?"

I answered: "I feel such calmness and peace in my soul that no words can express it."

"This, your Godliness," said Father Seraphim, "is that peace of which the Lord said to His disciples: 'My peace I give to you; not as the world gives do I give to you' (John 14:27). 'If ye were of the world, the world would love its own; but because I have chosen you out of the world, therefore the world hates you' (John 15:19). 'But be of good cheer; I have overcome the world' (John 16:33). And to those people whom this world hates but who are chosen by the Lord, the Lord gives that peace which you now feel within you, the peace which, in the words of the Apostle, 'passeth all understanding' (Phil. 4:7). The Apostle describes it in this way because it is impossible to express in words the spiritual well-being which it produces in those into whose hearts the Lord God has infused it. Christ the Savior calls it a peace which comes from His own generosity and is not of this world, for no temporary earthly prosperity can give it to the human heart; it is granted from on high by the Lord God Himself, and that is why it is called the peace of God."

"What else do you feel?" Father Seraphim asked me.

"An extraordinary sweetness," I replied.

And he continued: "This is that sweetness of which it is said in Holy Scripture: 'They will be inebriated with the fatness of Thy house; and Thou shalt make them drink of the torrent of Thy delight' (Ps. 36:8). And now this sweetness is flooding our hearts and coursing through our veins with unutterable delight. From this sweetness our hearts melt, as it were, and both of us are filled with such happiness as tongue cannot tell. What else do you feel?"

"An extraordinary joy in all my heart."

And Father Seraphim continued: "When the Spirit of God comes down to man and overshadows him with the fullness of His inspiration, then the human soul overflows with unspeakable joy, for the Spirit of God fills with joy whatever He touches. What else do you feel, your Godliness?"

I answered: "An extraordinary warmth."

"How can you feel warmth, my dear? Look, we are sitting in the forest. It is winter outdoors, and snow is underfoot. There is more than an inch of snow on us, and the snowflakes are still falling. What warmth can there be?"

I answered: "Such as there is in a bathhouse when the water is poured on the stone and the steam rises in clouds."

"And the smell," he asked me, "is it the same as in a bathhouse?"

"No," I replied. "There is nothing on earth like this fragrance. When in my dear mother's lifetime I was fond of dancing and used to go to balls and parties, my mother would sprinkle me with the scent which she bought at the best fashionshops in Kazan. But those scents did not exhale such fragrance."

And Father Seraphim, smiling pleasantly, said: "I know it myself just as well as you do, my dear, but I am asking you on purpose to see whether you feel it in the same way. It is absolutely true, your Godliness! The sweetest earthly fragrance cannot be compared with the fragrance which we now smell, for we are now enveloped in the fragrance of the Holy Spirit of God. What on earth can be like it? Mark, your Godliness, you have told me that around us it is as warm as in the bathhouse. But look, neither on you nor me does the snow melt, nor does it underfoot; therefore, this warmth is not in the air but in us. It is that very warmth about which the Holy Spirit in the words of prayer makes us cry to the Lord: 'Warm me with the warmth of Thy Holy Spirit!' By it the hermits of both sexes were kept warm and did not fear the winter frost, being clad, as in fur coats, in the grace-given clothing woven by the Holy Spirit."

During the whole of this time, from the moment when Father Seraphim's face began to shine, this illumination continued; and all that he told me from the beginning of the narrative until now, he said while remaining in one and the same position. The ineffable glow of the light which emanated from him I myself saw with my own eyes. And I am ready to vouch for it with an oath.

VI

Transparency

Now we see through a glass darkly,
but then face to face.

1 Corinthians 13:12

41

Filling Every Place

Jeremy Taylor

Let this thought often return, that God is omnipresent, filling every place. Say with David, "Whither shall I go from Thy Spirit, or whither shall I flee from Thy presence? If I ascend up into heaven, Thou art there: if I make my bed in Sheol, Thou art there" (Ps. 139:7-8). This thought, by being frequent, will give habitual awe and reverence towards God and a holy fear in all your actions.

When you begin a religious exercise, make an act of adoration; that is, solemnly worship God, place yourself in His presence, and behold Him with the eye of faith. Let your desires focus on Him as the object of your worship, the reason for your hope, and the source of your blessing. When you have placed yourself before Him and have knelt in His presence, it is most likely that all the rest of your devotion will be influenced by the wisdom of such an awareness and the glory of such a presence.

Let everything you see suggest to your spirit the presence, excellence, and power of God. Let your relationship with creatures lead you to the Creator. The more often you behold Him in the mirror of His creation, the more often your actions will be done with an actual eye to God's presence. In the face of the sun, you may see God's beauty; in the fire, you may feel His heat,

---

Jeremy Taylor (1613-67) was an Anglican chaplain to King Charles I and later the Bishop of Down and Connor in Ireland. His reputation as a gifted spiritual and devotional writer is based in large part on two famous treatises: *The Rule and Exercise of Holy Living*, from which this passage is taken, and *The Rule and Exercise of Holy Dying*.

in the water, His gentleness to refresh you. He it is who comforts your spirit when you have taken a cordial. It is the dew of Heaven that makes your field give you bread, and the fountains of God pour forth drink to your necessities. This idea, which is obvious to every man's experience, is a great help to our piety; and by this awareness, our wills are checked from violence and misbehavior.

Make frequent conversations between God and your own soul. David said, "Seven times a day do I praise Thee", and "my eyes are awake before the watches of the night, that I may meditate upon Thy promise" (Ps. 119:164, 148). Every act of complaint or thanksgiving, every act of rejoicing or of mourning, every petition and every return of the heart in these conversations, is going to God and appearing in His presence. Long ago a spiritual person called this "building a chapel to God in our heart". It reconciles Martha's employment with Mary's devotion, charity, and religion, and the necessities of our calling with the employment of devotion. Thus, in the midst of your daily work, you may retire into the chapel of your heart, and there converse with God.

Offer God acts of love and fear which are the proper results of this awareness and its consideration. As God is everywhere present by His power, He calls for reverence and godly fear. Since He is present to you in all your needs and relieves them, He deserves your love. And since, in every circumstance of our lives, we find either His power or His goodness apparent, and in most things we see both, it is a proper and fitting return that in every demonstration of His power and presence, we express our awareness of it by admiring His Divine goodness and trembling at His presence. We then obey Him because we love Him, and because we fear to offend Him. This is what Enoch did, who "walked with God" (Gen. 5:22).

God is in every place; think of every place as a church. Then the decency of conduct and piety of manner which you have been taught by religion, custom, civility, or public manners to use in church, use in all places, but with this difference: in church let your behavior be religious in external forms as is fitting, but everywhere else be religious in avoiding spiritual

indecencies and in making good actions. God is in every creature. Be cruel towards none, neither abuse any by intemper-
ance. Remember that the creatures and every member of your
own body are "receptacles of God", because God has blessed
them with His presence, hallowed them by His touch, and separated them from unholy use by making them to belong to His
dwelling.

He walks as in the presence of God who converses with Him
in frequent prayer and frequent communion; who runs to Him
in all necessities; who asks counsel of Him in all his doubtings;
who opens all his wants to Him; who weeps before Him for his
sins; who asks strength for his weakness; who fears Him as a
Judge, reverences Him as Lord, obeys Him as Father, and loves
Him as a Benefactor.

42

Virtues and Powers

Paracelsus

Having first invocated the name of the Lord Jesus Christ our Savior, we will enterprise this work, wherein we shall not only teach how to change any inferior metal into better, as iron into copper, this into silver, and that into gold, but also how to help all infirmities, whose cure to the opinionated and presumptuous physicians seems impossible.

This art was by our Lord God the Supreme Creator engraven as it were in a book in the body of metals from the beginning of the creation that we might diligently learn from them. Therefore, when any man desires thoroughly and perfectly to learn this art from its true foundation, it will be necessary that he learn the same from the Master thereof, that is, from God, who has created all things and alone knows what nature and property He Himself has placed in every creature. Wherefore He is able to teach every one certainly and perfectly; and from Him we may learn absolutely, as He has spoken, saying, "Of Me ye shall learn all things." For there is nothing found in Heaven nor in Earth so secret that its properties He does not perceive, and most exactly know and see, who has created all things. We will therefore take Him to be our Master,

---

Paracelsus (1493-1541)—the adopted name of Theophrastus Bombastus von Hohenheim—was a Swiss physician and alchemist, and for a time a professor of medicine at the University of Basle. Sickness, he taught, is a matter of forgetfulness, and knowledge—whether of oneself, of nature, or of God, each of these intimately linked with the others—is the root of good health. This passage is taken from the Prologue to his "Secrets of Alchemy, Discovered in the Nature of the Planets".

Operator, and Leader into this most true art. We will therefore imitate Him alone and through Him learn and attain to the knowledge of that nature which He Himself with His own finger has engraven and inscribed in the bodies of these metals. Hereby it will come to pass that the most high Lord God shall bless all the creatures unto us and shall sanctify all our ways, so that in this work we may be able to bring our beginning to its desired end, and in consequence thereof to produce exceeding great joy and love in our hearts.

This therefore has moved and induced us to write a peculiar book of Alchemy, founded not upon men, but upon nature itself, and upon those virtues and powers which God with His own finger has impressed in metals. Of this impression Hermes Trismegistus was an imitator, who is not undeservedly called the father of all wise-men and of all those that followed this art with love and with earnest desire, who demonstrates and teaches that God alone is the author, cause, and original of all creatures in this art. But he does not attribute the power and virtue of God to the creatures or visible things, as the heathen and such-like did.

Now seeing all art ought to be learned from the Trinity—that is, from God the Father, from God the Son of God, our Savior Jesus Christ, and from God the Holy Ghost, three distinct persons, but one God—we will therefore divide this our alchemistical work into three parts or treatises: in the first whereof we will lay down what the art contains in itself and what is the property and nature of every metal; secondly, by what means a man may work and bring the like powers and strength of metals to effect; and thirdly, what tinctures are to be produced from the sun and moon.

43

A Single Unified Science

Philip Sherrard

The fall may best be understood not as a moral deviation or as a descent into a carnal state, but as a drama of knowledge, as a dislocation and degradation of our consciousness, a lapse of our perceptive and cognitive powers—a lapse which cuts us off from the presence and awareness of other superior worlds and imprisons us in the fatality of our solitary existence in this world. It is to forget the symbolic function of every form and to see in things not their dual, symbiotic reality, but simply their non-spiritual dimension, their psycho-physical or material appearance.

Seen in this perspective, our crime, like that of Adam, is equivalent to losing this sense of symbols; for to lose the sense of symbols is to be put in the presence of our own darkness, of our own ignorance. This is the exile from Paradise, the condition of our fallen humanity; and it is the consequence of our ambition to establish our presence exclusively in this terrestrial world and to assert that our presence in this world, and exclusively in this world, accords with our real nature as human beings. In fact, we have reached the point not only of thinking that the world which we perceive with our ego-consciousness is the natural world, but also of thinking that our fallen, sub-human state is the natural human state, the state that accords

---

Philip Sherrard (1922-95) was an Orthodox theologian, spiritual writer, and co-translator of the *Philokalia*. His works include *The Sacred in Life and Art, The Eclipse of Man and Nature, Human Image, World Image,* and—his last book and the source of this passage—*Christianity: Lineaments of a Sacred Tradition.*

with our nature as human beings. And we talk of acquiring knowledge of the natural world when we do not even know what goes on in the mind of an acorn.

This dislocation of our consciousness which defines the fall is perhaps most clearly evident in the divorce we make between the spiritual and the material, the esoteric and the exoteric, the uncreated and the created, and in our assumption that we can know the one without knowing the other. If we acknowledge the spiritual realm at all, we tend to regard it as something quite other than the material realm and to deny that the Divine is inalienably present in natural forms or can be known except through a direct perception which bypasses the natural world—as though the existence of this world were, spiritually speaking, negative and of no consequence where our salvation is concerned.

This other-worldly type of esotericism only too often degenerates into a kind of spiritual debauchery, in the sense that it has its counterpart in the idea that it is possible to cultivate the inner spiritual life, and to engage in meditation, invocation, and other ritual practices, whether consecrated or counterfeit, while our outward life, professional or private, is lived in obedience to mental and physical standards and habits that not only have nothing spiritual about them but are completely out of harmony with the essential rhythms of being: Divine, human, and natural. We should never forget that an authentic spiritual life can be lived only on condition, first, that the way in which we represent to ourselves the physical universe, as well as our own place in it, accords with the harmony instilled into its whole structure through the Divine *fiat* which brings it into, and sustains it in, existence; and second, that insofar as is humanly possible, we conform every aspect of our life—mental, emotional, and physical—to this harmony, disengaging therefore from all activity and practice which patently clash with it. If we offend against the essential rhythms of being, then our aspirations to tap the wellspring of our spiritual life are condemned to fruitlessness, or in some cases may even lead to a state of psychic disequilibrium that can, in truth, be described as demonic.

The divorce between the spiritual and the material means that material forms are regarded as totally non-spiritual, and thus either as illusion or as only to be known through identifying their reality with their purely material aspects. Such a debasement of the physical dimension of things is tantamount not only to denying the spiritual reality of our own created existence, but also, through depriving natural things of their theophanic function, to treating a Divine revelation as a dead and soulless body. And in this case it is not only of a kind of suicide that we are speaking; we are also speaking of a kind of murder.

It is just as dangerous to think we can attain a knowledge of God while ignoring, or even denying, His presence in existing things and in their corresponding symbolic rituals as it is for us to think that we can attain a knowledge of existing things while ignoring, or even denying, the Divine presence that informs them and gives them their reality. In effect, there cannot be a knowledge of the outward appearance of things—of what we call phenomena—without a knowledge of their inner reality; just as there cannot be a knowledge of this inner reality which does not include a knowledge of the outer appearance. It is the same as with the Holy Book: the integrality of the revelation cannot be understood simply from its letter, from its outward literal sense; it can be understood only when interpreted by the spiritual science of its inner meaning. At the same time this inner meaning cannot be perceived except by means of the letter, of the outward literal sense. There is an unbreakable union between the esoteric and the exoteric, the feminine and the masculine, between the inner reality of a thing and its external appearance. And any genuine knowledge of either depends upon both being regarded as integers of a single unified science.

44

Practicing Presence

Brother Lawrence

That practice which is alike the most holy, the most general, and the most needful in the spiritual life is the practice of the Presence of God. It is the schooling of the soul to find its joy in His Divine companionship, holding with Him at all times and at every moment humble and loving converse, without set rule or stated method, in all time of our temptation and tribulation, in all time of our dryness of soul and disrelish of God, yes, and even when we fall into unfaithfulness and actual sin. We should apply ourselves unceasingly to this one end, to so rule all our actions that they be little acts of communion with God. But they must not be studied; they must come naturally, from the purity and simplicity of the heart.

We must do all things thoughtfully and soberly, without impetuosity or precipitancy, which denotes a mind undisciplined. We must go about our labors quietly, calmly, and lovingly, entreating Him to prosper the works of our hands; by thus keeping heart and mind fixed upon God, we shall bruise the head of the evil one, and beat down his weapons to the ground.

When we are busied, or meditating on spiritual things, even in our time of set devotion, whilst our voice is rising in prayer,

---

Brother Lawrence (1605-91)—Nicholas Herman of Lorraine—was a lay brother of the Carmelite monastery at Paris, where he had charge of the kitchen and led a life of nearly constant recollection. "The time of business does not with me differ from the time of prayer," he said, "and in the noise and clatter of my kitchen, I possess God in as great tranquility as if I were upon my knees before the Blessed Sacrament." This reading comes from his *Spiritual Maxims*, which were collected after his death by the Abbé de Beaufort.

we ought to cease for one brief moment, as often as we can, to worship God in the depth of our being, to taste Him though it be in passing, to touch Him as it were by stealth. Since you cannot but know that God is with you in all you undertake, that He is at the very depth and center of your soul, why should you not thus pause an instant from time to time in your outward business, and even in the act of prayer, to worship Him within your soul, to praise Him, to entreat His aid, to offer Him the service of your heart, and to give Him thanks for all His loving-kindnesses and tender mercies?

What offering is there more acceptable to God than thus throughout the day to quit the things of outward sense, and to withdraw to worship Him within the secret places of the soul? Besides, by so doing we destroy the love of self, which can subsist only among the things of sense, and of which these times of quiet retirement with God rid us well-nigh unconsciously. In very truth we can render to God no greater or more signal proofs of our trust and faithfulness than by thus turning from things created to find our joy, though for a single moment, in the Creator. Yet think not that I counsel you to disregard completely and for ever the outward things that are around us. That is impossible. Prudence, the mother of the virtues, must be your guide. Yet, I am confident, it is a common error among religious persons to neglect this practice of ceasing for a time that which they are engaged upon to worship God in the depth of their soul, and to enjoy the peace of brief communion with Him.

The Presence of God is an applying of our spirit to God, or a realization of God as present, which is borne home to us either by the imagination or by the understanding. I have a friend who these forty years past has been practicing through the understanding a realization of the Presence of God. To it he gives many other names: sometimes he calls it a simple act, or a clear and distinct knowledge of God; at other times, a view as through a glass, a loving gaze, an inward sense of God; yet again he terms it a waiting on God, a silent converse with Him, a repose in Him, the life and peace of the soul. Still, my friend tells me that all these ways in which he has expressed his sense of the Presence of God come to the same thing, and that the Presence fills his soul quite naturally.

He says that by unwearying efforts, by constantly recalling his mind to the Presence of God, a habit has been formed within him of such a nature that, so soon as he is freed from his ordinary labor, and not seldom even when he is engaged therein, his soul lifts itself up above all earthly matters, without care or forethought on his part, and dwells as it were firmly stayed on God, as in its center and place of rest, faith almost always being his companion at such times. Then his soul's joy is full; it is what he calls the actual Presence and includes all other kinds, and greatly more besides. Then he feels that only God and he are in the world; with Him he holds unbroken converse, asking from Him the supply of all his needs, and finding in His Presence fullness of joy. Let us mark well, however, that this intercourse with God is held in the depth of his being; there it is that the soul speaks to God, heart to heart, and over the soul thus holding converse there steals a great and profound peace. All that passes without concerns the soul no more than a fire of straw, which the more it flares, the sooner burns itself out; and rarely indeed do the cares of this world ever intrude to trouble the peace that is within.

But to come back to our consideration of the Presence of God, you must know that the tender and loving light of God's countenance kindles insensibly within the soul, which ardently embraces it, so great and so Divine a fire of love toward God that one is perforce compelled to moderate the outward expression of the feelings. Great would be our surprise if we but knew what converse the soul holds at these times with God, who seems so to delight in this communion that to the soul which would fain abide ever with Him He bestows favors past numbering; and as if He dreaded lest the soul should turn again to things of earth, He provides for it abundantly, so that the soul finds in faith a nourishment Divine, a joy that has no measure, beyond its utmost thought and desire; and this without a single effort on its part but simple consent.

45

Hidden and Glorified

Samuel Taylor Coleridge

I have at this moment before me, in the flowery meadow on which my eye is now reposing, one of the Book of Nature's most soothing chapters, in which there is no lamenting word, no one character of guilt or anguish. For never can I look and meditate on the vegetable creation without a feeling similar to that with which we gaze at a beautiful infant that has fed itself asleep at its mother's bosom, and smiles in its strange dream of obscure yet happy sensations. The same tender and genial pleasure takes possession of me, and this pleasure is checked and drawn inward by the like aching melancholy, by the same whispered remonstrance, and made restless by a similar impulse of aspiration.

It seems as if the soul said to herself: from this state hast thou fallen! Such shouldst thou still become, thy Self all permeable to a holier power! thy Self at once hidden and glorified by its own transparency, as the accidental and dividuous in this quiet and harmonious object is subjected to the life and light of nature which shines in it, even as the transmitted power, love, and wisdom of God over all fills, and shines through, nature. But what the plant is by an act not its own and unconsciously—*that* must thou *make* thyself to *become!* must by prayer and by a watchful and unresisting spirit *join* at least with the preventive

---

Samuel Taylor Coleridge (1772-1834) was an English poet, literary critic, and philosopher. Steeped like many another Anglican thinker in the traditions of Platonism and Hermeticism, he dedicated himself to the exposition of a Christian form of panentheism. When Coleridge speaks of Reason, as here in his *Statesman's Manual, or the Bible the Best Guide to Political Skill and Foresight*, he means the *Nous* or spiritual Intellect, our highest power of intuitive insight.

and assisting grace to *make* thyself, in that light of conscience which inflameth not, and with that knowledge which puffeth not up.

I feel it alike, whether I contemplate a single tree or flower, or meditate on vegetation throughout the world as one of the great organs of the life of nature. Lo! with the rising sun it commences its outward life and enters into open communion with all the elements, at once assimilating them to itself and to each other. At the same moment it strikes its roots and unfolds its leaves, absorbs and respires, steams forth its cooling vapor and finer fragrance, and breathes a repairing spirit, at once the food and tone of the atmosphere, into the atmosphere that feeds it. Lo! at the touch of light how it returns an air akin to light, and yet with the same pulse effectuates its own secret growth, still contracting to fix what expanding it had refined. Lo! how upholding the ceaseless plastic motion of the parts in the profoundest rest of the whole it becomes the visible *organismus* of the whole silent or elementary life of nature and, therefore, in incorporating the one extreme becomes the symbol of the other: the natural symbol of that higher life of Reason, in which the whole series (known to us in our present state of being) is perfected, in which, therefore, all the subordinate gradations recur, and are re-ordained "in more abundant honor" (1 Cor. 12:24).

We see each in its own cast, and we now recognize them all as co-existing in the unity of a higher form, the Crown and Completion of the earthly and the Mediator of a new and heavenly series. Thus finally the vegetable creation, in the simplicity and uniformity of its internal structure symbolizing the unity of nature, while it represents the omniformity of her delegated functions in its external variety and manifoldness, becomes the record and chronicle of her ministerial acts, and inchases the vast unfolded volume of the earth with the hieroglyphics of her history. O! if as the plant to the orient beam we would but open out our minds to that holier light, which "being compared with light is found before it, more beautiful than the sun, and above all the order of stars" (Wisd. of Sol. 7:29), ungenial, alien, and adverse to our very nature would appear all boastful wisdom.

46

As through a Mirror

St Bonaventure

ntering our very selves as if leaving the vestibule and entering into the sanctum—that is, the anterior part of the tabernacle, where after the manner of a candelabrum the light of Truth glitters upon the face of our soul—we should begin to see God as through a mirror. Enter therefore into yourself, and you will discover that your soul most fervently loves itself, nor can it love itself unless it knows itself, nor does it know itself unless it remembers itself; for we can understand nothing that is not present in our memory. And from this you will discover, not according to the eye of the flesh, but in the eye of the mind, that your soul has a threefold power. Therefore consider the activities and characteristics of these three powers, and you will see God through yourself as through an image, which is to see through a mirror in mystery.

The activity of the memory is retention and representation, not only of things present, corporeal, and temporal, but also of past and future things, simple and eternal. For the memory retains things past through remembrance, things present through receiving them, and things future through foresight. It also retains simple things, like the principles of continuous and discrete quantities, such as the point, the instant, and unity,

---

St Bonaventure (*c.* 1217-74), called the "Seraphic Doctor", was Minister General of the Franciscan Order and Cardinal Bishop of Albano. His greatest mystical work, *The Journey of the Mind into God*, divides the spiritual journey into six basic stages, the third of which consists in seeing God through the "mirror" of the self.

without which it is impossible to remember or think of those things which are derived by means of them. And it retains the principles and the axioms of the sciences as eternal things and in an eternal manner, because it can never forget them while it uses reason; on the contrary, it approves those things heard and assents to them, perceiving them not as something new, but recognizing them as things innate and familiar to itself, as is clear and self-evident when someone says: "One must either affirm or deny", or "Every whole is greater than its part", or whatever else cannot be rationally contradicted. Therefore from the first actual retention of all temporal things—things past, present, and future—it has a likeness to eternity, whose indivisible presence extends itself to all times. Thus through the activities of memory it appears that the soul itself is an image and similitude of God, so fully present to itself and having Him present that it is able to grasp Him by act and through power and to participate in Him.

The activity of the intellect consists in the understanding of terms, propositions, and inferences. It grasps what is signified by the understanding of terms when it comprehends what each thing is through its definition. But a definition must be based upon higher terms, and these latter have to be defined by things still higher, until one comes to things supreme and most general, without which lower things cannot be definitively understood. Therefore unless one becomes acquainted with what being itself is, there can be no complete definition of any special substance. Nor can one become acquainted with being itself unless one knows it together with its conditions: namely, the one, the true, the good. Since, however, being can be thought of as diminished or complete, as imperfect or perfect, as in potency or in act, as relative or absolute, as partial or whole, as transient or stable, as dependent or independent, as commingled with non-being or with pure being, as contingent or necessary, as posterior or prior, as mutable or immutable, as simple or composite; and since privations and defects can be known only through affirmations: it follows that our intellect cannot fully understand anything unless it is aided by the understanding of the most pure, most actual, most complete, and absolute being, which is being simple and eternal, in which are the reasons for all things in their purity. For in what manner would the intellect know that a being is defective and incomplete if it had no acquaintance with true being apart from all fault?

Furthermore, our intellect perceives the meaning of inference when it sees that a conclusion follows necessarily from the premises; this it sees not only in necessary terms, but also in those which are contingent: for example, if a man is running, a man is moving. Moreover it perceives this necessary characteristic not only in existing things, but also in non-existing ones. Thus if a man exists, it follows that if the man runs, he is moving; but the same thing follows even if the man is not existing. Therefore the necessity of such inferences does not come from the existence of a thing in matter, which is contingent, nor from the existence of a thing in the soul, which then would be a fiction if it did not also exist in the world: it comes instead from its archetype in the Eternal Mind of God, according to which everything has an aptitude and characteristic in relation to other things. As Augustine says in his *On True Religion*, the light of anyone who reasons truly is enkindled by the Truth and strives to return to it. From which it is obvious that our intellect has been conjoined to eternal Truth itself so that it cannot with certitude grasp anything truly except under its guidance. Therefore the Truth can be seen through yourself, the Truth which teaches you—if, that is, passions and phantasms do not impede you and do not interpose themselves as clouds between you and the ray of this Truth.

Finally, the activity of the power of choice is found in deliberation, judgment, and desire. Deliberation consists in inquiring which is better, this or that. But there is no consideration of "better" unless through comparison with the "best", and such comparison is by means of a degree of assimilation; therefore no one knows whether this is better than that unless he also knows that it is more assimilated to the best; and no one knows that anything is assimilated more to another unless he becomes acquainted with it, for I do not know that this is like Peter unless I know or become acquainted with Peter. Therefore, upon every deliberation there is necessarily impressed the idea of the Most High Good. Furthermore, certain judgment always comes through some law. No one, however, judges with certainty through law unless he is certain that that law is right and that one ought not judge it; but our mind judges about its very self: therefore since it cannot judge about the law through which it judges, that law must be superior to our mind, and it judges through this according to what is impressed upon itself. Nothing, however, is superior to the human mind except that One alone who made it; therefore, in judging, our deliberative power reaches upward to Divine laws in order to give a full explanation. As for desire, it is the power which especially moves one. Now that moves most which is most loved; happiness, however, is loved most of all; but happiness does not come about except through the best and last end: therefore, human desire seeks after nothing unless it is the Most High Good, or because it leads to that Good, or because it has some likeness to it. So great is the force of the Most High Good that nothing can be loved by a creature except through a desire for it, which creature thereby fails and errs when it accepts a likeness and imitation in place of the Truth.

See then in what manner the soul is nigh unto God, and in what manner the memory leads into Eternity, the intelligence into Truth, and the elective power into the Most High Goodness, according to their proper activities.

47

Recognition

The Gospel of Thomas

These are the secret sayings which the living Jesus spoke and which Didymos Judas Thomas wrote down. And He said, "Whoever finds the interpretation of these sayings will not experience death."

Jesus said, "Let him who seeks continue seeking until he finds. When he finds, he will become troubled. When he becomes troubled, he will be astonished, and he will rule over the All."

Jesus said, "If those who lead you say to you, 'See, the Kingdom is in the sky', then the birds of the sky will precede you. If they say to you, 'It is in the sea', then the fish will precede you. Rather, the Kingdom is inside of you, and it is outside of you. When you come to know yourselves, then you will become known, and you will realize that it is you who are the sons of the living Father. But if you will not know yourselves, you dwell in poverty, and it is you who are that poverty."

Jesus said, "The man old in days will not hesitate to ask a small child seven days old about the place of life, and he will live. For many who are first will become last, and they will become one and the same."

The Gospel of Thomas (*c.* 150), originally written in Greek, is one of several apocryphal gospels that were preserved in Coptic among the papyri excavated at Nag Hammadi in Upper Egypt in 1945-46. The sayings which it attributes to Jesus, whether one regards them as authentic or not, are entirely consistent with the insights of many later Christian mystics.

Jesus said, "Recognize what is in your sight, and that which is hidden from you will become plain to you. For there is nothing hidden which will not become manifest."

Jesus said, "This heaven will pass away, and the one above it will pass away. The dead are not alive, and the living will not die. In the days when you consumed what is dead, you made it what is alive. When you come to dwell in the light, what will you do? On the day when you were one you became two. But when you become two, what will you do?"

Jesus said to His disciples, "Compare me to someone and tell Me whom I am like." Simon Peter said to Him, "You are like a righteous angel." Matthew said to Him, "You are like a wise philosopher." Thomas said to Him, "Master, my mouth is wholly incapable of saying whom You are like." Jesus said, "I am not your master. Because you have drunk, you have become intoxicated from the bubbling spring which I have measured out." And He took him and withdrew and told him three things. When Thomas returned to his companions, they asked him, "What did Jesus say to you?" Thomas said to them, "If I tell you one of the things which He told me, you will pick up stones and throw them at me; a fire will come out of the stones and burn you up."

Jesus said, "I shall give you what no eye has seen and what no ear has heard and what no hand has touched and what has never occurred to the human mind."

The disciples said to Jesus, "Tell us how our end will be." Jesus said, "Have you discovered, then, the beginning that you look for the end? For where the beginning is, there will the end be. Blessed is he who will take his place in the beginning; he will know the end and will not experience death."

Jesus saw infants being suckled. He said to His disciples, "These infants being suckled are like those who enter the Kingdom." They said to Him, "Shall we then as children enter the Kingdom?" Jesus said to them, "When you make the two one, and when you make the inside like the outside and the outside like the inside, and the above like the below, and when you make the male and the female one and the same, so that the male not be male nor the female female; and when you fashion

159

an eye in place of an eye, and a hand in place of a hand, and a foot in place of a foot, and a likeness in place of a likeness, then will you enter the Kingdom."

His disciples said to Him, "Show us the place where You are, since it is necessary for us to seek it." He said to them, "Whoever has ears, let him hear. There is light within a man of light, and he lights up the whole world. If he does not shine, he is darkness."

Jesus said, "I took My place in the midst of the world, and I appeared to them in flesh. I found all of them intoxicated; I found none of them thirsty. And My soul became afflicted for the sons of men, because they are blind in their hearts and do not have sight; for empty they came into the world, and empty too they seek to leave the world. But for the moment they are intoxicated. When they shake off their wine, then they will repent."

Jesus said, "Where there are three gods, they are gods. Where there are two or one, I am with him."

His disciples said, "When will You become revealed to us and when shall we see You?" Jesus said, "When you disrobe without being ashamed and take up your garments and place them under your feet like little children and tread on them, then will you see the Son of the Living One, and you will not be afraid."

Jesus said, "Become passers-by."

Jesus said, "If they say to you, 'Where did you come from?', say to them, 'We came from the light, the place where the light came into being of its own accord and established itself and became manifest through their image.' If they say to you, 'Is it you?', say, 'We are its children, and we are the elect of the Living Father.' If they ask you, 'What is the sign of your Father in you?', say to them, 'It is movement and repose.'"

His disciples said to Him, "When will the repose of the dead come about, and when will the new world come?" He said to them, "What you look forward to has already come, but you do not recognize it."

Jesus said, "Whoever has come to understand the world has found only a corpse, and whoever has found a corpse is superior to the world."

Jesus said, "Take heed of the Living One while you are alive, lest you die and seek to see Him and be unable to do so."

Jesus said, "It is to those who are worthy of My mysteries that I tell My mysteries. Do not let your left hand know what your right hand is doing."

Jesus said, "It is I who am the light which is above them all. It is I who am the All. From Me did the All come forth, and unto Me did the All extend. Split a piece of wood, and I am there. Lift up the stone, and you will find Me there."

They said to Him, "Tell us who You are so that we may believe in You." He said to them, "You read the face of the sky and of the earth, but you have not recognized the One who is before you, and you do not know how to read this present moment."

48

Two Facades

C. S. Lewis

t Francis of Sales begins every meditation with the command *Mettez-vous en la présence de Dieu* [Place yourself in the presence of God]. I wonder how many different mental operations have been carried out in intended obedience to that?

What happens to me if I try to take it "simply" is the juxta-position of two "representations" or ideas or phantoms. One is the bright blur in the mind which stands for God. The other is the idea I call "me". But I can't leave it at that, because I know—and it's useless to pretend I don't know—that they are both phantasmal. The real I has created them both—or, rather, built them up in the vaguest way from all sorts of psychological odds and ends. Very often, paradoxically, the first step is to banish the "bright blur"—or, in statelier language, to break the idol. Let's get back to what has at least some degree of resistant reality. Here are the four walls of the room. And here am I. But both terms are merely the facade of impenetrable mysteries.

C. S. Lewis (1898-1963), Professor of Medieval and Renaissance Literature at Cambridge University and a member of the Church of England, is often described as the greatest Christian writer of the twentieth century. Although he more than once denied being a mystic—"for news of the fully waking world," he said, "you must go to my betters"—his books are filled with pene-trating spiritual insights. Among his most important works in this regard are *The Screwtape Letters, The Great Divorce,* and—the source of this reading—*Letters to Malcolm: Chiefly on Prayer.* For a selection from St Francis of Sales, see p. 51.

The walls, they say, are matter. That is, as the physicists will try to tell me, something totally unimaginable, only mathematically describable, existing in a curved space, charged with appalling energies. If I could penetrate far enough into that mystery, I should perhaps finally reach what is sheerly real. And what am I? The facade is what I call consciousness. I am at least conscious of the color of those walls. I am not, in the same way or to the same degree, conscious of what I call my thoughts: for if I try to examine what happens when I am thinking, it stops happening. Yet even if I could examine my thinking, it would, I well know, turn out to be the thinnest possible film on the surface of a vast deep. The psychologists have taught us that. Their real error lies in underestimating the depth and the variety of its contents. Dazzling lightness as well as dark clouds come up. And if all the enchanting visions are, as they rashly claim, mere disguises for sex, where lives the hidden artist who, from such monotonous and claustrophobic material, can make works of such various and liberating art? Here again, if I could dive deeply enough, I might again reach at the bottom that which simply is.

And only now am I ready, in my own fashion, to "place myself in the presence of God". Either mystery, if I could follow it far enough, would lead me to the same point—the point where something, in each case unimaginable, leaps forth from God's naked hand. The Indian, looking at the material world, says, "I am that." I say, "That and I grow from one root." *Verbum superne prodiens,* the Word coming forth from the Father, has made both, and brought them together in this subject-object embrace. And what, you ask, is the advantage of all this? Well, for me—I am not talking about anyone else—it plants the prayer right in the present reality. For whatever else is or is not real, this momentary confrontation of subject and object is certainly occurring: always occurring except when I am asleep. Here is the actual meeting of God's activity and man's—not some imaginary meeting that might occur if I were an angel or if God incarnate entered the room. There is here no question of a God "up there" or "out there"; rather, the present operation of God "in here", as the ground of my own being, and God "in there", as the ground of the matter that surrounds me, and God embracing and uniting both in the daily miracle of finite consciousness.

The two facades—the "I" as I perceive myself and the room as I perceive it—were obstacles as long as I mistook them for ultimate realities. But the moment I recognized them as facades, as mere surfaces, they became conductors. Do you see? A lie is a delusion only so long as we believe it; but a recognized lie is a reality—a real lie—and as such may be highly instructive. A dream ceases to be a delusion as soon as we wake. But it does not become a nonentity. It is a real dream: and it also may be instructive. A stage set is not a real wood or drawing room: it is a real stage set, and may be a good one. (In fact we should never ask of anything "Is it real?", for everything is real. The proper question is "A real *what?*", *e.g.,* a real snake or real *delirium tremens?*) The objects around me, and my idea of "me", will deceive if taken at their face value. But they are momentous if taken as the end-products of Divine activities. Thus and not otherwise the creation of matter and the creation of mind meet one another and the circuit is closed.

Or put it this way. I have called my material surroundings a stage set. A stage set is not a dream, nor a nonentity. But if you attack a stage house with a chisel you will not get chips of brick or stone; you'll only get a hole in a piece of canvas and, beyond that, windy darkness. Similarly, if you start investigating the nature of matter, you will not find anything like what imagination has always supposed matter to be. You will get mathematics. From that unimaginable physical reality my senses select a few stimuli. These they translate or symbolize into sensations, which have no likeness at all to the reality of matter. Of these sensations my associative power, very much directed by my practical needs and influenced by social training, makes up little bundles into what I call "things" (labeled by nouns). Out of these I build myself a neat little box stage, suitably provided with properties such as hills, fields, houses, and the rest. In this I can act. And you may well say "act". For what I call "myself" (for all practical, everyday purposes) is also a dramatic construction; memories, glimpses in the shaving glass, and snatches of the very fallible activity called "introspection" are the principal ingredients. Normally I call this construction "me", and the stage set "the real world".

Now the moment of prayer is for me—or involves for me as its condition—the awareness, the re-awakened awareness, that this "real world" and "real self" are very far from being rock-bottom realities. I cannot, in the flesh, leave the stage, either to go behind the scenes or to take my seat in the pit; but I can remember that these regions exist. And I also remember that my apparent self—this clown or hero or super—under his grease-paint is a real person with an off-stage life. The dramatic person could not tread the stage unless he concealed a real person: unless the real and unknown I existed, I would not even make mistakes about the imagined me. And in prayer this real I struggles to speak, for once, from his real being, and to address, for once, not the other actors, but—what shall I call Him? The Author, for He invented us all? The Producer, for He controls all? Or the Audience, for He watches, and will judge, the performance?

The attempt is not to escape from space and time and from my creaturely situation as a subject facing objects. It is more modest: to re-awake the awareness of that situation. If that can be done, there is no need to go anywhere else. This situation itself is, at every moment, a possible theophany. Here is the holy ground; the Bush is burning now.

Of course this attempt may be attended with almost every degree of success or failure. The prayer preceding all prayers is "May it be the real I who speaks. May it be the real Thou that I speak to." Infinitely various are the levels from which we pray. Emotional intensity is in itself no proof of spiritual depth. If we pray in terror we shall pray earnestly; it only proves that terror is an earnest emotion. Only God Himself can let the bucket down to the depths of us. And, on the other side, He must constantly work as the iconoclast. Every idea of Him we form, He must in mercy shatter. The most blessed result of prayer would be to rise thinking, "But I never knew before. I never dreamed . . ." I suppose it was at such a moment that Thomas Aquinas said of all his own theology, "It reminds me of straw."

Union

VII

Unity

That they all may be one:
as Thou, Father, art in Me and
I in Thee, that they also may be
one in Us.

John 17:21

49

A Higher School

Henry Suso

nce after matins, the servant sat in his chair, and as he meditated he fell into a trance. It seemed to his inner eye that a noble youth came down toward him, and stood before him saying: "Thou hast been long enough in the lower school and hast exercised thyself long enough in it; thou hast become mature. Come with me now! I will take thee to the highest school that exists in the world. There thou shalt learn diligently the highest knowledge, which will lead thee to Divine peace and bring thy holy beginning to a blessed fulfillment."

He was glad, and he arose. The youth took him by the hand and led him, as it seemed to him, to a spiritual land. There was an extremely beautiful house there, and it looked as if it was the residence of monks. Those who lived there were concerned with the higher knowledge. When he entered he was kindly received and affectionately welcomed by them. They hastened to their master and told him that someone had come who also wished to be his disciple and to learn their knowledge. He said, "First I will see him with my own eyes, to see if he pleases me." On seeing him, he smiled at him very kindly and said, "Know from me that this guest is quite capable of becoming a worthy master of our

---

Blessed Henry Suso (c. 1295-1366) was a German Dominican monk, a disciple of Meister Eckhart (see p. 249), and a spiritual father and pastor to many nuns of his order. Having lived an extremely ascetical life in his youth, he came to see that another method was needed if he was to attain inner purity and thereby full realization in God. His veneration began very shortly after his death, and he was beatified in 1831.

high learning, if he will only patiently submit to living in the narrow cage in which he must be confined."

The servant turned to the youth who had brought him there and said, "Ah, my dear friend, tell me what this highest school is and what this learning thou hast spoken of." The youth replied: "The highest school and the knowledge which is taught here is nothing but the complete, entire abandonment of one's self; a man must persist in self-abnegation, however God acts toward him, by Himself or by His creatures. He is to strive at all times, in joy and in sorrow, to remain constant in giving up what is his own, as far as human frailty permits, considering only God's praise and honor, just as the dear Christ did to His Heavenly Father."

When the servant had heard all this, he was well pleased, and he thought he would learn this knowledge, and that nothing could be so hard that he would fail to achieve it. He wanted to live there and find active occupation there. The youth forbade this, however, saying, "This learning demands unbroken leisure; the less one does here, the more one has done in reality." He meant that kind of activity with which a man hinders himself and does not strive purely for God's praise.

After these words the servant suddenly came to himself and sat still as he was. He began to think over the words deeply and noticed that they were the pure truths that Christ Himself taught. He then fell into an inner discussion with himself, saying: "Look carefully into thyself and thou wilt find that thou art still the slave of thyself, and thou wilt observe that in spite of all thy external actions, which indeed thou dost only carry out for thy own reasons, thou art not sufficiently composed to withstand the tribulations that confront thee from without. Thou art still like a timid hare that lies hidden in a bush and starts at every leaf that falls. Thus it is with thee: thou art afraid all thy days of imaginary sufferings that may befall thee. Thou dost turn pale at the very sight of thy adversary. When thou shouldst face them, thou dost flee; when thou shouldst surrender unarmed, thou dost conceal thyself. Then, when praised thou dost smile, when blamed thou dost grieve. It may well be true that thou dost need a higher school."

172

50

Flight to Greater Things

St Gregory of Nyssa

Our good Master, Jesus Christ, bestowed on us a partnership in His revered name, so that we get our name from no other person connected with us, and if one happens to be rich and well-born or of lowly origin and poor, or if one has some distinction from his business or position, all such conditions are of no avail because the one authoritative name for those believing in Him is that of "Christian". Now since this grace was ordained for us from above, it is necessary first of all for us to understand the greatness of the gift so that we can worthily thank the God who has given it to us. Then it is necessary to show through our life that we ourselves *are* what the power of this great name requires us to be.

The greatness of the gift of which we are deemed worthy through partnership with the Master becomes clear to us if we recognize the true significance of the name of Christ, so that when in our prayers we call upon the Lord of all by this name, we may comprehend the concept that we are taking into our soul. We must also understand reverently what we believe He is when He is called upon by this name. When we do understand

---

St Gregory of Nyssa (*c.* 330 - *c.* 395) was a bishop of the early Church and one of the Cappadocian Fathers. An outstanding exegete, homilist, and spiritual writer, he was among those attending the Second Ecumenical Council who spoke against the Apollinarian heresy, which taught that human nature, being subject to change, could not have been truly joined with the changeless Godhead in Christ. He is noted for the paradoxical idea, known in Greek as *epektasis* (a "reaching forward"), that perfection consists in an endless progress toward perfection.

this, we shall as a consequence also learn clearly what sort of persons we should be shown to be as a result of our zeal for this way of life and our use of His name as the instructor and the guide for our life. If we make St Paul our leader in these two undertakings, we shall have the safest guide to the plain truth of what we are seeking. For he most of all knew what Christ is, and he indicated by what he did the kind of person named for Him, imitating Him so brilliantly that he revealed his own Master in himself, his own soul being transformed through his accurate imitation of his Prototype, so that Paul no longer seemed to be living and speaking, but Christ Himself seemed to be living in him: "Do you seek a proof of the Christ who speaks in me?" (2 Cor. 13:3). "It is now no longer I that live but Christ lives in me" (Gal. 2:20).

This man knew the significance of the name of Christ for us, saying that Christ is "the power of God and the wisdom of God" (1 Cor. 1:24). And he called Him "peace" (Eph. 2:14) and "light inaccessible" (1 Tim. 6:16) in whom God dwells, and "sanctification and redemption" (1 Cor. 1:30) and "great high priest" (Heb. 4:14) and "passover" (1 Cor. 5:7) and "a propitiation" (Rom. 3:25) of souls, "the brightness of glory and the image of substance" (Heb. 1:3) and "maker of the world" (Heb. 1:2) and "spiritual food" (1 Cor. 10:3) and "spiritual drink and spiritual rock" (1 Cor. 10:4), "water" (John 4:14), "foundation" (1 Cor. 3:11) of faith, and "corner stone" (Matt. 21:42), and "image of the invisible God" (Col. 1:15) and "great God" (Tit. 2:13) and "head of the body of the Church" (*cf.* Col. 1:18) and "the first-born of every creature" (Col. 1:15) and "first-fruits of those who have fallen asleep" (1 Cor. 15:20), "firstborn from the dead" (Col. 1:18), "firstborn among many brethren" (Rom. 8:29), and "mediator between God and men" (1 Tim. 2:5), and "only-begotten Son" (John 3:16) and "crowned with glory and honor" (Heb. 2:7) and "Lord of glory" (*cf.* 1 Cor. 2:8) and "beginning" (Col. 1:18) of being, speaking thus of Him who is the beginning, "king of justice and king of peace" (Heb. 7:2) and "ineffable king of all, having the power of the kingdom" (*cf.* Luke 1:33), and many other such things that are not easily enumerated. When all of these phrases are put next to each other, each one of the terms makes its own contribution to a revelation of what is signified by being named after Christ.

What then is it necessary to do to be worthy of the name of Christ? What else than to distinguish in one's self the proper thoughts and words and deeds, asking whether they look to Christ or are at odds with Christ. Making the distinction is very easy. For whatever is done or thought or said through passion has no agreement with Christ, but bears the character of the adversary, who smears the pearl of the soul with the mud of the passions and dims the luster of the precious stone. What is free from every passionate inclination looks to the source of passionlessness, who is Christ. Drawing from Him as from a pure and uncorrupted stream, a person will show in his thoughts such a resemblance to his Prototype as exists between the water in the running water or stream and the water taken away from there in a jar. For the purity in Christ and the purity seen in the person who has a share in Him are the same, the One being the stream and the other drawn from it, bringing intellectual beauty to his life, so that there is agreement between the hidden and the visible man, since the graceful bearing of our life coincides with our thoughts which are put into motion in accordance with Christ. This therefore is perfection in the Christian life in my judgment, namely, the participation of one's soul and speech and activities in all of the names by which Christ is signified, so that perfect holiness, according to the eulogy of Paul, is taken upon oneself in "the whole body and soul and spirit" (1 Thess. 5:23), continuously safeguarded against being mixed with evil.

But what if someone should say that the good is difficult to achieve, since only the Lord of creation is immutable, whereas human nature is unstable and subject to change, and ask how it is possible for the fixed and unchangeable to be achieved in the changeable nature? We reply to such an argument that one cannot be worthily crowned "unless he has competed according to the rules" (*cf.* 2 Tim. 2:5). For how can there be a lawful contest if there is no opponent? If there is no opponent, there is no crown. Victory does not exist by itself, without there being a defeated party. Let us struggle, therefore, against this very unstable element of our nature, engaging in a close contest with our opponent, not becoming victors by destroying our nature, but by not allowing it to fall. For does man make a change only towards evil? Indeed it would not be possible for him to be on the side of the good if he were by nature inclined only to a single one of the opposites. In fact, the fairest product of change is the increase of good, the change to the better always changing what is nobly changed into something more Divine. Therefore, I do not think it is a fearful thing that our nature is changeable. The Logos shows that it would be a disadvantage for us not to be able to make a change for the better, as a kind of wing of flight to greater things. Therefore, let no one be grieved if he sees in his nature a penchant for change. Changing in everything for the better, let him exchange "glory for glory" (2 Cor. 3:18), becoming greater through daily increase, ever perfecting himself, and never arriving too quickly at the limit of perfection. For this is truly perfection: never to stop growing towards what is better and never placing any limit on perfection.

51

No Other Way

Theologia Germanica

Whthere are some men at the present time who take leave of imagery too soon, before truth and knowledge have shown them the way; hence they are scarcely or perhaps never after able to understand the Truth aright. For such men will follow no one, hold fast to their own understandings, and desire to fly before they are fledged. They would mount up to heaven in one flight even though Christ Himself did not do so, for after His resurrection He remained full forty days with His beloved disciples. No one can become perfect in a day. A man must first wholly deny himself and willingly forsake all things for God's sake, and must give up his own will, and all his natural inclinations, and purge and cleanse himself thoroughly from all sins and evil ways. After this let him humbly take up the cross and follow Christ. Also let him accept example and instruction, wise counsel and teaching, and permit devout and perfect servants of God to advise him, and not follow his own guidance; thus shall the work be established and come to a good end. And when a man has thus broken loose from and overleaped all tem-

The *Theologia Germanica* ("German Theology") is an anonymous treatise of the late fourteenth century which follows in the tradition of St Dionysios the Areopagite (see p. 223) and shares the fundamental mystical vision of Meister Eckhart (p. 249) and John Tauler (p. 189). Christian exclusivists, who may suppose that their condemnation of other religious traditions is justified by the words of Christ in John 14:6, should read this selection with particular care, as should those false mystics who may suppose that they can do without spiritual guidance and the protective framework of a revealed tradition.

poral things and creatures, he may afterward come to perfection in a life of contemplation. For he who will have the one must let the other go. There is no other way.

Christ therefore says: "No man cometh unto the Father but by Me" (John 14:6). Now mark how we must have come unto the Father through Christ. Over himself and all that belongs to him, within and without, the man shall set a watch, and shall so govern and guard himself, as far as in him lies, that neither will nor desire, love nor longing, wish nor thought shall spring up in his heart or have any abiding place in him, save such as belong to God and would be meet for him if God Himself were that man. And whenever he becomes aware of anything rising up within him that does not belong to God and is not meet for Him, he must resist it and root it out as thoroughly and as speedily as he may. And even so shall it be with his outward behavior also, whether he do or refrain, speak or keep silence, wake or sleep, go or stand still—in short, in all his ways and walks, whether touching his own business or his dealings with other men: to the end that he shall watch over all these, lest in him he suffer aught to spring up or dwell, inwardly or outwardly, or lest aught be done in him or through him other than what would belong to God and would be possible and meet for Him, if God Himself were that man.

Behold, he in whom it should be thus: whatever he had within or did without would be all of God, and the man would be a follower of Christ in his life, as we understand it and set it forth. And he who led such a life would go in and out through Christ, for he would be a follower of Christ. Therefore also he would come with Christ unto the Father, and through Christ. And he would also be a servant of Christ, for he who follows Him is His servant, as He Himself also says, "If any man serve Me, let him follow Me" (John 12:26)—as if He said, "He who follows Me not, neither does he serve Me." And he who is thus a servant and follower of Christ comes even to that place where Christ is, that is, unto the Father. So Christ Himself says: "Father, I will that My servants be with Me where I am" (John 17:24). Behold, he who walks in this way "entereth in by the door into the sheepfold", that is, into eternal life, "and to him the porter openeth" (John

10:1, 3). But he who walks in some other way, or imagines that he can come to the Father or to eternal blessedness otherwise than through Christ, is deceived; for he walks not in the right Way, nor enters in by the right Door. Therefore to him the porter opens not, for he is a thief and a murderer, as Christ names him. Lo, now consider whether a man may live in lawless freedom and license, disregarding virtue and vice, order and disorder, and the like; consider well whether, so living, he walks in the right Way and enters in by the right Door. Such heedlessness was not in Christ, neither is it in any of His true followers.

Christ says further: "No man cometh unto Me except the Father draw him" (John 6:44). Now mark: By the Father I understand the perfect, simple Good, which is All and above all, and without which and besides which there is no true Essence nor true Good, and without which no good work ever was or will be done. And in that it is All, it must be in all and above all. It cannot be any one of those things which the creature as creature can comprehend and understand. For whatever the creature as creature can comprehend and understand conforms to its creaturely nature; it is something, this or that, and therefore is likewise all creature. Now if the simple perfect Good were a something, this or that, which the creature understands, it would not be All and in all, and therefore also not perfect. Therefore we name it also "Nothing", meaning thereby that it is none of all the things which the creature can comprehend, know, conceive, or name in virtue of its creaturely nature. Now behold, when this Perfect and Unnamable flows into a person able to bring forth and brings forth the only-begotten Son in that person, and itself in Him, we call it the Father.

Now hear how the Father draws men to Christ. When somewhat of this perfect Good is discovered and revealed to the soul of man, as it were in a vision or an ecstasy, there is born in the man a longing to draw near to the perfect Goodness and unite himself with the Father. And the stronger this longing grows, the more is revealed to the man; and the more is revealed to him, the more he longs and is drawn. In such wise is a man drawn and called to a union with the eternal Goodness. And this is the drawing of the Father, and thus the man is taught of Him who draws him that he cannot come to that union except he come by the life of Christ. Behold, now he puts on that life, of which I have spoken before.

Now consider again those two sayings of Christ's. The one: "No man cometh unto the Father but by Me", that is, through My life, as set forth above. The other saying: "No man cometh unto Me", that is, he does not take My life upon him and follow Me, "except he be moved and drawn of My Father", that is, of the simple and perfect Good, of which Saint Paul says: "When that which is perfect is come, then that which is in part shall be done away" (1 Cor. 13:10). In whatever man this Perfect is known, felt, and tasted, so far as may be in this temporal world, to that man all created things seem as nothing compared with the Perfect, as in truth they are. For beside or without the Perfect is neither true Good nor true Essence. Whosoever then has, recognizes, and loves the Perfect has and recognizes all that is good. What more or else, then, should he want, or what is all that "is in part" to him, seeing that all the parts are united in the Perfect, in the one Essence? And thus the man comes wholly to poorness, and indeed he becomes nothing to himself, and in him becomes nothing all that is something, that is, all created things. Such is the first beginning of his true inward life; and thereafter God Himself becomes the man, so that nothing is left that is not God or of God, and nothing is left that arrogates anything to itself. And thus God Himself, that is, the one eternal Perfect alone, is, lives, knows, works, loves, wills, does, and refrains in the man. Thus should it be in truth, and where it is otherwise, let it be improved and rectified.

52

God's Own Breath

John Smith

Setting aside the Epicurean herd of brutish men who have drowned all their own sober reason in the deepest Lethe of sensuality, we shall divide the rest of men into four ranks with respect to a fourfold kind of knowledge.

The first is that complex and multifarious man that is made up of soul and body by a just equality, as it were, and arithmetical proportion of parts and powers in each of them. The knowledge of these men is a knowledge in which sense and reason are so twisted up together that it cannot easily be unraveled and laid out into its first principles, their life being steered by nothing else but opinion and imagination. Their higher notions of God and religion are so entangled with fleshly passions and mundane vanity that they cannot rise up above the surface of this dark earth or easily entertain any but earthly conceptions of heavenly things. Such souls as are here lodged, as Plato speaks, are heavy behind and are continually pressing down to this world's center; and though, like the spider, they may appear sometimes moving up and down aloft in the air, yet they but sit in the loom and move in that web of their own gross

John Smith (1618-52) was one of the Cambridge Platonists, an influential group of Protestant theologians and philosophers which included such writers as Ralph Cudworth, Benjamin Whichcote, and Henry More. Basing themselves on the teachings of Plato and Plotinus, as well as on the Scriptures and the Fathers of the Church, they taught that Reason is the immanent presence of the Logos or Word within man, and they agreed with St Clement of Alexandria (see p. 67) that the fulfillment of the spiritual life consists in the acquisition by this Reason of a deifying *gnosis* or knowledge of God.

fancies, which they fasten and pin to some earthly thing or other.

The second is the man who looks at himself rather by his soul than by his body, who thinks not fit to view his own face in any other glass but that of reason and understanding, who reckons his soul as that which was made to rule, his body as that which was born to obey and, like a handmaid, perpetually to wait upon his higher and nobler part. And in such a one the common principles of virtue and goodness are more clear and steady. To such a one we may allow more clear and distinct opinions, as being already in a method or course of purgation, or at least fit to be initiated into the lesser mysteries of religion. For though these innate notions of truth may be but poor, empty, and hungry things of themselves before they are fed and filled with the practice of true virtue, yet they are capable of being impregnated and exalted with the rules and precepts of it. And therefore the Stoic supposed that the doctrine of political and moral virtues was fit to be delivered to such as these; and though they may not be so well prepared for Divine virtue, which is of a higher emanation, yet they have the seeds of it already within themselves, which being watered by answerable practice may sprout up within them.

The third is he whose soul is already purged by this lower sort of virtue and so is continually flying off from the body and bodily passion and returning into himself. Such in St Peter's language are those "who have escaped the pollutions which are in the world through lust" (2 Pet. 1:4). To these we may attribute a lower degree of knowledge, their inward sense of virtue and moral goodness being far transcendent to all mere speculative opinions of it. But if this knowledge settles here, it may be quickly apt to corrupt. These forces with which the Divine bounty supplies us to keep a stronger guard against the evil spirit may be abused by our own rebellious pride, enticing them from their allegiance to heaven to strengthen itself in our souls and fortify them against heaven. They may make an airy heaven of these and wall it about with their own self-flattery and then sit in it as gods. And therefore if this knowledge is not attended with humility and a deep sense of self-penury and self-emptiness, we may easily fall short of that true knowledge of God which we seem to aspire after. We may carry such an image of ourselves constantly before us as will make us lose the clear sight of the Divinity and be too apt to rest in a mere logical life without any true participation of the Divine life—if indeed we do not relapse and slide back by vain-glory, popularity, or such vices into some mundane and external vanity or other.

The fourth is the true metaphysical and contemplative man, who running and shooting up above his own logical or self-rational life pierces into the highest life, who by universal love and holy affection abstracting himself from himself endeavors the nearest union with the Divine Essence that may be, knitting his own center, if he have any, into the center of Divine Being. To such a one the Platonists are wont to attribute a true Divine wisdom, powerfully displaying itself in an intellectual life, as they phrase it. Such knowledge, they say, is always pregnant with Divine virtue, which arises out of a happy union of souls with God and is nothing else but a living imitation of a Godlike perfection drawn out by a strong fervent love of it. This Divine knowledge makes us amorous of Divine beauty, beautiful and lovely, and this Divine love and purity reciprocally exalt Divine knowledge, both of them growing up together.

Such a life and knowledge as this peculiarly belongs to the true and sober Christian who lives in Him who is Life itself and is enlightened by Him who is the Truth itself and is made partaker of the Divine unction and knows all things. This Life is nothing else but God's own breath within him and an Infant-Christ—if I may use the expression—formed in his soul, the shining forth of the Father's glory. And yet we must not mistake: this knowledge is but here in its infancy; there is a higher knowledge or a higher degree of this knowledge that does not, that cannot, descend upon us in these earthly habitations; here we can see but "in a glass" (1 Cor. 13:12), and that darkly too. Our imaginative powers, which are perpetually attending the highest acts of our souls, continue to breathe a gross dew upon the pure glass of our understandings and so sully and besmear it that we cannot see the image of the Divinity sincerely in it. Nevertheless this knowledge, being a true heavenly fire kindled from God's own altar, begets an undaunted courage in the souls of good men and enables them to cast a holy scorn upon the poor petty trash of this life in comparison with Divine things and to pity those poor brutish Epicureans that have nothing but the mere husks of fleshly pleasure to feed themselves with. This sight of God makes pious souls breathe after that blessed time when mortality shall be swallowed up in Life, when they shall no more behold the Divinity through those dark mediums that eclipse the blessed sight of it.

53

The Very Marrow of the Bones

St Teresa of Avila

o not think it is a state in which we dream. I say "dream" because the soul sometimes seems to be drowsy, so that it neither is asleep nor feels awake. Here we are all asleep, and fast asleep, to the things of the world, and to ourselves. There is no need now for it to devise any method of suspending thought. Even in loving, if it is able to love, it cannot understand how or what it is that it loves, nor what it would desire; in fact, it has completely died to the world so that it may live more fully in God. This is a delectable death, a snatching of the soul from all the activities which it can perform while it is in the body—a death full of delight—for in order to come closer to God, the soul appears to have withdrawn so far from the body that I do not know if it has still life enough to be able to breathe. I have just been thinking about this, and I believe it has not; or at least, if it still breathes, it does so without realizing it. The mind would like to occupy itself wholly in understanding something of what it feels, and since it has not the strength to do this, it becomes so dumbfounded that, even if any consciousness remains to it, neither hands nor feet can move; as we commonly say of a person who has fallen into a swoon, it might be taken for dead.

St Teresa of Avila (1515-82) was a Spanish Carmelite nun and foundress of a Discalced convent, St Joseph's in Avila. Her most important work on the mystical life is the *Interior Castle*, which pictures the soul's journey as progressing from the outer courtyard of a crystal castle to the innermost of its seven "mansions" or rooms. Here she describes the Fifth Mansion, in which the soul begins to experience union with God. On the question of dreaming, see "What Dreams May Come" (p. 38) and "More than Ourselves" (p. 95).

Oh, the secrets of God! I should never weary of trying to describe them to you if I thought I could do so successfully. I do not mind if I write any amount of nonsense provided that just once in a while I can write sense, so that we may give great praise to the Lord.

I shall venture to affirm that, if this is indeed union with God, the devil cannot enter or do any harm; for His Majesty is in such close contact and union with the essence of the soul that the evil one does not dare to approach, nor can he even understand this secret thing. That much is evident: for it is said that he does not understand our thoughts; still less, therefore, will he understand a thing so secret that God will not even entrust our thoughts with it. Oh, what a great blessing is this state in which that accursed one can do us no harm! Great are the gains which come to the soul with God working in it, and neither we ourselves nor anyone else hindering Him. What will He not give who so much loves giving and can give all that He will?

I fear, however, that I may be leaving you confused by saying "if this is indeed union with God" and suggesting that there are other kinds of union. But of course there are! If we are very fond of vanities, the devil will send us into transports over them; but these are not like the transports of God, nor is there the same delight and satisfaction for the soul or the same peace and joy. That joy is greater than all the joys of earth, and greater than all its delights, and all its satisfactions, so that there is no evidence that these satisfactions and those of the earth have a common origin; and they are apprehended, too, very differently, as you will have learned by experience. I said once that it is as if the one kind had to do with the grosser part of the body, and the other kind penetrated to the very marrow of the bones; that puts it well, and I know no better way of expressing it.

But now you will say to me: How does the soul see it and understand it if it can neither see nor understand? I am not saying that it sees it at the time, but that it sees it clearly afterwards, and not because it is a vision, but because of a certainty which remains in the soul, which can be put there only by God. I know of a person who had not learned that God was in all things by presence and power and essence; God granted her a favor of this kind, which convinced her of this so firmly that, although one whom she asked in what way God was in us—until God granted him an understanding of it he knew as little of it as she—told her that He was in us only by grace, she had the truth so firmly implanted within her that she did not believe him, and asked others, who told her the truth, which was a great consolation to her.

Do not make the mistake of thinking that this certainty has anything to do with bodily form—with the presence of our Lord Jesus Christ, for example, unseen by us, in the Most Holy Sacrament. It has nothing to do with this—only with His Divinity. How, you will ask, can we become so convinced of what we have not seen? That I do not know; it is the work of God. But I know I am speaking the truth; and if anyone has not that certainty, I should say that what he has experienced is not union of the whole soul with God but only union of one of the faculties or some one of the many other kinds of favor which God grants the soul. In all these matters we must stop looking for reasons why they happened; if our understanding cannot grasp them, why should we try to perplex it? It suffices us to know that He who brings this to pass is all-powerful, and as it is God who does it and we, however hard we work, are quite incapable of achieving it, let us not try to become capable of understanding it either.

With regard to what I have just said about our incapability, I recall that, as you have heard, the Bride in the Song of Songs says: "The King brought me" (or "put me", I think the words are) "into the cellar of wine" (Song of Sol. 1:4, 2:4). It does not say that she "went". It also says that she was wandering about in all directions seeking her Beloved. This, as I understand it, is the cellar where the Lord is pleased to put us when He wills and as He wills. But we cannot enter by any efforts of our own; His Majesty must put us right into the center of our soul, and must enter there Himself; and, in order that He may the better show us His wonders, it is His pleasure that our will, which has entirely surrendered itself to Him, should have no part in this. Nor does He desire the door of the faculties and senses, which are all asleep, to be opened to Him; He will come into the center of the soul without using a door, as He did when He came in to His disciples and said "Peace to you" (John 20:19), and when He left the sepulcher without removing the stone.

54

Christmas in the Soul

John Tauler

oday the church celebrates three births, each of which is
such a source of joy and delight that we should break forth
into jubilation, love, and thanksgiving, and whoever does not
feel such sentiments should mistrust himself. The first birth,
and the most sublime, is that in which the Heavenly Father
begets His only Son in the Divine Essence and in the distinction
of the Divine persons. The second birth is that which made
Mary a mother in virginity most pure and inviolate. The third is
that by which every day and every hour God is truly and spiritually begotten in our souls by grace and love.

These three births are shown forth by the three masses of
Christmas Day. The first is sung at midnight, commencing with
the words: "Thou art My Son; this day have I begotten Thee"
(Ps. 2:7), that is to say, in eternity. This brings home to us the
hidden birth accomplished in the darksome mystery of the inaccessible Divinity. The second mass begins with these words:
"Today light has shined upon us" (Isa. 9:2). It figures the glory
of human nature divinely influenced by its union with the Word.
That mass is celebrated partly in the night and partly in the day,
because the birth it represents is partly known to us and partly
unknown. The third mass is sung in the daytime, and begins

John Tauler (*c.* 1300-1361), the "Illuminated Doctor", was a popular
Dominican preacher and widely sought-after spiritual father who was well
known for his tireless work among the sick and dying during the Black Death.
His homilies, which include this "First Sermon for the Feast of Christmas",
were much admired by Martin Luther, who said that he had "found more true
theology in him than in all the doctors of all the universities".

with the words: "A Child is born to us, and a Son is given to us" (Isa. 9:6). It figures that mysterious birth which should happen, and does happen, every day and every instant in holy souls when they dispose themselves for it by deep attention and sincere love, for one can never experience that birth except by the recollection of all one's powers. In that nativity God belongs to us and gives Himself to us so completely that nothing whatever is more our own than He is. And that is what those words say to us: "A Child is born to us, and a Son is given to us." He is, therefore, our own; He is ours totally and everywhere, for He is always being begotten within us.

Let us speak first of the ineffable birth represented by the third mass of Christmas, and let us explain how it may be brought about in us in a manner the most perfect and efficacious. To that end let us consider the qualities of that first generation, by which the Father begets the Son in eternity. The ineffable riches of the Divine good are so overflowing that God cannot contain Himself, and by His very nature He is forced to expend and communicate Himself. "It is God's nature to expend Himself," says St Augustine. The Father has thus poured Himself out into the other two Divine persons; after that He communicated Himself to creatures. The same saint says further: "It is because God is good that we are good, and all the good that the creature has is good with the essential goodness of God."

What then is the peculiar character of the Divine generation? The Father, inasmuch as He is Father, turns inward to Himself and His Divine intelligence; He sees Himself and penetrates Himself with a gaze which wholly embraces His Divine Essence, and then, just as He sees and knows Himself, so does He utter Himself completely; and the act whereby He knows Himself and the Word whereby He utters Himself is also the act whereby He begets His Son in eternity. Thus the Father Himself remains within Himself in the unity of His Essence and goes out of Himself in the distinction of persons. Again He returns into Himself, and therein He rests in unspeakable self-delight, and that self-delight goes forth and overflows in ineffable love which is the Holy Spirit. Thus does God dwell within Himself and go forth out of Himself to return again into Himself. Therefore is all outgoing for the sake of ingoing again. And hence in the material universe the movement of the heavenly spheres is most noble and most perfect, because it unceasingly returns again to the origin and beginning from which it first set forth. And so also the course of man is ever noblest and most perfect when it returns again upon its source and origin. The quality which the Heavenly Father has in this His incoming and outgoing, the same should every man have who will become the spiritual mother in this Divine bringing forth.

If we would be born again with the Divine birth, then we need to start back again, earnestly struggle inwardly, and there gather up all our powers, lower and higher, restoring all dissipation of mind to unity, since united forces are ever the strongest, and they become united when drawn back from multiplicity. When a hunter would hit the mark he shuts one eye in order that with the other he may look straighter; when one would think deeply about anything, he closes all his senses and unites all his powers in his inmost soul, out of which, as branches from a tree, all the senses go forth into activity. When all our powers of sense and motion are thus by an inward movement assembled together in the highest power, which is the force and foundation of them all, then there happens an outward, indeed an overflowing, movement beyond and above self, by which we renounce all ownership of will, of appetite, and of activity. There remains then only a pure and clear intention to be of God and of God's purposes, to be nothing whatever of self or ever to become anything of self, to be for Him alone, to give room to Him alone, whether in things high or low, so that He may work His will in us and bring about His birth in us and therein remain unhindered by us to the end. When a man thus clears the ground and makes his soul ready, without doubt God must fill up the void. The very heavens would fall down to fill up empty space, and much rather will God not allow you to remain empty, for that would be against His nature, His attributes, and indeed against His justice. If you go out of self, He without doubt goes in, and so it will be much or little of His entering in according to much or little of your going out.

We have so far spoken of the first and last births and how by the last we learn a lesson about the first. And now we shall instruct you about the second birth, in which this night the Son of God is born of His Mother and becomes our Brother. In eternity He was born a Son without a mother, and in time He was born a Son without a father. Now St Augustine tells us: "Mary is much more blessed because God was born spiritually in Her soul than because He was born Her fleshly Son." Whosoever would experience this spiritual and blessed birth in his soul, as Mary did in Her soul, should consider the qualities of Mary, that Mother of God both fleshly and spiritual. She was a virgin, all chaste and pure, and yet She was retired and separated from all things, and so the angel found Her. It is thus that one must be who would bring forth God in his soul. That soul must be chaste and pure. If it has strayed away from purity, then must it come back and be made pure again; for the meaning of virginity in this teaching is to be outwardly unfruitful and inwardly very fruitful. And this virgin soul must close its outward senses, having little external occupation, for from such it can have little fruit. Mary thought of nothing else but of Divine things. Inwardly the soul must have much fruit: "The beauty of the King's daughter is all within" (Ps. 45:13). Hence must this virgin soul live in detachment in all its habits, senses, behavior, and speech.

Mary lived retired, and so must the soul espoused to God be in retirement if it will experience the interior regeneration. But not alone from those wanderings after temporal things which appear to be faulty, but even from the sensible devotion attached to the practice of virtue, must the soul refrain. It must establish rest and stillness as an enclosure in which to dwell, hiding from and cutting off nature and the senses, guarding quiet and interior peace, rest, and repose. It is of this state of the soul that we shall sing next Sunday in the introit of the mass: "While all things were in quiet silence, and the night was in the midst of her course, Thine Almighty Word, O Lord, came down from Heaven, out of Thy royal throne" (Wisd. of Sol.18:14-15). That was the Eternal Word going forth from the Father's heart. It is amid this silence, when all things are hushed in eternal silence, that in very truth we hear this Word; for when God would speak, you must be silent. When God would enter in, all things must go out. When our Lord entered Egypt, all the idols in the land fell down. However good or holy anything may seem, if it hinders the actual and immediate Divine generation within you, it is an idol. Our Lord tells us that He has come bringing a sword, cutting off all that clings to men, even mother, brother, sister, for whatever is intimately joined to you without God is your enemy, forming as it does a multitude of imaginations covering and hiding the Divine Word.

Although this tranquility may not as yet wholly possess you, nor last all the time within you, yet you should so constantly cultivate interior silence as a means of experiencing the Divine birth that it shall finally become a spiritual habit. What is easy to a well-practiced man may seem impossible to an unpracticed one, for practice makes perfect. May God grant us all the grace of inner stillness, and thereby the birth of His Divine Word in our souls. Amen.

55

High Fantasy Lost Power

Dante

The piercing brightness of the living ray
Which I endured, my vision had undone,
I think, if I had turned my eyes away.

And I recall this further led me on,
Wherefore my gaze more boldness yet assumed
Till to the Infinite Good it last had won.

O grace abounding, whereby I presumed
So deep the eternal light to search and sound
That my whole vision was therein consumed!

In that abyss I saw how love held bound
Into one volume all the leaves whose flight
Is scattered through the universe around;

How substance, accident, and mode unite,
Fused, so to speak, together, in such wise
That this I tell of is one simple light.

Yea, of this complex I believe mine eyes
Beheld the universal form—in me,
Even as I speak, I feel such joy arise.

Dante Alighieri (1265-1321) was an Italian poet and Catholic philosopher
whose *Divine Comedy* is often regarded as one of the greatest poems ever
written. This selection is taken from the very end of "Paradise", the third and
final part of the *Comedy*, and describes Dante's vision of the Trinity and of man
in its midst.

Dante

One moment brings me deeper lethargy
Than twenty-five centuries brought the quest that dazed
Neptune when Argo's shadow crossed the sea.

And so my mind, bedazzled and amazed,
Stood fixed in wonder, motionless, intent,
And still my wonder kindled as I gazed.

That light doth so transform a man's whole bent
That never to another sight or thought
Would he surrender, with his own consent;

For everything the will has ever sought
Is gathered there, and there is every quest
Made perfect, which apart from it falls short.

Now, even what I recall will be exprest
More feebly than if I could wield no more
Than a babe's tongue, yet milky from the breast;

Not that the living light I looked on wore
More semblances than one, which cannot be,
For it is always what it was before;

But as my sight by seeing learned to see,
The transformation which in me took place
Transformed the single changeless form for me.

That light supreme, within its fathomless
Clear substance, showed to me three spheres, which bare
Three hues distinct, and occupied one space;

The first mirrored the next, as though it were
Rainbow from rainbow, and the third seemed flame
Breathed equally from each of the first pair.

How weak are words, and how unfit to frame
My concept—which lags after what was shown
So far 'twould flatter it to call it lame!

Unity

Eternal light, that in Thyself alone
Dwelling, alone dost know Thyself, and smile
On Thy self-love, so knowing and so known!

The sphering thus begot, perceptible
In Thee like mirrored light, now to my view—
When I had looked on it a little while—

Seemed in itself, and in its own self-hue,
Limned with our image; for which cause mine eyes
Were altogether drawn and held thereto.

As the geometer his mind applies
To square the circle, nor for all his wit
Finds the right formula, howe'er he tries,

So strove I with that wonder—how to fit
The image to the sphere; so sought to see
How it maintained the point of rest in it.

Thither my own wings could not carry me,
But that a flash my understanding clove,
Whence its desire came to it suddenly.

High fantasy lost power and here broke off;
Yet, as a wheel moves smoothly, free from jars,
My will and my desire were turned by love,

The love that moves the sun and the other stars.

56

Motionless Circling

Nikitas Stithatos

*E*xalt the One over the dyad—the single over the dual—and free its nobility from all commerce with dualism, and you will consort immaterially with immaterial spirits; for you will yourself have become a noetic spirit, even though you appear to dwell bodily among other men.

Once you have brought the dyad into subjection to the dignity and nature of the One, you will have subjected the whole of creation to God, for you will have brought into unity what was divided and will have reconciled all things. So long as the nature of the powers within us is in a state of inner discord and is dispersed among many contrary things, we do not participate in God's supra-natural gifts. And if we do not participate in these gifts, we are also far from the mystical eucharist of the heavenly sanctuary, celebrated by the intellect through its spiritual activity. When through assiduous ascetic labor we have purged ourselves of the crudity of evil and have reconciled our inner discord through the power of the Spirit, we then participate in the ineffable blessings of God and worthily concelebrate the

---

Nikitas Stithatos, an eleventh-century Orthodox monk, entered the monastery of Studios at Constantinople *c.* 1020 and may have become abbot in his old age, sometime between 1076-92. A disciple and biographer of St Symeon the New Theologian (see p. 79), he took an active part in defending the Orthodox Church against Rome during the confrontations of 1054. The *Philokalia* preserves three of his centuries, corresponding to the three principal stages of the Way: "On the Practice of the Virtues", "On the Inner Nature of Things", and—the source of this selection—"On Spiritual Knowledge".

Divine mysteries of the intellect's mystical eucharist with God the Logos in His supra-celestial and spiritual sanctuary; for we have become initiates and priests of His immortal mysteries.

Souls that have attained total purity and have reached the heights of wisdom and spiritual knowledge resemble the Cherubim. By virtue of their unmediated cognition they draw close to the source of all beauty and goodness, and in this way they are directly and fully initiated into the vision of secret things. Among the spiritual powers it is said that only the Cherubim are illuminated in this direct manner by the source of Divinity itself and thus possess this vision in the highest degree. Among the highest angelic powers, some are more ardent and clear-sighted in their devotion to the Divine realities around which they unceasingly circle; others are more contemplative, gnostic, and imbued with wisdom, this being the Divine state that impels them unceasingly to circle around these realities. Similarly, angel-like souls are ardent and clear-sighted in their devotion to the Divine realities, as well as wise, gnostic, and exalted in mystical contemplation. Potentially and actually they too unceasingly circle around things Divine, firmly rooted in them alone. Immutably receptive of Divine illuminations, and thus participating in Him who truly is, they also unstintingly communicate His irradiance and grace to others through their teaching.

God is Intellect and the activating agent of everything. All intellects have both their permanent abode and their eternal mobility in this primary Intellect. Such is the experience of all whose activity is not adulterated by materiality but is pure and unsullied as a result of sacred ascetic labor. They experience this when, ardent with Divine love, they communicate to each other and to themselves the illumination bestowed on them by the Divinity, generously transmitting to others the wisdom of God's mysteries concealed within it; and in this way they unceasingly extol the Divine love that inspires them. Souls whose intelligence has been freed from material preoccupation, and in whom the self-warring appetitive and incensive aspects have been restored to harmony and harnessed to their heaven-bound, well-reined chariot, both revolve around God and yet stand fixedly. They revolve incessantly around God as the center and cause of their circular movement. They stand steadfast and unwavering as fixed points on the circumference of the circle and cannot be diverted from this fixed position by the sense-world and the distraction of human affairs. This is therefore the perfect consummation of stillness, and it is to this that stillness leads those who truly achieve it, so that while moving they are stationary, and while steadfast and immobile they move around the Divine realities. So long as we do not experience this we can only be said to practice an apparent stillness, and our intellect is not free from materiality and distraction.

When through great diligence and effort we recover the original beauty of the intelligence, and through the abiding presence of the Holy Spirit participate in supernal wisdom and knowledge, we can then perceive things as they are by nature and hence can recognize that the source and cause of all things is itself wise and beautiful. We see that we cannot hold it in any way responsible for the evil that destroys created things when they deviate towards what is base. When we are so deflected and dragged downwards, we are sundered from the pristine beauty of the Logos and forfeit our deification, while the evil that has invaded us disfigures us into its own obtuse and witless form. When, on the other hand, through the practice of the virtues we attain a spiritual knowledge of created things, we have achieved the first stage on the path of deification. We achieve the second stage when—initiated through the contemplation of the spiritual essences of created things—we perceive the hidden mysteries of God. We achieve the third stage when we are united and interfused with the primordial Light. It is then that we reach the goal of all ascetic and contemplative activity. By means of these three stages all intellects are brought, in a way that accords with their own nature, into unity with themselves and with Him who truly is. They can then illumine their fellow intellects, initiating them into Divine realities, through celestial wisdom perfecting them as spirits already purified, and uniting them with themselves and with the One.

Deification in this present life is the spiritual and truly sacred rite in which the Logos of unutterable wisdom makes

Himself a sacred offering and gives Himself, so far as is possible, to those who have prepared themselves. God, as befits His goodness, has bestowed this deification on beings endowed with intelligence so that they may achieve the union of faith. Those who as a result of their purity and their knowledge of things Divine participate in this dignity are assimilated to God, "conformed to the image of His Son" (Rom. 8:29), through their exalted and spiritual concentration upon the Divine. Thus they become as gods to other men on earth. These others in their turn, perfected in virtue by purification through their Divine intelligence and through sacred intercourse with God, participate according to their proficiency and the degree of their purification in the same deification as their brethren, and they commune with them in the God of unity. In this way all of them, joined together in the union of love, are unceasingly united with the one God; and God, the source of all holy works and totally free from any indictment because of His work of creation, abides in the midst of gods (*cf.* Ps. 82:1, LXX), God by nature among gods by adoption.

VIII

Unicity

Why callest thou Me good?
None is good save One, that is,
God.

Luke 18:19

57

A Reply to Active Persons

The Cloud of Unknowing

In the Gospel of St Luke, we read that our Lord came to Martha's house, and while she set about at once to prepare His meal, her sister Mary did nothing but sit at His feet. She was so intent upon listening to Him that she paid no attention to what Martha was doing. Now certainly Martha's chores were holy and important; indeed they are the works of the first degree of the active life. But Mary was unconcerned about them. Neither did she notice our Lord's human bearing, the beauty of His mortal body, or the sweetness of His human voice and conversation, although this would have been a holier and better work; it represents the second degree of the active life and the first degree of the contemplative life. But she forgot all of this and was totally absorbed in the highest wisdom of God concealed in the obscurity of His humanity.

Mary turned to Jesus with all the love of her heart, unmoved by what she saw or heard spoken and done about her. She sat there in perfect stillness with her heart's secret, joyous love intent upon that cloud of unknowing between her and her God. Even when Martha complained to Jesus about her, scolding Him for not bidding her to get up and help with the work, Mary remained there quite still and untroubled, showing not the least

---

The Cloud of Unknowing is an anonymous mystical treatise from fourteenth-century England. Influenced by the teachings of St Dionysios the Areopagite (see p. 223), its author insists that true knowledge of God can be attained only on the far side of a great "cloud of unknowing", within whose darkness the seeming clarity of all discursive modes of consciousness is deliberately left behind.

resentment against Martha for her grumbling. But this is not surprising really, for she was utterly absorbed in another work, all unknown to Martha, and she did not have time to notice her sister or defend herself.

"Mary has chosen the best part" (Luke 10:42). What does this mean? Whenever we speak of the best, we imply a good and a better. The best is the superlative degree. What then are the options from which Mary chose the best? They are not three ways of life since Holy Church only speaks of two, the active and the contemplative. No, the deeper meaning of the Gospel story is that Martha represents the active life and Mary the contemplative life, the first of which is absolutely necessary for salvation. So when a choice narrows down to two, one of them may not be called best. Nevertheless, although the active and the contemplative are the two ways of life in Holy Church, yet within them, taken as a whole, there are three parts, three ascending stages. The first stage is the good and upright Christian life in which love is predominantly active in corporal works of mercy. In the second, a person begins to meditate on spiritual truths regarding his own sinfulness, the Passion of Christ, and the joys of eternity. The first way is good but the second is better, for here the active and contemplative life begin to converge. They merge in a sort of spiritual kinship, becoming sisters like Martha and Mary. This is as far as an active person may advance in contemplation except for the occasional intervention of special grace. And to this middle ground a contemplative may return—but no farther—to take up some activity. He should not do so, however, except on rare occasions and at the demand of great need.

In the third stage, a person enters the dark cloud of unknowing where in secret and alone he centers all his love on God. The first stage is good, the second is better, but the third is best of all. This is the best part belonging to Mary. It is surely obvious now why our Lord did not say to Martha, "Mary has chosen the best *life*." There are only two ways of life, and as I said, when a choice is between only two, one may not be called best. But our Lord says, "Mary has chosen the best *part*, and it shall not be taken from her." The first and second parts are good and holy, but they will cease with the passing of this mortal life. For in eternity there will be no need for the works of mercy as there is now. People will not hunger or thirst or die of cold or be sick, homeless, and captive. No one will need Christian burial, for no one will die. In heaven it will no longer be fitting to mourn for our sins or for Christ's Passion. So then, if grace is calling you to choose the third part, choose it with Mary. Or rather let me put it this way. If God is calling you to the third part, reach out for it; work for it with all your heart. It shall never be taken from you, for it will never end. Though it begins on earth, it is eternal.

Let the words of the Lord be our reply to active persons who complain about us. Let Him speak for us as He did for Mary when He said, "Martha, Martha" (Luke 10:41). He is saying, "Listen, all you who live the active life. Be diligent in the works of the first and second parts, working now in one, now in another. Or if you are so inclined, courageously undertake both together. But do not interfere with my contemplative friends, for you do not understand what afflicts them. Leave them in peace. Do not begrudge them the leisure of the third and best part, which is Mary's."

58

Closing to a Bud Again

Lilian Staveley

As the loving creature progresses, he will find himself ceasing to live in things, or thoughts of things or of persons, but his whole mind and heart will be concentrated upon the thought of God alone. Now Jesus, now the High Christ, now the Father, but never away from one of the aspects or personalities of God, though his conditions of nearness will vary. For at times he will be in a condition of great nearness, at times in a condition of some farness, or, more properly speaking, of obscurity. He will be in a condition of waiting—this exceedingly frequent, the most frequent of all; a condition of amazing happiness; a condition of pain, of desolation at being still upon the earth instead of with God. He will be in a condition of giving love to God, or a condition of receiving love, of remembrance and attention. He will be in a condition of immeasurable glamour, an extraordinary illumination of every faculty, not by any act of his own, but poured through him until he is filled with the elixir of some new form of life, and feels himself before these experiences never to have lived; he but existed as a part of Nature. But now, although he has become more united to Nature than ever before, he also is mysteriously drawn apart from her; without being in any way presumptuous,

---

Lilian Staveley (1878-1928) was an Anglican laywoman whose inward spiritual life remained hidden even from her closest friends and family members until after her death, when it was discovered that she was the author of three anonymous works concerning the mystical journey, including an autobiography, *The Prodigal Returns*, and *The Golden Fountain*, the source of this selection.

he feels himself to be above her, not by any merits, but by intention of Another. He has become lifted up into the spirit and essence of Nature, and the heavy and more obvious parts of her bind him no more. He is in a condition of freedom; he is frequently in a condition of great splendor, and is wrapped perpetually round about with that most glorious mantle: the consciousness of God.

These are man's right and proper conditions. These are the lovely will of God for us. And too many of us have the will to go contrary to Him. Oh, the tragedy of it! If only the whole world of men and women could be gathered and lifted into this garden of love, persuaded to rise from lesser loves into the bosom of His mighty Love. For the truly loving soul here on earth there are no longer heavens, nor conditions of heavens, nor grades, nor crowns, nor angels, nor archangels, nor saints, nor holy spirits; but, going out and up and on, we reach at last the One, and for unspeakably glorious moments we know Him. This is life: to be in Him, and He in us, and know it.

These beautiful flights of the soul cannot be taken through idleness, though they are taken in what would outwardly appear to be a great stillness. This stillness is but the necessary abstraction from physical activity, even from physical consciousness; but inwardly the spirit is in a great activity, a very ferment of secret work. This is frequently produced by the beautiful in Nature, the spirit involuntarily passing at the sight of beauty into a passionate admiration for the Maker of it. This high, pure emotion, which is also an intense activity of the spirit, would seem so to etherealize the creature that instantly the delicate soul is able to escape her loosened bonds and flies towards her home, filled with ineffable, incomparable delight, praising, singing, and joying in her Lord and God until the body can endure no more, and swiftly she must return to bondage in it. But the most wonderful flights of the soul are made during a high adoring contemplation of God. We are in high contemplation when the heart, mind, and soul, having dropped consciousness of all earthly matters, have been brought to a full concentration upon God—God totally invisible, totally un-imaged, and yet focused to a center point by the great power of love. The soul, while she is able to maintain this most difficult height of contemplation, may be visited by an intensely vivid perception, inward vision, and knowledge of God's attributes or perfections, very brief; and this as a gift, for she is not able to will such a felicity to herself, but being given such she is instantly consumed with adoration, and enters ecstasy.

Having achieved these degrees of progress, the heart and mind will say: "Now I may surely repose, for I have attained!" And so we may repose, but not in idleness, which is to say, not without abundance of prayer. For only by prayer is our condition maintained and renewed; but without prayer, by which I mean an incessant inward communion, quickly our condition changes and wears away. No matter to what degree of love we have attained, we need to pray for more; without persistent but short prayer for faith and love, we might fall back into strange woeful periods of cold obscurity. To the accomplished lover, great and wonderful is prayer; the more completely the mind and heart are lifted up in it, the slower the wording. The greater the prayer, the shorter in words, though the longer the saying of it, for each syllable needs to be held up upon the soul before God, slowly and, as it were, in a casket of fire, and with marvelous joy. And there are prayers without words, and others without even thoughts, in which the soul in a great stillness passes up like an incense to the Most High. This is very pure, great love; wonderful, high bliss.

The mode of entrance into active contemplation I would try to convey in this way. The body must be placed either sitting or kneeling, and supported, or flat on the back as though dead. Now the mind must commence to fold itself, closing forwards as an open rose might close her petals to a bud again, for every thought and image must be laid away and nothing left but a great forward-moving intention of love. Out glides the mind all smooth and swift, and plunges deep, then takes an upward curve, and up and on till willingly it faints, the creature dies, and consciousness is taken over by the soul, which, quickly coming to the trysting place, spreads herself, and there awaits the revelations of her God. To my feeling this final complete passing over of consciousness from the mind to the soul is by act and will of

God alone, and cannot be performed by will of the creature, and is the fundamental difference between the contemplation of Nature and the contemplation of God. The creature worships, but the soul alone knows contact. And yet the mode of contemplation is a far simpler thing than all these words; it is the very essence of simplicity itself; and in this sublime adventure, we are really conscious of no mode nor plan nor flight—nothing but the mighty need of spirit for Spirit and love for Love.

59

The Joyful Instant

St Augustine

When the day on which my mother was to depart from this life was near at hand—Thou knewest the day, but we did not—I believe it happened by Thy management, in Thy hidden ways, that she and I were standing alone, leaning on a window from which the garden inside the house we occupied could be viewed. It was at Ostia on the Tiber, where, far removed from the crowds after the hardship of a long journey, we were resting in preparation for the sea voyage. We were talking to each other alone, very sweetly, "forgetting what is behind, straining forward to what is before" (Phil. 3:13). Between us, "in the present truth" (2 Peter 1:12) which Thou art, we tried to find out what the eternal life of the saints would be, which "eye hath not seen nor ear heard, nor hath it entered into the heart of man" (1 Cor. 2:9). But we also yearned with the mouth of our heart for the supernal flood from "Thy Fountain, the Fountain of Life, which is with Thee" (Ps. 36:9), so that, having been sprinkled from it as much as our capacity would permit, we might think in some way about such a great thing.

When our talk had reached the conclusion that the greatest delight of the bodily senses, in the brightest bodily light, was not capable of comparison with the joy of that life and, moreover,

---

St Augustine (354-430) was the greatest of the western Church Fathers and an immensely influential figure in the history of Christian theology and spirituality. His *Confessions*, which takes the form of an extended prayer, includes this famous description of mystical elevation that he was blessed to share with his mother, St Monica, shortly before her death.

did not seem worthy of being mentioned, then, lifting ourselves up in the yet greater ardor of our feeling toward the Selfsame, we advanced step by step through all bodily things up to the sky itself, from which the sun, moon, and stars shine out over the earth, and we ascended still farther in our interior cogitation, conversation, and admiration of Thy works and came to our own minds. Then we transcended them, so that we might touch that realm of unfailing abundance in which Thou feedest Israel eternally on the food of truth. There, life is wisdom, through which all these things come into being, both those which have been and those which will be. Yet it is not made, but is as it was, and thus it will be forever. Or, rather, to have been in the past, or to be in the future, does not pertain to it, but simply *to be,* for it is eternal. To be in the past, or to be in the future, is not to be eternal.

And while we were so speaking and panting for it, we did touch it a little, with an all-out thrust of our hearts. We sighed and left behind "the first fruits of the spirit" (Rom. 8:23) which were bound there, and we came back to the clattering of our mouths, where the spoken word has its beginning and end. How is it like Thy Word, our Lord, "remaining ageless in itself and renewing all things" (*cf.* Wisd. of Sol. 7:27)? We were saying then: Suppose, for any person, that the tumult of the flesh be silenced—silenced, the images of earth and water and air; silenced, the very heavens; silenced, his very soul unto himself, when, having passed beyond himself, he ceases to think of himself by means of images; silenced, his dreams and imaginary apparitions, every tongue and every sign, and whatever comes to be by transition: if he be granted this complete silence (since, if one can hear, all these things are saying: "We did not make ourselves, but He who endureth forever made us" [Ps. 100:3-5])—and if, having said this, they become quiet, once they have lifted up his ear to Him who made them—then, if He alone speak, not through them, but through Himself, so that we might hear His Word, not through fleshly speech, or through the voice of an angel, or through the crash of thunder, or through the darkness of a similitude, but *Himself* whom we love in these things, and if we might hear Him, without these things, just as now we reached out and, with the speed of thought, touched the Eternal Wisdom abiding above all things—and if this could continue, and other visions of a much lower type were taken away, and this one vision were to enrapture, absorb, and enclose its beholder in inner joys, so that life might forever be like that instant of understanding for which we had sighed—then, surely, this is the meaning of: "Enter into the joy of thy Master" (Matt. 25:21-23).

60

One and the Same Mind

Origen

We believe that the goodness of God through Christ will restore His entire creation to one end, even His enemies being conquered and subdued. For so says the Holy Scripture: "The Lord said unto my Lord, Sit Thou on my right hand, until I make Thine enemies the footstool of Thy feet" (Ps. 110:1). And if it is not very evident what the prophetic language here means, let us learn from Paul the Apostle, who says more openly, "Christ must reign, till He hath put all His enemies under His feet" (1 Cor. 15:25). But if even this clear declaration of the Apostle is not sufficient to inform us what is the meaning of "putting enemies under His feet", hear further what he says in the words that follow: "For all things must be made subject to Him" (1 Cor. 15:27, 28). What then is this "subjection" by which "all things must be made subject" to Christ? In my opinion, it is the same subjection by which we too desire to be subjected to Him, and by which the apostles and all the saints who have followed Christ were subject to Him. For the word "subjection", when used of our subjection to Christ, implies the salvation, pro-

---

Origen (*c.* 185 - *c.* 254)—the greatest, if also the most controversial, of the early Church Fathers—came under a shadow of suspicion at the Fifth Ecumenical Council (553) for his teachings concerning, among other things, universal salvation, mystically linked in this passage to the recovery of unity through "sleepless attention". Even so, no less a figure than St Vincent of Lérins—whose well-known canon concerning "what has been believed everywhere, always, and by all" is the very definition of orthodoxy—was bold enough to admit, "I would rather be wrong with Origen than right with the world." This selection is taken from the most important of his theological works, *On First Principles.*

ceeding from Christ, of those who are subject; as David also said, "Shall not my soul be subject to God? For of Him cometh my salvation" (Ps. 62:1).

Seeing then that such is the end when "all enemies shall have been subjected to Christ", when "the last enemy shall be destroyed, that is, death", and when "the kingdom shall be delivered up to God and the Father by Christ, to whom all things have been subjected" (1 Cor. 15:24-27), let us, from such an end as this, contemplate the beginning of things. For the end is always like the beginning. As therefore there is one end of all things, so we must understand that there is one beginning of all things, and as there is one end of many things, so from one beginning arise many differences and varieties, which in their turn are restored, through God's goodness—through their subjection to Christ and their unity with the Holy Spirit—to one end, which is like the beginning. I refer to all those who, by "bending the knee at the name of Jesus" (Phil. 2:10), have through this very fact displayed the sign of their subjection. These are they who dwell "in heaven and on earth and under the earth" (Phil. 2:10), the three terms indicating the entire universe, that is, all those beings who started from one beginning but were drawn in various directions by their own individual impulses and were distributed throughout the different ranks of existence in accordance with their merit; for in them goodness does not rest essentially, as it does in God and His Christ and in the Holy Spirit. For only in this Trinity, which is the source of all things, does goodness reside essentially. Others possess it as an accident, liable to be lost, and only then do they live in blessedness when they participate in holiness and wisdom and in the Divine nature itself.

In the case of those who do not pay sleepless attention to themselves, changes of condition take place, more quickly or more slowly, and to a greater or less extent, according to their individual fault. So, arising out of this fault, by a Divine judgment corresponding to the better or worse movements of each and in accordance with merit, one will have in the future order of things the rank of angel, or the power of a ruler, or authority over certain beings, or a throne over subjects, or lordship over slaves. Others, however, who have not been utterly cast out, will have a subordinate position assigned them below those above mentioned. And thus, from among those who have been set under the rulers and authorities and thrones and lordships, even from these the human race will one day be constituted in the world in unity, which the Lord Jesus promises when He prays to God the Father for His disciples, "I pray not for these alone, but also for all who shall believe on Me through their word, that they all may be one; as I, Father, am in Thee, and Thou art in Me, that they may be one in Us" (John 17:20, 21); and again when He says, "That they may be one, as We are one, I in them, and Thou in Me, that they also may be perfected in one" (John 17:22, 23). The Apostle Paul also confirms this when he says, "Till we all come to the unity of the faith, to a perfect man, to the measure of the stature of the fullness of Christ" (Eph. 4:13), and the same apostle also exhorts us, who even now in the present life have been placed in the Church, in which we see an imitation of the future kingdom, to strive after the same pattern of unity, when he prays "that ye all say the same things, and that there be no divisions among you, but that ye be perfected in one and the same mind and in one and the same judgment" (1 Cor. 1:10).

61

Awareness and Return

Swami Abhishiktananda

$\mathcal{T}$he highest times of prayer are certainly those which are devoted to the contemplation of the mystery of God in itself. There is no doubt that it is by becoming more and more aware of the Divine Presence in the secret place of our hearts that we become more and more aware of that same Divine Presence surrounding us on all sides. Was it not the promise of God to the prophet Hosea (Hos. 2:7) that he would take the soul into solitude, would hedge up all the ways whereby she used to run after her "lovers"—all the desires and thoughts of this world—and bring her to the place where she would be alone with Him, face to face?

Truly speaking there is no outside and no inside, no without and no within, in the mystery of God and in the Divine Presence. Yet the mind is so much distracted through the senses that it needs first of all to be withdrawn from external things: hence the need of recollecting and gathering towards their center all thoughts and all desires. Then, after we have been inwardly fully illumined by the glory of the Presence, we realize that there are no limits to that glory, no limits to that Presence.

Abhishiktananda (1910-73)—"Bliss of the Anointed One"—was the adopted Indian name of Dom Henri Le Saux, a French Benedictine monk who lived for many years in a hermitage at Gyansu in the Himalayas near the source of the Ganges. Having first gone to India as a missionary, he became convinced after an encounter with the great *jnâni* master Sri Ramana Maharshi that traditional Christian doctrine and Hindu *Advaita Vedânta* are but two forms of an identical Truth. "Whoever sees difference here goes from death to death" (*Katha Upanishad*, 4:10-11).

In the light of this spiritual endeavor our very I, however personal it may be, seems no longer to know any boundary: it encompasses, as it were, everything on earth, attains to everything in creation, even to the core of every being, even to the center of each heart, of each soul of each man, though of course without losing its own individuality. Nothing then is foreign or strange to it in creation, for nothing is strange or foreign to God, and in God Himself we have at long last found our home.

Jesus teaches us: "You shall love the Lord your God" and "You shall love your neighbor as yourself" (Matt. 22:37-9); He goes on to say that the second commandment is similar to the first, for it is in loving our brothers that we love God (1 John 3:17, 4:20). Each one is responsible before God for all his brothers, spiritually and temporally. He can be indifferent to none of them. They are his own flesh (Gen. 37:27); they can even be said to be his own soul. Those who will most truly succeed in loving their neighbors as themselves are those who have realized through their experience of the Presence within that all men are one, as the Holy Spirit Himself is one, and that therefore no other man can be a stranger to them. So also only those can understand that the love of God and the love of man are one single love who in the same experience have realized that there is only one Son of God. Jesus is "the man for others", as we are often reminded today. But in the first place Jesus is "the Man for God". He is effectually the man for others because in the depth of His heart He has realized that God alone is and that He Himself is His only Son. There is no within or without, properly speaking, in that experience of the Divine Presence which Jesus came to the world to make known to us and to share with us. As with Jesus, so with us: the hearing of God's unique Word makes us to be and to realize that God is everywhere and in all things—and that finally He alone is. According to the Scriptures, Christ's return to glory will bring about the summing up of all things in God. The universe, including the whole history of mankind, is moving towards that final consummation. This is true also of each individual man in his own unique development. Each man is a microcosm and sums up in himself the whole world. The world is reaching its fulfillment whenever any conscious being passes into God, and for the Christian the Eucharist is the clearest sign that the fulfillment is already present. "The hour is coming", said Jesus, "and now is" (John 5:25). In every moment of his life—in every act performed with due awareness—man is reaching his fulfillment, which is God alone, and with him and in him the whole world is reaching it also. As soon as he hears the voice of the Son of Man (John 5:25), and in it also the voice of the Father who calls him from His eternity, then man with Christ, beyond time and history, is born again, rises from the dead, and together with his Lord reaches the very place from which he originally comes, the infinite glory of God.

62

Waylessness

John of Ruysbroeck

When we go out in love beyond and above all things and die to all observation in ignorance and in darkness, then we are wrought and transformed through the eternal Word, who is the image of the Father. In this idleness of our spirit we receive the incomprehensible Light, which enwraps us and penetrates us, as the air is penetrated by the light of the sun. And this Light is nothing else than a fathomless staring and seeing. What we are, that we behold; and what we behold, that we are: for our thought, our life, and our being are uplifted in simplicity and made one with the Truth, which is God. And therefore in this simple staring we are one life and one spirit with God: and this I call a contemplative life.

As soon as we cleave to God through love, we practice the better part; but when we gaze thus into our super-essence, we possess God utterly. With this contemplation there is bound up an exercise that is wayless, that is, a noughting of life; for where we go forth out of ourselves into darkness and the abysmal waylessness, there shines perpetually the simple ray of the splendor of God in which we are grounded, and which draws us out of

Blessed John of Ruysbroeck (1293-1381) was the prior of a Belgian community of Augustinian canons. His works, originally written in Flemish and translated into Latin, include *Spiritual Espousals, The Book of Supreme Truth,* and *The Sparkling Stone: A Treatise of the Perfection of the Sons of God,* from which this selection is taken. He was deeply influenced by a number of earlier mystics, including St Augustine (see p. 210), St Bernard of Clairvaux (p. 41), St Dionysios the Areopagite (p. 223), and Meister Eckhart (p. 249), and was beatified in 1908.

ourselves into the super-essence and into the immersion of love. And with this sinking into love there is always bound up a practice of love which is wayless; for love cannot be lazy, but would search through and through and taste through and through the fathomless richness which lives in the ground of her being, and this is a hunger which cannot be appeased. But a perpetual striving after the unattainable—this is swimming against the stream. One can neither leave it nor grasp it, neither do without it nor attain it, neither be silent on it nor speak of it, for it is above reason and understanding, and it transcends all creatures; and therefore we can never reach nor overtake it. But we should abide within ourselves: there we feel that the Spirit of God is driving us and enkindling in us this restlessness of love. And we should abide above ourselves. And then we feel that the Spirit of God is drawing us out of ourselves and burning us to nothingness in his Selfhood, that is, in the super-essential Love with which we are one, and which we possess more deeply and more widely than all else.

This possession is a simple and abysmal tasting of all good and of eternal life; and in this tasting we are swallowed up above reason and without reason in the deep quiet of the Godhead, which is never moved. That this is true we can know only by our own feeling and in no other way. For how this is, or where, or what, neither reason nor practice can come to know; and therefore our ensuing exercise always remains wayless, that is, without manner. For that abysmal good which we taste and possess, we can neither grasp nor understand; neither can we enter into it by ourselves or by means of our exercises. And so we are poor in ourselves, but rich in God; hungry and thirsty in ourselves, drunken and fulfilled in God; busy in ourselves, idle in God. And thus we shall remain throughout eternity. But without the exercise of love, we can never possess God; and whosoever thinks or feels otherwise is deceived. And thus we live wholly in God, where we possess our blessedness; and we live wholly in ourselves, where we exercise ourselves in love toward God. And though we live wholly in God and wholly in ourselves, yet it is but one life; but it is twofold and opposite according to our feeling; for poor and rich, hungry and satisfied, busy and idle—these things are wholly contrary to one another.

Yet with this our highest honor is bound up, now and in eternity: for we cannot wholly become God and lose our created being—this is impossible. Did we, however, remain wholly in ourselves, sundered from God, we should be miserable and unblest. And therefore we should feel ourselves living wholly in God and wholly in ourselves; and between these two feelings we should find nothing else but the grace of God and the exercise of our love. For out of our highest feeling the brightness of God shines into us, which teaches us truth and moves us toward every virtue and in eternal love toward God. If we follow this brightness without pause, back into that Source from whence it comes forth, there we feel nothing but a quenching of our spirit and an irretrievable down-sinking into simple and fathomless love. Could we continue to dwell there with our simple gaze, we should always so feel it; for our immersion and transformation in God continues without ceasing in eternity if we have gone forth from ourselves, and God is ours in the immersion of love. For if we possess God in the immersion of love—that is, if we are lost to ourselves—God is our own, and we are His own; and we sink ourselves eternally and irretrievably in our own possession, which is God. This immersion is essential and is closely bound up with the state of love: and so it continues whether we sleep or whether we wake, whether we know it or whether we know it not.

And so it does not earn for us any new degree of reward, but it maintains us in the possession of God and of all that good which we have received. And this down-sinking is like a river, which without pause or turning back ever pours into the sea, since this is its proper resting place. So likewise when we possess God alone, the down-sinking of our being, with the love that belongs to it, flows forth without return into a fathomless experience which we possess, and which is our proper resting place. Were we always simple, and could we always contemplate with the same recollection, we should always have the same experience. Now this immersion is above all virtues, and above every exercise of love; for it is nothing else than an eternal going out from ourselves with a clear looking forward into an otherness or difference toward which, outside ourselves, we tend as toward our blessedness. For we feel an eternal yearning toward something other than what we are ourselves. And this is the most inward and hidden distinction which we can feel between God and ourselves, and beyond it there is no difference any more. But our reason abides here with open eyes in the darkness, that is, in an abysmal ignorance; and in this darkness, the abysmal splendor remains covered and hidden from us, for its overwhelming unfathomableness blinds our reason. But it enwraps us in simplicity and transforms us through its Selfhood: and thus we are brought forth by God out of our selfhood into the immersion of love, in which we possess blessedness and are one with God.

When we are thus made one with God, there abides within us a quickening knowledge and an active love; for without our own knowledge we cannot possess God; and without the practice of love we cannot be united with God, nor remain one with Him. For if we could be blessed without our knowledge, then a stone, which has no knowledge, could also be blessed. Were I lord over all the world and knew it not, how would it profit me? And therefore we shall ever know and feel that we taste and possess; and this is testified by Christ Himself where He speaks thus of us to His Father: "This," he says, "is life eternal, that they should know Thee, the only true God, and Jesus Christ, whom Thou has sent" (John 17:3).

63

Hidden Beauty

St Dionysios the Areopagite

Ⓞ Trinity, who exceeds all Being, Deity, and Goodness—who instructs Christians in heavenly wisdom—guide us to that topmost height of mystic lore which surpasses light and more than surpasses knowledge, where the simple, absolute, and unchangeable mysteries of heavenly Truth lie hidden in the dazzling obscurity of the secret Silence, outshining all brilliance with the intensity of their darkness, and surcharging our blinded intellects with the utterly impalpable and invisible fairness of glories which exceed all beauty.

Such is my prayer; and you I counsel, dear Timothy, that in the earnest exercise of mystic contemplation, you leave the senses and the activities of the intellect and all things that the senses or the intellect can perceive, and all things in this world of nothingness or in that world of being, and that, your understanding being laid to rest, you strain—as far as you can— towards a union with Him whom neither being nor understanding can contain. For by unceasing and absolute

---

According to tradition, St Dionysios the Areopagite was an Athenian judge who was converted by St Paul's famous speech on Mars Hill (the Areopagus): "When they heard of the resurrection of the dead . . . some men joined [Paul] and believed, among them Dionysios the Areopagite" (Acts 17:32, 34). Scholars believe the author of the Dionysian *corpus* to have been an anonymous Syrian monk of the early sixth century, who accentuated the *via negativa*—that is, the method of attaining to God through the negation of all images and concepts— as he does here in his *Mystical Theology*, which takes the form of an epistle addressed to Timothy, St Paul's missionary companion; the master Bartholomew is not otherwise known to history.

renunciation of yourself and all things, you shall in pureness cast all things aside and be released from all and so shall be led upwards to the ray of that Divine Darkness which exceeds all existence. These things you must not disclose to any of the uninitiated, by whom I mean those who cling to the objects of human thought and imagine there is no super-essential reality beyond, and fancy that they know by human understanding Him that has made Darkness His secret place. And if the Divine initiation is beyond such men as these, what can be said of others yet more incapable, who describe the Transcendent Cause of all things by qualities drawn from the lowest order of being while they deny that It is in any way superior to the various ungodly delusions which they fondly invent in ignorance of this truth? For while It possesses all the positive attributes of the universe—being the universal Cause—yet in a stricter sense It does not possess them since It transcends them all; there is thus no contradiction between affirming and denying that It has them inasmuch as It precedes and surpasses all deprivation, being beyond all positive and negative distinctions.

Such at least is the teaching of the blessed Bartholomew. For he says that the subject matter of the Divine Science is vast and yet minute, and that the Gospel combines in itself both width and straitness. He has shown by his words how marvelously he has understood that the good Cause of all things is eloquent yet speaks few words, or rather none, possessing neither speech nor understanding because It exceeds all things in a super-essential manner and is revealed in Its naked truth to those alone who pass right through the opposition of fair and foul, and pass beyond the topmost altitudes of the holy ascent and leave behind them all Divine enlightenment and voices and heavenly utterances and plunge into the Darkness where truly dwells, as says the Scripture, that One which is beyond all things. For not without reason is the blessed Moses bidden first to undergo purification himself and then to separate himself from those who have not undergone it; and after all purification he hears the many-voiced trumpets and sees many lights flash forth with pure and diverse-streaming rays, and then stands separate from the multitudes and with the chosen priests presses forward to the topmost pinnacle of the Divine ascent. Nevertheless he meets not with God Himself, and yet he beholds—not Him indeed (for He is invisible)—but the place in which He dwells. And this I take to signify that the highest and most Divine of the things perceived by the eyes of the body or the mind are but the symbolic language of things subordinate to Him who Himself transcends them all. Through these things His incomprehensible Presence is shown walking upon those heights of His holy places that are perceived by the mind; and then It breaks forth even from the things that are beheld and from those that behold them and plunges the true initiate into the Darkness of unknowing, in which he renounces all the apprehensions of his understanding and is enwrapped in that which is wholly intangible and invisible, belonging wholly to Him that is beyond all things and to none else—whether himself or another—and being through the passive stillness of all his reasoning powers united by his highest faculty to Him that is wholly unknowable, of whom thus by a rejection of all knowledge he possesses a knowledge that exceeds his understanding.

Unto this Darkness which is beyond light we pray that we may come and may attain unto vision through the loss of sight and knowledge, that in ceasing thus to see or to know we may learn to know that which is beyond all perception and understanding—for this emptying of our faculties is true sight and knowledge—and that we may offer Him that transcends all things the praises of a transcendent hymnody, which we shall do by denying or removing all things that are, like men who, carving a statue out of marble, remove all the impediments that hinder the clear perception of the latent image and by this mere removal display the hidden statue itself in its hidden beauty.

64

Essence Is Simple

St Nikolai Velimirovich

O my soul, my eternal surprise! What happened once in heaven and once on earth must happen to you. You must become a virgin so that you can conceive the Wisdom of God. You must be a virgin so that the Spirit of God may fall in love with you. All the miracles in heaven and on earth originate from the Virgin and the Spirit. A virgin gives birth to creative wisdom. A wanton woman creates barren knowledge. Only a virgin can see truth, while a wanton woman can recognize only things. O triune Lord, cleanse the vision of my soul and bow down Your face over her so that my soul may glisten with the glory of her Lord, so that the wondrous history of heaven and earth may be unsealed in her, so that she may be filled with glittering like my lake when the sun hovers above it at noon.

Once I bound myself to You, my love, all other bonds broke. I see a swallow distraught over its demolished nest, and I say: "I am not bound to my nest." I see a son mourning for his father, and I say: "I am not bound to my parents." I see a fish expiring as soon as it is taken out of the water, and I say: "That is me! If

---

St Nikolai Velimirovich (1880-1956), a Serbian Orthodox bishop and a survivor of Dachau, held doctorates from the University of Berne and Oxford. His four-volume *Prologue from Ochrid*, a compendium of homilies, "considerations", and saints' lives for every day of the year, is widely used among Orthodox Christians. The present selection comes from his *Prayers by the Lake*, a century of meditations penned while he lived in retreat near Lake Ochrid in southern Yugoslavia. *Hypostases* (sing. *hypostasis*) is the Greek term for the "Persons" of the Holy Trinity; the "Ultimate Man" is the Bishop's phrase for Christ, the "last Adam" (1 Cor. 15:45), in whom all men may regain their "ultimate humanity".

they take me out of Your embrace, I shall die in seconds, like a fish tossed onto the sand." Yet how could I have plunged so far into You, with no way back, and lived if I had not been in You before? Truly, I was in You from Your first awakening, because I sense that You are my home. Eternity exists in eternity just as duration exists in time. In one eternity, O Lord, You were in ineffable sameness and vesperal blessedness. At that time Your *Hypostases* were the truth within You, for it was impossible for them not to be in You. But they did not recognize one another, for they were unconscious of their diversity. In a second eternity You were in Your matinal blessedness, and the three *Hypostases* recognized themselves as such.

The Father was not before the Son, nor was the Son before the Father, nor was the All-Holy Spirit before or after the Father and the Son. As a man while waking suddenly opens both eyes at the same time, so did the three *Hypostases* within. You suddenly open at the same time. There is no Father without the Son and no Son without the Holy Spirit. When I lie beside my lake and sleep unconsciously, neither consciousness, nor desire, nor action dies within me—rather they all flow into one blessed, nirvana-like, indistinguishable unity. When the sun pours out its gold over the lake, I awaken not as a nirvana-like unity, but as a tri-unity of consciousness, desire, and action. This is Your history in my soul, O Lord, interpreter of my life. Is not the history of my soul the interpreter of the history of everything created, everything divided and everything united? And of You as well, my Homeland, my soul is—forgive me, O Lord—the interpreter of You. O my Homeland, save me from the assaults of foreigners upon me. O my Light, chase the darkness out of my blood. O my Life, burn up all the death in my soul and my body.

The Ultimate Man is the child of the Father's mercy and the Spirit's light. All creation is merely a story about Him. The mighty sun in the heavens and the smallest drops of water in the lake carry in themselves one part of the story about Him. All the builders of heaven and earth, from the exceedingly mighty seraphim to rulers and thence to the tiniest particle of dust, tell the very same story about Him, their fore-essence and fore-source. What are all the things on the earth and the moon except the sun in stories? Truly, in this way all visible and invisible creation is the Ultimate Man in stories. Essence is simple, but there is no end or number to the stories about Essence.

My neighbors, how can I tell you about Essence when you do not understand even stories? If you only knew how great the sweetness, the expanse, and the strength are when one reaches the bottom of all the stories—there, where the stories begin and where they end. There, where the tongue is silent and where everything is told at once. How boring all the lengthy and tedious stories of creatures then become! Truly, they become just as boring as it is for one who is accustomed to seeing lightning to hear stories about lightning. Receive me into Yourself, O Only-Begotten Son, so that I may be one with You as I was before Creation and the Fall. Let my long and weary story about You end with a moment's vision of You. Let my self-deception die, which would have me think that I am something without You, that I am something else outside of You. My ears are stuffed with stories. My eyes no longer seek to see any display of clothing but You, my Essence, over-laden with stories and clothing.

White doves fly over my blue lake like white angels over the blue heaven. The doves would not be white nor would the lake be blue if the great sun did not open its eye above them. O my heavenly Mother, open Your eye in my soul, so that I may see what is what—so that I may see who is dwelling in my soul and what sort of fruits are growing in her. Without Your eye, I wander hopelessly through my soul like a wayfarer in the night, in the night's indistinguishable gloom. The wayfarer falls and picks himself up, and what he encounters along the way he calls "events". You are the only event of my life, O Lamp of my soul. When a child scurries to the arms of his mother, events do not exist for him. When a bride races to meet her bridegroom, she does not see the flowers in the meadow, nor does she hear the rumbling of the storm, nor does she smell the fragrance of the cypresses, or sense the mood of the wild animals—she sees only the face of her bridegroom; she hears only the music from his lips; she smells only his soul. When love goes to meet love, no events befall it. Time and space make way for love.

Aimless wanderers and loveless people have events and have history. Love has no history, and history has no love. When someone makes his way down a mountain or climbs up a mountain without knowing where he is going, events are imposed upon him as though they were the aim of his journey. Truly, events are the aim of the aimless and the history of the pathless. Therefore the aimless and the pathless are blocked by events and squabble with events. But I tranquilly hasten to You, both up the mountain and down the mountain, and despicable events angrily move out of the way of my footsteps. If I were a stone and were rolling down a mountain, I would not think about the stones against which I was banging, but about the abyss at the bottom of the steep slope. If I were a mountain stream, I would not be thinking about my uneven course, but about the lake that awaited me. Truly terrifying is the abyss of those who are in love with the events that are dragging them downward.

O heavenly Mother, my only love, set me free from the slavery of events, and make me Your slave. O most radiant Day, dawn in my soul, so that I may see the aim of my tangled path. O Sun of suns, the only event in the universe that attracts my heart, illuminate my inner self.

IX

Identity

It is no longer I who live,
but Christ who lives in me.

Galatians 2:20

65

The Flight of the Eagle

John Scotus Eriugena

The blessed theologian John flies beyond not only what may be thought and spoken, but also beyond all mind and meaning. Exalted by the ineffable flight of his spirit beyond all things, he enters into the very *arcanum* of the one Principle of all. There he clearly distinguishes the super-essential unity and the super-substantial difference of the Beginning and the Word—that is, of the Father and the Son, both incomprehensible—and begins his Gospel saying: "In the beginning was the Word" (John 1:1).

To whom among theologians is given what is given to you? Namely, to penetrate the hidden mysteries of the highest good and to intimate to human mind and senses what was there revealed and declared unto you. To whom else, I pray, was given grace so great and of such a kind? Perhaps some will say such a grace was given to the chief of the Apostles—I mean to Peter— who, when the Lord asked him who he thought He was, replied, "Thou art the Christ, the Son of the living God" (Matt. 16:16). It may be said without fear, however, that Peter in answering thus spoke more as the figure of faith and action than as that of knowledge and contemplation. Peter is always presented as the model of faith and action, while John portrays the type of con-

---

John Scotus Eriugena (*c.* 810 - *c.* 877) was an Irish theologian and philosopher whose translations were instrumental in bringing St Dionysios the Areopagite (see p. 223) and St Maximos the Confessor (p. 72) to the attention of the Latin West. Best known for his metaphysical treatise *On the Division of Nature*, he also wrote a number of exegetical works, including a short "Homily on the Prologue to the Gospel of St John", from which this reading is taken.

templation and knowledge. The one indeed leans on the bosom of the Lord, which is the sacrament of contemplation, while the other often hesitates, which is the symbol of restless action. For the execution of Divine commands, before it becomes habitual, may shatter the pure brilliance of virtue and fall short in its judgments, clouded by the fog of sense-bound thinking. The keenness of profoundest contemplation, on the other hand, once it has perceived the countenance of the truth, neither hesitates nor slips, nor is ever darkened by any cloud.

Both Apostles, however, run to the tomb. Christ's tomb is Holy Scripture, in which the mysteries of His Divinity and humanity are secured by the weight of the letter, just as the tomb is secured by the stone. But John runs ahead and arrives before Peter, for contemplation, being deeply purified, penetrates more sharply and speedily into the secret power of the Divine intent than action, which still needs purification. Nevertheless—although they have both run to the tomb and both enter into it—Peter enters first, and John enters only after him. For if Peter symbolizes faith, John signifies the Intellect. Therefore, since it is written, "Unless you believe you will not understand" (Isa. 7:9), faith necessarily enters first into the tomb of Holy Scripture, followed by the Intellect, for which faith has prepared the entry. Peter, who recognized the Christ, now made human and Divine in time, and said, "Thou art the Christ, the Son of the living God", flew very high, but higher still flew the one who, having known this same Christ as God, born of God before time, said, "In the beginning was the Word."

Let it not be thought, however, that we prefer John to Peter. For who could do so? Who indeed among the Apostles could be higher than he who is, and is called, their chief? We do not prefer John to Peter; we only compare action and contemplation—the soul still needing purification to the soul that is already purified. We only compare virtue that is still in the process of ascending to an immutable state to virtue that has already attained it. We do not here consider the personal dignity of the Apostles, but only investigate the beautiful distinctions that are made in the Divine mysteries. Thus Peter, action practicing virtue, perceives, through the virtue of faith and action, the Son of God confined in the flesh in a wonderful and ineffable manner. But John, who is the highest contemplation of the truth, wonders at the Word of God in itself, before the flesh, in its Principle or absolute and infinite Origin—that is, in the Father. Peter, truly, when he observes eternity and time made one in Christ, is led by Divine revelation; but it is John alone who leads the faithful among souls to knowledge of what in Christ is eternal.

The spiritual bird therefore, fast-flying, God-seeing—I mean John the Theologian—ascends beyond all visible and invisible creation, passes through all thought and Intellect, and, deified, enters into God, who deifies him. O blessed Paul, you were caught up, as you yourself assert, into the third heaven, to paradise; but you were not caught up beyond every heaven and every paradise. John, however, went beyond every heaven formed and paradise created, beyond every human and angelic nature. In the third heaven, O vessel of election and teacher of the gentiles, you heard words not lawful for a human being to utter. But John, the observer of the inmost truth, in the paradise of paradises, in the very Cause of all, heard the one Word through which all things are made. It was permitted to him to speak this Word, and to proclaim it, as far as it may be proclaimed, to human beings. Therefore most confidently he cried out, "In the beginning was the Word."

John, therefore, was not a human being but more than a human being when he flew above himself and all things which are. Transported by the ineffable power of wisdom and by purest keenness of mind, he entered into that which is beyond all things—namely, into the secret of the single Essence in three substances and the three substances in the single Essence. He would not have been able to ascend into God if he had not first become God. For as the gaze of our eyes cannot feel the forms and colors of sensible things unless it is first mixed and united with the sun's rays, so the souls of saints cannot receive the pure knowledge of spiritual things transcending all intelligence unless they have first been made worthy of participation in the incomprehensible truth. Thus the holy theologian, transmuted into God, and participating in the truth, proclaims that God the

Word subsists in God, the Beginning: that is, that God the Son subsists in God the Father. "In the beginning", he says, "was the Word."

And in case you are tempted to say that it is impossible that mortals should become immortals, that corruptible beings should become free of corruption, that simple human beings should become sons of God, and that temporal creatures should possess eternity—whichever of these doubts poses the greatest temptation for you—accept the argument which faith prepares for what you doubt: "And the Word was made flesh" (John 1:14). If what is greatest has undoubtedly already gone before, why should it seem incredible that what is less should be able to come after? If the Son of God is made a human being, which none of those who receive Him doubt, why is it astonishing that a human being who believes in the Son of God should become a son of God? For this very purpose, indeed, the Word descended into the flesh: that in Him the flesh—the human being—believing through the flesh in the Word, might ascend; that through Him who was the only-begotten Son by nature, many might become sons by adoption. It was not on His account that the Word was made flesh, but on our account, for it is only through the flesh of the Word that we can be transmuted into sons of God. Alone He came down; but with many He goes up. He who from God made Himself a human being makes gods from human beings.

66

More God than a Soul

St John of the Cross

To understand the nature of union, one should first know that God sustains every soul and dwells in it substantially, even though it may be that of the greatest sinner in the world. This union between God and creatures always exists. By it He conserves their being so that if the union would end they would immediately be annihilated and cease to exist. Consequently, in discussing union with God, we are not discussing the substantial union which always exists, but the union and transformation of the soul in God.

This union does not always exist, but we find it only where there is likeness of love. We shall call it "the union of likeness" and the former "the essential or substantial union". The union of likeness is supernatural, the other natural. The supernatural union exists when God's will and the soul's are in complete conformity so that nothing in the one is repugnant to the other. When the soul completely rids itself of what is repugnant and unconformed to the Divine will, it rests transformed in God through love. It is true that God is ever present in the soul, as we said, and thereby bestows and preserves its natural being by

---

St John of the Cross (1542-91) was a Spanish priest and co-founder, with St Teresa of Avila (see p. 185), of the Discalced Carmelites. His works on the mystical life consist in part of commentaries on his own poems. The present prose selection from his *Ascent of Mount Carmel* aims to assist in explaining the following stanza, which alludes to one of his most distinctive ideas, the "dark night of the soul": "In darkness and secure/ By the secret ladder, disguised/— Ah, the sheer grace!—/ In darkness and concealment/ My house being now all stilled."

His sustaining presence. Yet He does not always communicate supernatural being to it. He communicates supernatural being only through love and grace, which not all souls possess. And those who do, do not have it in the same degree. Some have attained higher degrees of love; others remain in lower degrees. God communicates Himself more to the soul more advanced in love, that is, more conformed to His will. A person who has reached complete conformity and likeness of will has attained total supernatural union and transformation in God. Manifestly, then, the more a person through attachment and habit is clothed with his own abilities and with creatures, the less disposed he is for this union. For he does not afford God full opportunity to transform his soul into the supernatural. As a result, a man has nothing more to do than strip his soul of these natural contrarieties and dissimilarities so that God, who is naturally communicating Himself to it through nature, may do so supernaturally through grace.

This is what St John meant when he said, "He gives power for becoming the children of God, for being transformed in God, only to those who are born not of blood—not of natural complexion and humors; nor of the will of the flesh—the free will included in the natural aptitude and capacity; nor even less of the will of man—which includes every mode and manner by which the intellect judges and understands. To none of these has He conferred the power of becoming the children of God, but only to those who are born of God—those who, in their rebirth through grace and death to everything of the old man, rise above themselves to the supernatural and receive from God this rebirth and sonship which transcends everything imaginable" (*cf.* John 1:12-13). St John affirms elsewhere, "He who is not reborn in the Holy Spirit will be unable to see the kingdom of God, which is the state of perfection" (*cf.* John 3:5). To be reborn in the Holy Spirit during this life is to become most like God in purity, without any mixture of imperfection. Accordingly, pure transformation can be effected, although not essentially, through the participation of union.

Here is an example that will provide a better understanding of this explanation. A ray of sunlight shining upon a smudgy window is unable to illumine that window completely and transform it into its own light. It could do this if the window were cleaned and polished. The less the film and stain are wiped away, the less the window will be illumined; and the cleaner the window is, the brighter will be its illumination. The extent of illumination is not dependent upon the ray of sunlight but upon the window. If the window is totally clean and pure, the sunlight will so transform and illumine it that to all appearances the window will be identical with the ray of sunlight and shine just like the sun's ray. Although obviously the nature of the window is distinct from that of the sun's ray—even if the two seem identical—we can assert that the window is the ray or light of the sun by participation. The soul upon which the Divine light of God's being is ever shining—or better, in which it is always dwelling by nature—is like this window.

A man makes room for God by wiping away all the smudges and smears of creatures, by uniting his will perfectly to God's; for to love is to labor to divest and deprive oneself for God of all that is not God. When this is done the soul will be illumined by and transformed in God. And God will so communicate His supernatural being to it that it will appear to be God Himself and will possess all that God Himself has. When God grants this supernatural favor to the soul, so great a union is caused that all the things of both God and the soul become one in participant transformation, and the soul appears to be God more than a soul. Indeed, it is God by participation. Yet truly, its being—even though transformed—is naturally as distinct from God's as it was before, just as the window, although illumined by the ray, has an existence distinct from the ray.

67

Unencumbered

Marguerite Porete

This soul has her right name from the nothingness in which she rests. And since she is nothing, she is concerned about nothing, neither about herself, nor about her neighbors, nor even about God Himself, for she is so small that she cannot be found, and every created thing is so far from her that she cannot feel it. And God is so great that she can comprehend nothing of Him. On account of such nothingness, she has fallen into the certainty of knowing nothing and into the certainty of willing nothing. And this nothingness of which we speak gives her the All, and no one can possess it in any other way.

This soul is imprisoned and held in the country of complete peace, for she is always in full sufficiency, in which she swims and bobs and floats, and she is surrounded by Divine peace without any movement in her interior and without any exterior work on her part. These two things would remove this peace from her if they could penetrate to her, but they cannot, for she is in the sovereign state where they cannot pierce or disturb her about anything. If she does any exterior thing, it is always

---

Marguerite Porete (*c.* 1250 - 1310) belonged to a French *beguinage*, a philan- thropic sisterhood of devout women who lived an austere communal life, but without special vows. Her *Mirror of Simple Souls*, from which this reading has been taken, was the source of much controversy. Defended by some— including Godfrey of Fontaines, a widely respected theologian at the University of Paris—it was nonetheless eventually condemned as heretical, and when its author refused to respond to the Inquisitors' charges, she was burned at the stake. Compare this selection with "Go Not but Stay" (p. 51) and "Leading Strings" (p. 92).

without herself. If God does His work in her, it is by Him in her without herself for her sake. Such a soul is no more encumbered by this than is her angel by guarding her. No more is an angel encumbered by guarding us than if he never guarded us at all. So also neither is such a soul encumbered by what she does without herself than if she had never done it at all, for she has nothing of herself. She has given all freely without a why, for she is the lady of the Bridegroom of her youth (*cf.* Isa. 62:5). He is the Sun who shines and warms and nourishes the life of being separate from His Being. This soul has retained neither doubt nor anxiety any longer.

This soul, who is what she is perfectly, is unencumbered in her four aspects. For four aspects are required in a noble person before he might be called a gentleman and thus of a spiritual intellect. The first aspect in which this soul is unencumbered is that she has no reproach in her at all, even though she does not do the work of the virtues. Ah, for the sake of God! Give attention, you who hear, if you can. How could Love have her practice along with the works of the virtues when it is necessary that works cease when Love has her practice? The second aspect is that she has no longer any will, no more than the dead in the sepulchers have, but only the Divine will. Such a soul is not concerned about either justice or mercy. She places and plants everything in the will alone of the One who loves her. The third aspect is that she believes and maintains that there never was, nor is there, nor will there ever be anything worse than she, nor any better loved by the One who loves her according to what she is. Note this and do not grasp it poorly. The fourth aspect is that she believes and maintains that it is no more possible for God to be able to will something other than goodness than it is for her to will something other than His Divine will. Love has so adorned the soul with Herself that She makes her maintain this about Him who by His goodness has transformed her into such goodness through His goodness, who by His love has transformed her into such love through love, and who by His will has purely transformed her into such will through Divine will. He is of Himself in her for her sake this same One. And this she believes and maintains. She would not be unencumbered in all her aspects by any other means.

Grasp the gloss, readers of this book, for the kernel is there which nourishes the bride. This is so as long as she is in the Being by which God makes her to be—there where she has given her will—and thus cannot will except the will of the One who has transformed her of Himself for her sake into His goodness. And if she is thus unencumbered in all aspects, she loses her name, for she rises in sovereignty. And therefore she loses her name in the One in whom she is melted and dissolved through Himself and in Himself. Thus she is like a body of water which flows from the sea, which has some name, as one would be able to say Aisne or Seine or another river. And when this water or river returns into the sea, it loses its course and its name with which it flowed in many countries in accomplishing its task. Now it is in the sea where it rests and thus has lost all labor. Likewise it is with this soul. You have from this enough of an example to gloss the intention of how this soul came from the sea and had a name, and how she returns into the sea and so loses her name and has a name no longer, except for the name of Him into whom she is perfectly transformed, that is, into the love of the Bridegroom of her youth, who has transformed the bride completely into Himself. He is—therefore this soul is. And this satisfies her marvelously—thus she is marvelous; and this is pleasing to Love, and so this soul is love, and this delights her.

68

Other Suns

St Gregory Palamas

The grace of deification transcends nature, virtue, and knowledge; as St Maximos the Confessor says, all these things are inferior to it. Every virtue and imitation of God on our part indeed prepares those who practice them for Divine union, but the mysterious union itself is effected by grace. It is through grace that the entire Divinity comes to dwell in fullness in those deemed worthy, and all the saints in their entire being dwell in God, receiving Him in His wholeness, and gaining no other reward for their ascent to Him than God Himself.

He is conjoined to them as a soul is to its body, to its own limbs, judging it right to dwell in believers by authentic adoption, according to the gift and grace of the Holy Spirit. So when you hear that God dwells in us through the virtues, or that by means of the memory He comes to be established in us, do not imagine that deification is simply the possession of the virtues, but rather that it resides in the radiance and grace of God,

St Gregory Palamas (*c.* 1296-1359) is one of the most important theologians of the Orthodox East. Having lived over twenty years as a hermit, much of it on the Holy Mountain of Athos, he spent the last part of his life as the Metropolitan of Thessaloniki. He is perhaps best known for his vigorous defense of the psycho-somatic contemplative techniques employed by the monks of Athos—see "Descending with the Breath" (p. 33)—and of their claim to have experienced in their very bodies the uncreated light of Mt Tabor. This selection comes from that work, the *Triads in Defense of the Holy Hesychasts,* and includes his important distinction between the Divine Essence, which always remains beyond human grasp, and the Divine energies, in which man may come to share fully and visibly. See also "Uncreated Light" (p. 134) and "Ascent to Tabor" (p. 255).

which really comes to us through the virtues. As St Basil the Great says, a soul which has curbed its natural impulses by a personal spiritual discipline and the help of the Holy Spirit becomes worthy, according to the just judgment of God, of the splendor granted to the saints. This splendor is light, as you may learn from this text: "The just will shine like the sun" (Matt. 13:43). God will stand in the midst of them, distributing and determining the dignities of blessedness, for they are gods and kings. No one will deny that this relates to supra-celestial and supra-cosmic realities, for it is possible to receive the supra-celestial light among the promises of good things. Solomon declares, "Light shines always for the just" (Prov. 13:9), and the Apostle Paul says, "We give thanks to God, who has counted us worthy to participate in the heritage of the saints in light" (Col. 1:12).

The Lord dwells in men in different and varied ways according to the worthiness and way of life of those who seek Him. He appears in one way to an active man, in another to a contemplative, in another again to the man of vision, and in yet different ways to the zealous or to those already divinized. There are numerous differences in the Divine vision itself: among the prophets, some have seen God in a dream, others when awake by means of enigmas and mirrors; but to Moses He appeared "face-to-face, and not in enigmas" (Num. 12:8). When you hear of the vision of God face-to-face, recall the testimony of St Maximos: "Deification is a direct illumination which has no beginning, but appears in those worthy as something exceeding their comprehension. It is indeed a mystical union with God, beyond intellect and reason, in the age when creatures will no longer know corruption. Thanks to this union, the saints, observing the light of the hidden and more-than-ineffable glory, become themselves able to receive the blessed purity, in company with the celestial powers."

The great St Dionysios the Areopagite, who elsewhere terms this light a "super-luminous and theurgic ray", also calls it the "deifying gift and principle of the Divinity", that is, of deification. To one who asks how God can transcend the thearchy—the very principle of Divinity—he replies: You have heard that God permits Himself to be seen face-to-face and not in enigmas;

that He becomes attached to those worthy as is a soul to its body, to its own members; that He unites Himself to them to the extent of dwelling completely in them, so that they too dwell entirely in Him; that "through the Son, the Spirit is poured out in abundance on us" (Tit. 3:6) and not as something created; and that we participate in Him and He speaks through us—all this you know. But you should not consider that God allows Himself to be seen in His super-essential Essence, but according to His deifying gift and energy, the grace of adoption, the uncreated deification. You should think that that is the principle of the Divinity, the deifying gift, in which one may supernaturally communicate, which one may see and with which one may be united. But the Essence of God, which is beyond principle, transcends this principle, too.

The Principle of deification, Divinity by nature—the imparticipable Origin whence the deified derive their deification, Beatitude itself, transcendent over all things and supremely thearchic—is inaccessible to all sense perception and to every mind, to every incorporeal or corporeal being. It is only when one or another of these beings goes out from itself and acquires a superior state that it is deified. For it is only when it is hypostatically united to a mind or body that we believe the Divinity to have become visible, even though such union transcends the proper nature of mind and body. Only those beings united to it are deified by the total presence of the Anointer; they have received an energy identical to that of the deifying Essence, and possessing it in absolute entirety, they reveal it through themselves. For as the Apostle says, "In Christ the fullness of the Divinity dwells bodily" (Col. 2:9).

As for us, "it is of His fullness that we have all received" (John 1:16). The Essence of God is everywhere, for as it is said, "the Spirit fills things" (Wisd. of Sol. 1:7) according to Essence. Deification is likewise everywhere ineffably present in the Essence and inseparable from it, as its natural power. But just as one cannot see fire if there is no matter to receive it, nor any sense organ capable of perceiving its luminous energy, in the same way one cannot contemplate deification if there is no matter to receive the Divine manifestation. But if with every veil

removed it lays hold of appropriate matter, that is, of any purified rational nature, freed from the veil of manifold evil, then it
becomes itself visible as a spiritual light, or rather it transforms
these creatures into spiritual light. The prize of virtue, it is said,
is to become God, to be illumined by the purest of lights, by
becoming a son of that day which no darkness can dim. For it is
another Sun which produces this day, a Sun which shines forth
the true light. And once it has illumined us, it no longer hides
itself in the West, but envelops all things with its powerful light.
It grants an eternal and endless light to the worthy, and transforms those who participate in this light into other suns.

69

No Self to Forgive

Bernadette Roberts

J called this great void and state of unknowing a passageway.
It was during this time—when I was doing my utmost to
acclimate or get used to this state—that a distant voice broke
through the silence. I had been walking on a secluded road and
stopped to look around at my old friends: the hills, trees, and
wild grasses, now so empty and void; it was a look of complete
unbelievability. How could I have been so duped, hood-
winked—and all my life! It was impossible, and yet it had to be:
there was nothing there.

Then, above the trees, I heard a distant voice asking His
Father why He had abandoned Him, and with that, the door of
my understanding began to give way. Christ had a Divine self—
not like the self we know—and though He knew God in a sub-
jective way as being inseparable from Himself, it was still
God-as-object, analogous perhaps to the knowledge of our own
union with the Divine. His agony and death were the foregoing
of His Divine self, His union with God, a prospect which is more
than giving up the self as we know it; it is the giving up of a self
made one with God. In this way His life is parallel to our own,

---

Bernadette Roberts (1931-), a Roman Catholic nun for ten years, has since
raised a family of four. Here she looks back on her attempts, beginning as a
child of twelve, to find the Christian meaning in what she calls, in her book by
that name, *The Experience of No-Self*—a state of "unknowing" that she first experienced when camping with her parents in the Sierra Nevada: "The surroundings gave way to an unknown immensity, to something that had no
description because it was invisible, formless, and un-localized. I felt a leap of
joy that took me by surprise, and instantly I knew what I had seen: it was God."

wherein our first movement is coming to this union in which God is still object and other than ourselves, and the second movement is the relinquishing of this union, and a coming upon God as He is in Himself—God as pure subject.

That Christ knew this second movement and entered the gap between object and subject—into the state of unknowing— is truly the death of God, but only God-as-object, not God-as-subject. In many ways this state of unknowing is a descent into hell, a great void and the passageway to seeing: the resurrection. Evidently not even a Divine self, or a self that is one with God, can avoid making this transition or entering the gap between object and subject. Nevertheless, I do not regard the resurrection as the final step; to see and know is not enough. Greater than this is the ascension, or final dissolution into the fullness of God. With the dissolution of His human form—seemingly into thin air—Christ suddenly becomes everywhere: the God within and without, as well as all form in which the manifested and unmanifested have fruition and become one.

I am as convinced today as I was momentarily convinced as a child that the real tragedy of Christ's death is that so few understand it. The general interpretation is that Christ gave up His self so that the rest of us would not have to do so. He did it, so now the rest of us are free. That we should have a liberated self when Christ had no self, however, makes no sense. Self is not our true life or our real nature; it is but a temporary mechanism, useful for a particular way of knowing, and in every way equivalent to our notion of original sin. Self may not *be* sin, but certainly it is the cause of sin, and what needs to be overcome is not the effects but the cause itself. To be forgiven is not enough. We must put an end to the very need to be forgiven.

70

To Be Quit of God

Meister Eckhart

lessedness opened the mouth that spake wisdom and said: "Blessed are the poor in spirit, for theirs is the kingdom of heaven" (Matt. 5:3). All the angels and all the saints and all that were ever born must keep silence when the Eternal Wisdom of the Father speaks; for all the wisdom of angels and creatures is pure nothing before the bottomless Wisdom of God. And this Wisdom has spoken and said that the poor are blessed.

Now there are two kinds of poverty. One is external poverty, and it is good and much to be praised in people who take it upon themselves willingly for the love of our Lord Jesus Christ, for He himself practiced it in the earthly realm. Of this poverty I shall say nothing more, for there is still another kind of poverty, an inward poverty, with reference to which this saying of our Lord is to be understood: "Blessed are the poor in spirit, or of spirit." I pray you that you may be like this, so that you may understand this address; for by the eternal truth I tell you that if you do not have this truth of which we are speaking in yourselves, you cannot understand me. Bishop Albert says: "To be

---

Meister Eckhart (c. 1260-1327), perhaps the greatest of all Christian esoterists, was a Dominican teacher and preacher, whose deliberately provocative formulations were, and are, troubling to many Christians. He was brought up on charges of heresy and tried before the court of the Archbishop of Cologne in 1326, but died before the proceedings concluded. Eckhart maintained his innocence to the end, but agreed to revoke certain propositions attributed to him "insofar as they could generate in the minds of the faithful a heretical opinion or one erroneous and hostile to the true faith". The Bishop Albert of whom he speaks is Albert the Great (c. 1200-1280), and the "great authority" is Plato.

poor is to take no pleasure in anything God ever created," and that is well said. But we shall say it better and take poverty in a higher sense. He is a poor man who wants nothing, knows nothing, and has nothing. I shall speak of these three points.

In the first place, let us say that he is a poor man who wants nothing. Some people do not understand very well what this means. They are people who continue very properly in their penances and external practices of piety (popularly considered of great importance—may God pardon them!), and still they know very little of the Divine Truth. To all outward appearances, these people are to be called holy, but inwardly they are asses, for they understand not at all the true meaning of the Divine Reality. They say well that to be poor is to want nothing, but they mean by that living so that one never gets his own way in anything, but rather so displeases himself as to follow the all-loving will of God. These persons do no evil in this, for they mean well, and we should praise them for that; may God keep them in His mercy.

I tell you the real truth, however, that these people are not poor, nor are they even like poor people. They pass for great in the eyes of people who know no better, and yet I say that they are asses, who understand the truth of the Divine not at all. For their good intentions they may possibly receive the kingdom of heaven, but of this poverty, of which I shall now speak, they have no idea. If I were asked, then, what it is to be a poor man who wants nothing, I should answer and say: As long as a person keeps his own will, and thinks it his will to fulfill the all-loving will of God, he has not that poverty of which we are talking, for this person has a will with which he wants to satisfy the will of God, and that is not right. For if one wants to be truly poor, he must be as free from his creaturely will as when he had not yet been born. For by the everlasting truth, as long as you will do God's will, and yearn for eternity and God, you are not really poor; for he is poor who wills nothing, knows nothing, and wants nothing. Back in the Womb from which I came, I had no "God" and merely was, myself. I did not will or desire anything, for I was pure being, a knower of myself by Divine Truth. Then I wanted myself and nothing else. And what I wanted I was, and what I was I wanted; and thus I existed untrammeled by "God" or anything else. But when I parted from my free will and received my created being, then I had a "God". For before there were creatures, God was not "God", but rather He was what He was. When creatures came to be and took on creaturely being, then God was no longer God as He is in Himself, but "God" as He is with creatures.

God insofar as He is only "God" is not the highest goal of creation, nor is His fullness of being as great as that of the least of creatures, themselves in God. If a flea could have the intelligence by which to search the eternal abyss of Divine being out of which it came, we should say that "God", together with all that "God" is, could not give fulfillment or satisfaction to the flea. Therefore, we pray that we may be rid of "God", and taking the truth, break into eternity, where the highest angels and souls too are like what I was in my primal existence, when I wanted what I was, and was what I wanted. Accordingly, a person ought to be poor in will, willing as little and wanting as little as when he did not exist. This is how a person is poor, who wills nothing.

Again, he is poor who knows nothing. We have sometimes said that man ought to live as if he did not live, neither for self, nor for the truth, nor for God. But regarding that same point, we shall say something else and go further. The man who is to achieve this poverty shall live as having what was his when he did not live at all, neither his own, nor the truth, nor "God". More: he shall be quit and empty of all knowledge, so that no knowledge of "God" exists in him; for when a man's existence is in God's very being, there is no other life in him: his life is Himself. Therefore we say that a man ought to be empty of his own knowledge, as he was when he did not exist, and let God achieve what He will and be as untrammeled by humanness as he was when he came from God.

Now the question is raised: In what does happiness consist most of all? Certain authorities have said that it consists in loving. Others say that it consists in knowing and loving, and this is a better statement. But we say that it consists neither in knowledge nor in love, but in that there is something in the soul from which both knowledge and love flow and which, like the agents of the soul, neither knows nor loves. To know this is to know what blessedness depends on. This something has no "before" or "after", and it waits for nothing that is yet to come, for it has nothing to gain or lose. Thus, when God acts in it, it is deprived of knowing that He has done so. What is more, it is the same kind of thing that, like God, can enjoy itself. Thus I say that man should be so disinterested and untrammeled that he does not know what God is doing in him. Thus only can a person possess that poverty.

The authorities say that God is a being, an intelligent being who knows everything. But I say that God is neither a being nor intelligent, and He does not "know" either this or that. God is free of everything, and therefore He is everything. He then who is to be poor in spirit must be poor of all his own knowledge, so that he knows nothing of God, or creatures, or of himself. This is not to say that one may not desire to know and to see the way of God, but it *is* to say that he may thus be poor in his own knowledge.

In the third place, he is poor who has nothing. Many people have said that this is the consummation—that one should possess none of the corporeal goods of this world—and this may well be true in case one thus becomes poor voluntarily. But this is not what I mean. Thus far I have said that he is poor who does not want to fulfill the will of "God", but who so lives that he is empty of his own will *and* the will of "God", as much so as when he did not yet exist. We have said of this poverty that it is the highest poverty. Next we said that he is poor who knows nothing of the action of "God" in himself. When a person is as empty of "knowledge" and "awareness" as God is innocent of all things, this is the purest poverty. But the third poverty is the most inward and real of all, and I shall now speak of it. It consists in *having* nothing.

Now pay earnest attention to this. I have often said, and great authorities agree, that to be a proper abode for God and fit for God to act in, a man should also be free from all things and actions, both inwardly and outwardly. But we shall say something else. If it is the case a man is emptied of things, creatures, himself, and "God", and if still "God" could find a place in him to act, then we say: as long as that place exists, this man is not poor with the most intimate poverty. For God does not intend that man shall have a place reserved for Him to work in, since true poverty of spirit requires that man shall be emptied of "God" and all His works, so that if God wants to act in the soul, He Himself must be the place in which He acts. For if God once found a person as poor as this, He would take the responsibility of His own action and would Himself be the scene of action, for God is one who acts within Himself. It is here, in this poverty, that man regains the eternal being that once he was, now is, and evermore shall be.

There is the question of the words of St Paul: "All that I am, I am by the grace of God" (1 Cor. 15:10), but our argument soars above grace, above intelligence, and above all desire. How is it to be connected with what St Paul says? It is to be replied that what St Paul says is true, not that this grace was in him, but the grace of God had produced in him a simple perfection of being, and then the work of grace was done. When, then, grace had finished its work, Paul remained as he was. Thus we say that a man should be so poor that he is not and has not a place for God to act in. To reserve a place would be to maintain distinctions. Therefore I pray God that He may quit me of "God", for unconditioned Being is above "God" and all distinctions. It was here that I was myself, wanted myself, and knew myself to be this person, and therefore I am my own First Cause, both of my eternal being and of my temporal being. To this end I was born, and by virtue of my birth being eternal, I shall never die. It is of the nature of this eternal birth that I have been eternally, that I am now, and shall be forever. What I am as a temporal creature is to die and come to nothingness, for it came with time and so with time it will pass away. In my eternal birth, however, everything was begotten. I was my own First Cause as well as the First Cause of everything else. If I had willed it, neither I nor the world would have come to be. If I had not been, there would have been no "God". There is, however, no need to understand this.

A great authority says, "His bursting forth is nobler than His efflux." When I flowed forth from God, creatures said, "He is a god!" This, however, did not make me blessed, for it indicates that I too am a creature. In bursting forth, however, when I shall be free within God's will and free therefore of the will of "God" and all His works, and even of "God" Himself, then I shall rise above all creaturely kinds, and I shall be neither "God" nor creature, but I shall be what I was once, now, and forevermore. I shall thus receive an impulse which shall raise me above the angels. With this impulse, I receive wealth so great that I could never again be satisfied with a "God", or anything that is a "God's", nor with any Divine activities, for in bursting forth I discover that God and I are One. Now I am what I was, and I neither add to nor subtract from anything, for I am the Unmoved Mover, which moves all things. Here then a "God" may find no "place" in man, for by his poverty the man achieves the being that was always his and shall remain his eternally. Here too God is identical with the spirit, and that is the most intimate poverty discoverable.

If anyone does not understand this discourse, let him not worry about it, for if he does not find this truth in himself he cannot understand what I have said, for it is a discovered truth that comes immediately from the heart of God. That we all may so live as to experience it eternally, may God help us. Amen.

71

Ascent to Tabor

Hierotheos Vlachos

Sunset on Mount Athos—the sun was about to set, but I was ascending in order to rise. The setting of the sun found me climbing with great difficulty a narrow and steep path towards the East. I was walking bent over, the Jesus Prayer on my lips, in my heart, within my *nous*. For this is the way one should visit the Holy Mountain, having the feeling of a simple pilgrim. A short distance away from the path among the rocks one can see small houses, which are the cells of the hermit-monks. Some of them are within caves, others project a little from the face of the cliff, and you think when you look at them that they will fall into the sea. It is within these small caves that the spiritual bees live, making the sweetest honey of *hesychia*.

I continued my way to the heights, to the mountain of my transfiguration. After a while I reached with great effort the cell which I wanted to visit. I stood outside for a little to cool down. The cell of a hermit, I thought, is not only a place of mystery but also a heavenly place. He who dwells within and is occupied with *hesychia* and prayer is an Apostle of Christ. St Gregory Palamas says this in a homily to the Thessalonians. His starting-point is the case of the Apostle Thomas, who was not able to see the res-

---

Hierotheos Vlachos (1945 -) is the Orthodox Metropolitan of Nafpaktos in Greece and a widely-acclaimed spiritual writer. This description of his encounter with a contemporary Athonite *gerondas* or spiritual elder (*starets* in Russian) is taken from his book *A Night in the Desert of the Holy Mountain*. *Nous* is the Greek term for "spiritual intellect"; *hesychia* means "silence" or "stillness".

urrected Christ on the Sunday of Resurrection because he was absent from the group of the disciples. When however he was with the Apostles, after eight days, he saw the Lord. And this saint of God recommends: "On Sunday, after the Divine Liturgy, take great care to find someone who imitates the Apostles of Christ and stays inside, and who through prayer in quietness and the chanting of hymns desires Christ. If you find him, enter his cell in faith as a heavenly place, because it has the sanctifying power of the Holy Spirit. And remain there as long as possible and talk with him about God and Divine things and ask guidance with humility and invoke help through his blessing. Then the Lord Jesus will come to you too, invisibly, as in the case of Thomas. He will grant peace to the soul, He will add faith and give you support, and He will count you among the chosen ones in the heavenly Kingdom."

Following the saint's instruction, I approached that cell, taking it for a heavenly place. Inside I had the sense that the *gerondas* was an Apostle of Christ who had already seen Christ and was now in the upper room of Jerusalem. He was then deified. He was participating in the uncreated energies of God and had everything that God has, yet without having His Essence. "All that God has," wrote St Gregory, "he who is deified through grace acquires also without being identified with Him in Essence." How could I see him differently since the God-seeing St Gregory spoke about him like that? I had the desire like Thomas to see Christ; that is why I decided to approach the *gerondas* with great humility and contrition and to put into practice whatever he would tell me.

I knocked on the outer door of the cave. Endless peace reigned, which scared me a little. Some slow steps were heard. The door opened quietly, and one of the disciples who lived there appeared in front of me.

"Your blessing," I said.

"The Lord bless you," he replied.

I was moved by his presence in this wild area—by his life, his youth, in that hard place. Although I did not know him, I felt admiration for him. "Are there many of you here?" I asked.

"The *gerondas* and his three disciples."

256

"I would like to discuss a few things that occupy my mind; that is why I came here to this solitary place."

"What you have done is good," he said. "Pilgrims should come here with this sort of feeling. Some of them come here simply because of an external curiosity. They come to see the *gerondas* externally, and then they boast of having seen him. These people make him exceedingly tired. He feels they are like visitors to a zoo, like tourists. It is good that you ask about spiritual questions and problems that concern you. And you should know that you will not hear theories. He speaks out of experience. The *gerondas* has had his experiences, and he speaks about some of them to his visitors to help them."

"I would like, if it is possible, to see the *gerondas*. Is he busy?" You should be very discreet when you visit a hermit. You may stop him from prayer. He may be in Divine rapture on Mount Tabor, and you bring him down to the noisy earth. At the same time, however, that would be the best thing you could do for yourself, because it would fill you with Divine fragrance. The brilliance he has absorbed will blind you. He emerges from prayer like a being aflame, as Moses shone when he went down from Sinai and the Israelites could not see him and as the iron is red-hot when you take it from the fire.

"I will ask," the disciple said.

He returned after a few minutes. "The *gerondas* is ill, but he will get up to see you. Let us go in, if you wish."

No sooner had he finished than the old man appeared in front of me. It was like a sun which rose suddenly, like a spring which cascaded joy, like lightning in the night. His white beard fell like a waterfall from his face. His eyes were penetrating, shining, brilliant. I had rarely seen such transfigured eyes. St Gregory Palamas says that the Apostles, seeing the uncreated light on Mount Tabor, had their eyes first transformed by the power of the Holy Spirit so that they were able to see it: "Do you understand? In front of this light, the eyes of those who see according to nature are blind. This light is not perceptible if it comes before the eyes of simple gazes, but it is perceptible only by those whose eyes are transfigured by the power of the Holy Spirit. They have been changed, and it is by this change that

257

they can see. Our mortal nature has received it from God, by union with the Word." The *gerondas*, who had seen the light of Tabor often, had eyes transformed by this experience. The change was easy to see and good to see.

"Your blessing," I said, bending low to kiss his hand, which showed the marks of many prostrations. Yet he bent lower than I did, and was the first to give the kiss.

72

Be Thyself the Book

Angelus Silesius

What hath been said of God
sufficeth not my mind.
The more-than-God is where
my life and light I find.

God giveth naught to none,
to all He standeth free;
So that, if thou but wilt,
thine will He wholly be.

Deny'st thou that perfection,
as it is God's, is mine?
Thou first must break me off
from that perfection's vine!

Who is as he were not—
nay, as he had never been—
He hath become pure God.
O blessedness supreme!

Angelus Silesius (1624-77)—Johannes Scheffler—the son of a Lutheran Polish nobleman, was court physician to the Duke of Oels in Silesia before converting to Catholicism. He was later ordained a priest and named coadjutor to the prince bishop of Breslau. This final selection comes from one of his mystical poems, *The Cherubinic Wanderer*, written under the pen name of "The Silesian Angel".

Identity

See, where thou nothing seest;
go, where thou canst not go;
Hear, where there is no sound;
then where God speaks art thou.

Wouldst thou know the new man,
and what name him becometh?
Then first ask God the name
by which Himself He nameth.

Who in his neighbor seeth
nothing but God and Christ
Seeth truly with the light
the Godhead's self doth cast.

To me, God is God and man;
to Him, I am man and God;
I soothe and quench His thirst;
He helps me in my need.

Because the Godhead was
in childhood shown to me,
To Godhead and to childhood
I am drawn equally.

Child, God—'tis all the same:
if thou me "child" hast called,
Thou hast but known the God
in me, the child in God.

God is my final end:
if in me He begin,
His being comes from me,
and I do cease in Him.

Angelus Silesius

I am God's other self;
He findeth but in me
His equal and His like
for all eternity.

In God is nothing known;
He is undivided One.
What we would know in Him,
we must ourselves become.

Christian, 'tis not enough
if I but be in God.
I must draw in God's sap
if I would grow and bud.

Go out—and God goes in;
die—and thou livest God;
Be not—and He will be;
do naught—and obey His word.

I am not I nor Thou;
but Thou art I in me;
Wherefore, my God, I give
all honor unto Thee.

No man shall ever know
what is true blessedness
Till oneness overwhelm
and swallow separateness.

Die thou before thou diest,
that so thou shalt not diest
When thou dost come to die;
else thou diest utterly.

Identity

Here, as a brook of time,
I still flow on to God;
There, I become, myself,
the sea of beatitude.

Reader, it is enough.
But if thou still wouldst read,
Then be thyself the book,
in thought, word, life, and deed.

Sources of Readings and Recommendations for Further Study

We are most grateful to the following publishers, translators, and editors. It is recommended that the reader turn to these helpful books for further study and meditation concerning the Christian mystical journey.

I. Severity

1. "Breaking the Chains": Jakob Boehme, "Dialogue of the Supersensual Life", *The Signature of All Things and Other Writings* (London: James Clarke, 1969), pp. 227-31, 243-44.

2. "The Ladder of Graces": Theophanis the Monk, "The Ladder of Divine Graces which Experience Has Made Known to Those Inspired by God", *The Philokalia*, Vol. 3, trans. G. E. H. Palmer, Philip Sherrard, and Kallistos Ware (London: Faber and Faber, 1984), pp. 67-68.

3. "Transposition": Lorenzo Scupoli, *Unseen Warfare*, ed. Nikodimos of the Holy Mountain, trans. Theophan the Recluse (Crestwood, New York: St Vladimir's Seminary Press, 1987), pp. 128-30, 133-34.

4. "Death": St Thomas à Kempis, *The Imitation of Christ*, trans. Leo Sherley-Price (New York: Penguin, 1952), pp. 57-60.

5. "Pure Fire": Hugh of St Victor, "The Grades of Knowledge", *Late Medieval Mysticism*, ed. Ray C. Petry (Philadelphia: The Westminster Press, 1957), pp. 90-91.

6. "What More Must I Do?": *The Desert Fathers*, trans. Helen Waddell (Ann Arbor, Michigan: University of Michigan Press, 1957), pp. 108, 111, 112, 125-26, 127-28.

7. "The Ceremony of Substitution": Charles Williams, "The Cross", *Charles Williams: Essential Writings in Spirituality and Theology*, ed. Charles Hefling (Cambridge, Massachusetts: Cowley Publications, 1993), pp. 198-201.

8. "My Desire Has Been Crucified": St Ignatios of Antioch, "Letter to the Ephesians", "Letter to the Romans", *Early Christian Fathers*, ed. Cyril C. Richardson (New York: Collier Books [Macmillan Publishing Company], 1970), pp. 93, 104-105.

II. Simplicity

9. "Drawn by the Flames": Thérèse of Lisieux, *The Story of a Soul*, trans. John Beevers (New York: Image Books [Doubleday], 1957), pp. 149-50, 152-53.

10. "Descending with the Breath": Nikiphoros the Athonite, "On Watchfulness and the Guarding of the Heart", *The Philokalia*, Vol. 4, trans. G. E. H. Palmer, Philip Sherrard, and Kallistos Ware (London: Faber and Faber, 1995), pp. 205-206.

11. "So Many Names": Jean-Pierre de Caussade, "Abandonment to Divine Providence", *Silent Fire: An Invitation to Western Mysticism*, ed. Walter Holden Capps and Wendy M. Wright (New York: Harper and Row, 1978), pp. 212-14.

12. "What Dreams May Come": St Diadochos of Photiki, "On Spiritual Knowledge and Discrimination: One Hundred Texts", *The Philokalia*, Vol. 1, trans. G. E. H. Palmer, Philip Sherrard, and Kallistos Ware (London: Faber and Faber, 1979), pp. 262, 263-65.

13. "I Sleep but My Heart Waketh": St. Bernard of Clairvaux, "Sermon Fifty-Two", *On the Song of Songs III*, trans. Kilian Walsh and Irene M. Edmonds (Kalamazoo, Michigan: Cistercian Publications, 1979), pp. 49-54.

14. "Nakedness and Sacrifice": Jean Borella, *The Secret of the Christian Way: A Contemplative Ascent through the Writings of Jean Borella*, trans. G. John Champoux (Albany, New York: State University of New York Press, 2001), pp. 120-22.

15. "The Tao": Hieromonk Damascene, *Christ the Eternal Tao* (Platina, California: St Herman of Alaska Brotherhood, 1999), pp. 84-86, 143-44.

16. "Go Not but Stay": St Francis of Sales, "Abandonment to God's Pleasure", *An Anthology of Mysticism*, ed. Paul de Jaegher, S.J. (Westminster, Maryland: The Newman Press, 1950), pp. 174-77.

III. Purity

17. "The Center of the Soul": William Law, *Selected Mystical Writings of William Law*, ed. Stephen Hobhouse (London: Salisbury Square, 1948), pp. 67-68, 81-82.

18. "True Prayer": Evagrios the Solitary (Evagrius Ponticus), "Chapters on Prayer", *The Praktikos and Chapters on Prayer*, trans. John Eudes Bamberger, O.C.S.O. (Kalamazoo, Michigan: Cistercian Publications, 1981), pp. 61-79.

19. "The Tabernacle of the Covenant": Richard of St Victor, *The Twelve Patriarchs, The Mystical Ark, Book Three of the Trinity*, trans. Grover A. Zinn (New York: Paulist Press, 1979), pp. 344-46.

20. "Rank upon Rank": St Clement of Alexandria, "On Spiritual Perfection", *Alexandrian Christianity*, trans. John Ernest Leonard Oulton and Henry Chadwick (Philadelphia: The Westminster Press, 1954), pp. 98-101.

21. "Ignorance Is Bliss": Nicholas of Cusa, *The Vision of God* (New York: Frederick Ungar, 1928), pp. 76-79.

22. "Opening the Tomb": St Maximos the Confessor, "Two Hundred Texts on Theology and the Incarnate Dispensation of the Son of God", *The Philokalia*, Vol. 2, trans. G. E. H. Palmer, Philip Sherrard, and Kallistos Ware (London: Faber and Faber, 1981), pp. 126-28, 155-56.

23. "The Virginal Paradise": St Louis Marie de Montfort, *True Devotion to the Blessed Virgin, or Preparation for the Reign of Jesus Christ* (Bay Shore, New York: Montfort Publications, 1980), pp. 78, 130-136.

24. "Clothed in Christ": St Symeon the New Theologian, *Hymns of Divine Love*, trans. George A. Maloney, S.J. (Denville, New Jersey: Dimension Books, n.d.), pp. 54-57.

IV. Clarity

25. "Two Ways": St Thomas Aquinas, *Summa Theologica*, Vol. 4, trans. Fathers of the English Dominican Province (Westminster, Maryland: Christian Classics, 1981), Part II-II, Question 180, Article 5, pp. 1928-29.

26. "Dispelling Darkness": Boethius, *The Consolation of Philosophy*, trans. W. V. Cooper (London: J. M. Dent, 1902), pp. 2-6.

27. "Leading Strings": François de Salignac de La Mothe Fénelon, *Christian Perfection*, trans. Mildred Whitney Stillman (New York: Harper and Brothers, 1947), pp. 145-48.

28. "More than Ourselves": Sir Thomas Browne, *Religio Medici*, ed. James Winny (Cambridge: Cambridge University Press, 1963), pp. 89-92.

29. "No Fixed Abode": Giovanni Pico della Mirandola, "Oration on the Dignity of Man", *The Renaissance Philosophy of Man*, ed. Ernst Cassirer, Paul Oskar Kristeller, John Herman Randall, Jr (Chicago: University of Chicago Press, 1948), pp. 223-25.

30. "Today": St Patrick of Ireland, "The Deer's Cry", *Celtic Christianity: Ecology and Holiness,* ed. Christopher Bamford and William Parker Marsh (West Stockbridge, Massachusetts: Lindisfarne Press [Inner Traditions], 1987), pp. 47-49.

31. "The Teacher": St Gregory of Sinai, "On Commandments and Doctrines", *The Philokalia,* Vol. 4, trans. G. E. H. Palmer, Philip Sherrard, and Kallistos Ware (London: Faber and Faber, 1995), pp. 245-46.

32. "True Imagination": George MacDonald, *Unspoken Sermons: Third Series* (Eureka, California: Sunrise Books, 1996), pp. 61-69.

V. Luminosity

33. "Nothing Amiss": Julian of Norwich, *Revelations of Divine Love,* comp. Roger L. Roberts (Wilton, Connecticut: Morehouse-Barlow, 1982), pp. 20-23.

34. "Sweet Delight in God's Beauty": Jonathan Edwards, "Personal Narrative", *Selected Writings of Jonathan Edwards,* ed. Harold P. Simonson (New York: Frederick Ungar, 1970), pp. 29-34.

35. "Thinking the Unthinkable": St Anselm, *Proslogion,* trans. M. J. Charlesworth (Oxford: The Clarendon Press, 1965), pp. 111, 117, 135, 136.

36. "Prayer of the Heart": *The Way of a Pilgrim,* trans. Helen Bacovcin (Garden City, New York: Image Books [Doubleday], 1978), pp. 38-41, 85.

37. "The Religion of Light": Martin Palmer, *The Jesus Sutras: Rediscovering the Lost Scrolls of Taoist Christianity* (New York: Ballantine, 2001), pp. 225-26.

38. "In the Eyes of a Child": Thomas Traherne, *Centuries* (Oxford: The Clarendon Press, 1960), pp. 12-15, 109-110.

39. "Saving Loveliness": "The Life of St Pelagia", *The Desert Fathers*, trans. Helen Waddell (Ann Arbor, Michigan: University of Michigan Press, 1957), pp. 178-79.

40. "Uncreated Light": St Seraphim of Sarov, "The Acquisition of the Holy Spirit", *Little Russian Philokalia: Vol. I, Saint Seraphim of Sarov* (Ouzinkie, Alaska: New Valaam Monastery, 1991), pp. 109-14, 119.

VI. Transparency

41. "Filling Every Place": Jeremy Taylor, *Holy Living*, ed. Hal M. Helms (n.p.: Paraclete Press, 1988), pp. 24-27.

42. "Virtues and Powers": Paracelsus, "Of the Supreme Mysteries of Nature", *The Archidoxes of Magic* (London: Askin Publishers, 1975), pp. B1-B2.

43. "A Single Unified Science": Philip Sherrard, *Christianity: Lineaments of a Sacred Tradition* (Brookline, Massachusetts: Holy Cross Orthodox Press, 1998), pp. 226-28.

44. "Practicing Presence": Brother Lawrence, *The Practice of the Presence of God* (Grand Rapids, Michigan: Spire Books [Baker House], 1958), pp. 71-72, 77-79.

45. "Hidden and Glorified": Samuel Taylor Coleridge, *Lay Sermons*, ed. R. J. White (Princeton: Princeton University Press, 1972), pp. 71-73.

46. "As through a Mirror": St Bonaventure, *The Journey of the Mind into God*, trans. Alexis Bugnolo (The Franciscan Archive: www.franciscan-archive.org, 1999), Chapter 3 (no page numbers).

47. "Recognition": The Gospel of Thomas, *The Nag Hammadi Library in English*, trans. Members of the Coptic Gnostic Library Project of the Institute for Antiquity and Christianity (James M.

Robinson, Director) (New York: Harper and Row, 1977), pp. 118-28.

48. "Two Facades": C. S. Lewis, *Letters to Malcolm: Chiefly on Prayer* (New York: Harcourt, Brace, Jovanovich, 1963), pp. 78-82.

VII. Unity

49. "A Higher School": Henry Suso, "The Life of the Servant", *Late Medieval Mysticism*, ed. Ray C. Petry (Philadelphia: The Westminster Press, 1957), pp. 259-60.

50. "Flight to Greater Things": St Gregory of Nyssa, "On Perfection", *Saint Gregory of Nyssa: Ascetical Works*, trans. Virginia Woods Callahan (Washington, D.C.: Catholic University of America Press, 1967), pp. 95-97, 98, 99, 120-22.

51. "No Other Way": *Theologia Germanica* in *Late Medieval Mysticism*, ed. Ray C. Petry (Philadelphia: The Westminster Press, 1957), pp. 335-36, 346-48.

52. "God's Own Breath": John Smith, "A Discourse Concerning the True Way or Method of Attaining to Divine Knowledge", *The Cambridge Platonists*, ed. E. T. Campagnac (Oxford: The Clarendon Press, 1901), pp. 93-98.

53. "The Very Marrow of the Bones": St Teresa of Avila, *Interior Castle*, trans. E. Allison Peers (London: Sheed and Ward, 1974), pp. 48-52.

54. "Christmas in the Soul": John Tauler, "First Sermon for the Feast of Christmas", *Silent Fire: An Invitation to Western Mysticism*, ed. Walter Holden Capps and Wendy M. Wright (New York: Harper and Row, 1978), pp. 124-28.

55. "High Fantasy Lost Power": Dante, *The Comedy of Dante Alighieri the Florentine, Cantica III: Paradise*, trans. Dorothy L.

Sayers and Barbara Reynolds (New York: Penguin, 1962), pp. 345-47.

56. "Motionless Circling": Nikitas Stithatos, "On Spiritual Knowledge", *The Philokalia*, Vol. 4, trans. G. E. H. Palmer, Philip Sherrard, and Kallistos Ware (London: Faber and Faber, 1995), pp. 143-48.

VIII. Unicity

57. "A Reply to Active Persons": *The Cloud of Unknowing*, ed. William Johnston (Garden City, New York: Image Books [Doubleday], 1973), pp. 71-72, 75-77.

58. "Closing to a Bud Again": Lilian Staveley, *The Golden Fountain, or the Soul's Love of God: Being Some Thoughts and Confessions of One of His Lovers* (Bloomington, Indiana: World Wisdom Books, 1982), pp. 64-69.

59. "The Joyful Instant": St Augustine, *Confessions*, Bk. 9, Ch. 10, trans. Vernon J. Bourke (New York: Fathers of the Church, 1953), pp. 250-53.

60. "One and the Same Mind": Origen, *On First Principles*, trans. G. W. Butterworth (Gloucester, Massachusetts: Peter Smith, 1973), pp. 52-56.

61. "Awareness and Return": Swami Abhishiktananda, *Prayer* (Philadelphia: Westminster Press, 1967), pp. 22-24.

62. "Waylessness": John of Ruysbroeck, "How We May Become Hidden Sons of God, and Attain to the God-seeing Life", *Late Medieval Mysticism*, ed. Ray C. Petry (Philadelphia: The Westminster Press, 1957), pp. 307-10.

63. "Hidden Beauty": St Dionysios the Areopagite, *The Mystical Theology*, trans. C. E. Rolt (London: Society for Promoting Christian Knowledge, 1920), pp. 191-95.

64. "Essence Is Simple": St Nikolai Velimirovich, *Prayers by the Lake*, trans. Todor Mika and Stevan Scott (Grayslake, Illinois: The Free Serbian Orthodox Diocese of the United States of America and Canada, n.d.), pp. 20-24, 27-28.

IX. Identity

65. "The Flight of the Eagle": John Scotus Eriugena, *The Voice of the Eagle: Homily on the Prologue to the Gospel of St John*, trans. Christopher Bamford (Hudson, New York: Lindisfarne Press, 1990), pp. 21-26, 54-55.

66. "More God than a Soul": St John of the Cross, *The Ascent of Mount Carmel* in *The Collected Works of St John of the Cross*, trans. Kieran Kavanaugh, O.C.D. and Otilio Rodriguez, O.C.D. (Washington, D.C.: Institute of Carmelite Studies, 1979), pp. 115-18.

67. "Unencumbered": Marguerite Porete, *The Mirror of Simple Souls*, trans. Ellen L. Babinsky (New York: Paulist Press, 1993), pp. 156-58.

68. "Other Suns": St Gregory Palamas, *The Triads*, trans. Nicholas Gendle (New York: Paulist Press, 1983), pp. 83-85, 87-89.

69. "No Self to Forgive": Bernadette Roberts, *The Experience of No-Self: A Contemplative Journey* (Boston: Shambhala, 1985), pp. 129-30, 132-33.

70. "To Be Quit of God": Meister Eckhart, "Blessed Are the Poor", *Meister Eckhart: A Modern Translation*, trans. Raymond Bernard Blakney (New York: Harper and Brothers, 1941), pp. 227-32.

71. "Ascent to Tabor": Hierotheos Vlachos, *A Night in the Desert of the Holy Mountain: Discussion with a Hermit on the Jesus Prayer*,

trans. Effie Mavromichali (Levadia, Greece: Birth of the Theotokos Monastery, 1991), pp. 26-27, 31-34.

72. "Be Thyself the Book": Angelus Silesius, *The Cherubinic Wanderer*, trans. Willard R. Trask (New York: Pantheon, 1953), pp. 15, 21, 22, 27, 29, 30, 31, 33, 37, 39, 43, 45, 46, 53, 56, 57, 61.

Index

Abhishiktananda, Swami, 216n
Adam, 59, 78, 100, 130, 146, 226n
Advaita Vedânta, 216n
Albert the Great, 249n
alchemy, 5n, 144n, 145
Alexandria, 67n
Angelus Silesius, 259n
Anselm, 119n
Anthony the Great, 21n
apatheia, 60, 60n
appetite, 191, 198
Aquinas, Thomas, 32, 87n, 165
Archimedes, 32
Aristotelian philosophy, 87
Aristotle, 97
Arsenios, 22
ascesis, 104n
asceticism, 10n, 21n, 40, 60n, 72n,
    76, 105, 122n, 134n, 171n, 197-99
Asclepius, 98
Athos, Mount, 33n, 104n, 243n, 255
attention, 13-14, 19, 34, 52, 62, 190,
    206, 213n, 214, 241, 252
Augustine, 14, 32, 88, 156, 190, 192,
    210n, 219n
Augustinian Order, 16n, 19n, 219n
awakening, 41, 57, 59, 62, 96-97, 142,
    164, 185, 221, 227, 244
awareness, 38, 42, 60, 124-25, 135,
    141-42, 146, 165, 178, 216, 218,
    252
Baptism, 81, 101
Bartholomew, 223n
Basil the Great, 244
beauty, xiii, 14-15, 49, 73, 75, 79, 89,
    93, 99, 115-16, 118, 131-33, 141,
    175, 183, 192, 198-99, 203, 207,
    225, 267
beguilement, 40
beguinage, 240n
Benedictine Order, 216n
Bernard of Clairvaux, 41n, 219n
Boehme, Jakob, 5n, 57n
Boethius, 89n
Bonaventure, 154n
Borella, Jean, 44n

breath, breathing, 33, 48, 50, 122n,
    124, 153, 181, 183, 243n
Brethren of the Common Life, 16n
bride, bridegroom, 41, 43, 187, 228,
    242
Browne, Thomas, 95n
Cappadocian Fathers, 79n, 173n
Carmel, Mount, 237
Carmelite Order, 31n, 149n, 185n,
    237n
Cassian, John, 60n
Caussade, Jean-Pierre de, 35n
Celtic Church, 101
Cherubim, 101, 131, 198
child, childhood, 8-9, 29, 46, 48-50,
    51-53, 75, 94, 106-108, 118, 128,
    130-31, 158-60, 190, 227-28, 248,
    260
Christensen, Damascene, 47n
Christmas, 189-90
Cistercian Order, 41n
Clement of Alexandria, xvii, 67n,
    181n
Coleridge, Samuel Taylor, 152n
Communion, Holy. *See* Eucharist
contemplation, contemplative, 14-
    15, 19-20, 41-42, 61, 64-66, 68, 74,
    76, 87-89, 99, 104-105, 115-17,
    178, 183, 198-99, 203-205, 207-
    209, 214, 216, 219, 223, 233-35,
    244-45
councils, ecumenical, xviii, 72n,
    132n, 173n, 213n
Counter-Reformation, 12, 51
crucifixion, 23, 26-27, 46, 73, 101
Cudworth, Ralph, 181n
Daniel, 47n
Dante Alighieri, 107, 194n
death, dead, xix, 3, 13, 16-18, 21, 23-
    25, 27, 41-42, 46, 50, 58-59, 74,
    126-27, 130, 148, 158-160, 185,
    214, 216n, 218, 223n, 227, 238,
    247-48
deification, xvi, xviii, 46, 72n, 181n,
    199-200, 235, 243-45, 256
delusion, 57, 71, 96, 164, 224

demons, 39-40, 62, 73, 102
Desert Fathers, 21n, 60n
desire, 7-8, 13, 17, 26-27, 34-36, 42,
    44-45, 49, 50, 57, 62, 70-71, 93,
    96, 120, 126, 131, 141, 145, 151,
    156-57, 178, 196, 216, 227
devil. *See* Satan
devils. *See* demons
devotion, devotions, xvi-xvii, 73, 75,
    96, 141-42, 149, 192, 198
Diadochos of Photiki, 38n
dianoia, 33n
Dionysios the Areopagite, xx, 19n,
    177n, 203n, 219n, 223, 233n, 244
discernment, 9, 64, 90, 92, 98, 135
discrimination, 40
dispassion, 60n
Divinity, 22, 61, 78-80, 95, 183-84,
    187, 189, 198, 234, 243-45
Dominican Order, 87n, 171n, 189n,
    249n
Donne, John, 25
dream, dreaming, 39-40, 57, 96, 122-
    23, 152, 164, 185, 211, 244
dryness of soul, 149
dualism, 197
Eckhart, Meister, xix, 171n, 177n,
    219n, 249n
Edwards, Jonathan, 115n
ego, ego-consciousness, 44-46, 146
Egypt, 21n, 60n, 158n, 193
elder, spiritual, 104, 122-23, 134n,
    136, 255n, 256-58
Elijah, 75
Eliot, T. S., 23n
emotion, emotions, 124, 165, 207
emptiness, 37, 48-49, 93, 126, 160,
    182-83, 191, 225, 247, 251-52
enlightenment, 41-42, 80, 104, 125-
    26, 183, 224
Enoch, 142
epektasis, 173n
Eriugena, John Scotus, 233n
esotericism, esoterism, 44n, 147,
    249n
essence, Divine, 87-88, 179-80, 183,
    189-90, 219-20, 227-28, 235,
    243n, 245, 256
Eucharist, 31, 143, 149n, 197-98, 218

Evagrios the Solitary, 60n
Evagrius Ponticus. *See* Evagrios the
    Solitary
exotericism, exoterism, xviii, 147-48
experience, experiences, xvii, 10-11,
    34, 38-39, 60, 62, 79n, 104, 116,
    120-21, 123-25, 130, 142, 185n,
    186, 190, 192, 198-99, 206, 217,
    221, 254, 257-58
Ezekiel, 47n
fall of man, 25, 44, 59, 146-47, 152,
    228
fantasy, xiii, 38-39, 196
Fénelon, François, 92n
foreseeing, Divine, 113
forgiveness, 248
form, forms, 47, 100, 146-48, 235
formlessness, 62, 105
Francis of Sales, 51n, 162
Franciscan Order, 154n
Galen, 97
Gerhoh of Reichersberg, xx
gerondas. *See* elder, spiritual
gnosis, xvi, xvii, xix, 67n, 181n
gnostic, 69, 198
Gnosticism, xvii
Godfrey of Fontaines, 240n
Gospels, 25, 32, 79n, 158n
Gregory Nazianzos, 79n, 87-88
Gregory of Nyssa, 173n
Gregory of Sinai, 104n
Gregory Palamas, xix, 243n, 255, 257
Guénon, René, 44n
Guyon, Madame, 92n
Heaven, xvii, 8, 11, 18, 22, 34, 36-37,
    48-49, 52, 58, 96, 99-100, 102,
    108, 115, 117, 127, 130-31, 141-
    42, 144, 159, 177, 182, 192, 205,
    214, 226-28, 235, 249-250
hell, 57-58, 141, 248
heresy, heretic, xv, xviii, 72n, 98n,
    102, 173, 240, 249n
Herman of Lorraine, Nicholas. *See*
    Lawrence, Brother
Hermes Trismegistus, 98, 145
Hermeticism, 152n
hermit, hermitage, 21n, 104n, 134n,
    135, 138, 216n, 243n, 255, 257
hesychast, 33n, 122n, 243n

hesychia, 255n
Horeb, Mount, 75-76
Hugh of St Victor, 19n
hypostasis, hypostases, 226n, 227
idol, idolatry, 103, 162, 193
Ignatios of Antioch, 26n
illumination, 10, 136, 138, 189, 198-
99, 206, 216, 229, 239, 244, 246
illusion, 38, 44-46, 77, 93, 148
imagination, 5-6, 88, 106n, 109, 116,
123, 150, 164, 181, 193
immortals, immortality, 127, 236
incarnation, 25, 73
infinity, infinitude, 59, 70-71, 106
initiate, initiation, 67, 73, 105, 182,
198-99, 224-25
intellect, 5, 10, 33, 33n, 34, 38-40,
46, 70-71, 74-76, 104-105, 152n,
155-56, 197-99, 223, 234-35, 238,
241, 244, 255n
intelligence, 19, 62, 98, 127, 157,
190, 198-200, 235, 251, 253
intuition, 130
invocation, 101, 103, 144, 147
Irenaeus of Lyons, xvii
Jacob, 87
Jesus Prayer, 124, 255
Jingjing, 126n
Job, 36
John of Ruysbroeck, 57n, 219n
John of the Cross, 32, 237n
John the Evangelist, 25, 79n, 233-235
Johnson, Samuel, 57n
Judas, 25
Julian of Norwich, 113n
Kabala, 98n
Kallistos of Constantinople, 123
knowledge, 15, 20, 32, 58, 61-62, 68,
72-73, 75-76, 87n, 104-105, 125,
130, 134, 144n, 145-48, 150, 153,
171-72, 177, 181-83, 196-200,
203n, 208, 222-23, 225, 229, 233-
35, 243, 247, 251-52
Lady Wisdom, 89n
Lao Tzu, 47n
Law, William, 57n
Lawrence, Brother, 149n
Lazarus, 41

Le Saux, Henri. *See*
Abhishiktananda, Swami
Lewis, C. S., 23n, 106n, 162n
liturgy, 256
Logos, 72-76, 104, 176, 181n, 198-99
love, xiii, xvii, 9, 14, 17, 31-32, 34, 37-
40, 45, 48, 60, 68, 70, 92-94, 99,
101, 105, 107-109, 114, 116-18,
124-25, 128-29, 134, 142, 150-52,
178, 183, 185, 189-90, 194, 196,
198, 200, 203-204, 206-209, 211,
217, 219-22, 228-29, 237-39, 241-
42, 249, 251
MacDonald, George, 106n
magic, magician, 26, 98
Maharshi, Ramana, 216n
Makarios of Corinth, 10n
Martha, 142, 203-205
Mary of Bethany, 142, 203-205
Mary the Mother of God, 26, 32, 46,
51, 77-78, 127, 189, 192, 226
Maximos the Confessor, 72n, 233n,
243-44
meditation, 19-20, 22, 34-35, 115,
117-18, 147, 149, 152-53, 162, 171
microcosm, 95, 217
mind, 9, 14-15, 19, 40, 42-43, 47-50,
57, 63, 65, 80-81, 88, 90, 95, 119-
20, 124-25, 147, 156-57, 159, 162,
164, 185-86, 191, 195-96, 206-208,
215-16, 225, 233, 235, 245, 259
miracle, 25, 98-99, 164, 226
Monica, 210n
Montfort, Louis Marie de, 77n
More, Henry, 181n
Motovilov, Nicholas Alexandrovich,
134n
mystery, mysteries, 10, 73, 81, 98n,
130, 154, 161, 182, 189, 198-99,
216, 223, 233-34, 255
Nag Hammadi, 158n
Nicholas of Cusa, 70n
Nikiphoros the Athonite, 33n
Nikodimos of the Holy Mountain,
10n, 12n, 38n
Nirvana, 227
non-being, 70, 155, 164
Nonnus, 132n

nothingness, 46, 77, 93, 121, 220, 223, 240, 253

nous, 33n, 152n, 255, 255n

panentheism, 152n

Paracelsus, 144n

paradise, 59, 78, 87n, 130, 146, 194n, 235

participation, 175, 183, 238-39

passion, 27, 40, 44, 50, 61, 68-69, 73, 156, 175, 181-82, 204-205

passionlessness, 175

Patrick of Ireland, 101n

Paul the Apostle, 15, 32, 39-40, 42, 76, 87n, 88, 122, 174-75, 180, 213, 215, 223n, 235, 244, 253

peace, 10, 20, 34, 43, 61, 118, 124, 130, 136, 150-51, 171, 174, 186, 188, 192, 205, 240, 256

Pelagia, 132n

perfection, 10-11, 31n, 44-45, 63, 67, 77-78, 92, 94, 173n, 175-76, 178, 183, 238, 253, 259

Peter, 26n

phantasms, 87, 96, 156

phantoms, 162

phenomena, 148

Philokalia, 10n, 12n, 38n, 122-24, 197n

philosopher, philosophy, 104-105, 159

Pico Della Mirandola, Giovanni, 98n

Pius IX, Pope, 51n

Plato, 181n, 249n

Platonism, Platonists, 128n, 152n, 181n, 183

Plotinus, 181n

Porete, Marguerite, 240n

poverty, 35, 93, 96, 99, 118, 158, 249-54

prânâyâma, 33n

prayer, 9-10, 22, 32, 34, 36, 38n, 60-62, 96, 122-25, 135, 138, 143, 149n, 150, 152, 162-63, 165, 173, 208, 216, 255-57

preoccupation, 92

prepossession, 73

presence of God, 18, 92, 143, 149-151, 162-163

principle, 67, 74-76, 105, 181-82, 233, 235, 244-45

proof, 119n, 174

prophets, 21, 101-102, 244

psyche, 44, 46

psychosomatic method, 33n, 243n

purification, 37, 50, 94, 127, 224, 234

purity, 39, 42-43, 47, 116, 118, 121, 124, 127, 149, 156, 171n, 175, 183, 192, 198, 200, 224, 238, 244

rapture, 88, 118, 257

reason, 15, 35-36, 90, 98, 130, 152n, 153, 155, 181n, 181, 182, 220, 222, 244

recognition, 36

recollection, 149n, 190, 221

religion, 117, 127, 142, 156, 181-82

resurrection, xix, 24, 73, 101, 177, 223n, 248, 256

revelation, 106-107, 109, 124-25, 148, 175, 235

Richard of St Victor, 63n

rite, ritual, 148, 199

Roberts, Bernadette, 247n

sanctification, 65, 94, 145, 174

Satan, 40, 126, 186

Scheffler, Johannes. *See* Angelus Silesius

Schuon, Frithjof, 44n

Scripture, Holy, 36, 73, 75-76, 81, 87n, 115, 125, 127, 134, 137, 181n, 213, 217, 224, 234

Scupoli, Lorenzo, 12n

self, selfhood, xviii, 5, 12, 43, 45, 59, 64, 77, 92, 94, 109, 150, 152, 154, 157, 165, 172, 175, 191, 220, 222, 229, 247-48, 251, 260-61

self-deception, 228

self-denial, xvi, 17, 36, 94, 172

self-interest, 92-94

sensations, sense-perception, 6, 76, 152, 164

Seraphim of Sarov, 134n

Severinus. *See* Boethius

sheol. See hell

Sherrard, Philip, 146n

silence, 20, 26, 47, 90, 132, 178, 192-193, 211, 223, 247, 249, 255n

sin, sinfulness, sinner, 13, 16, 41, 44, 46, 58, 73, 93, 113, 115, 124, 126, 130, 132, 143, 149, 177, 204-205, 237, 248
sleep, 41-42, 96-97, 221, 227
Smith, John, 181n
Socrates, 70
solitude, 43, 216
Solomon, 15, 20, 244
Son of God, xviii, 34, 67, 100, 145, 192, 217, 235-236
Son of Man, 17, 218
sons of God, 236
space, 163, 165, 191, 195, 229
stages, spiritual, xix, 11, 154n, 197n, 199, 204
starets. See elder, spiritual
Staveley, Lilian, 206n
Stithatos, Nikitas, 197n
Stoic, 182
suffering, 23, 36, 72, 80, 91, 93, 172, 178
Suso, Henry, 171n
symbolism, 23, 46, 73, 75, 78, 109, 146, 148, 153, 164, 225, 234
Symeon the New Theologian, 79n, 123, 197n
Tabor, Mount, 243n
Taoism, 47n, 126n
Tauler, John, 57n, 177n, 189n
Taylor, Jeremy, 141n
temptation, 42, 73, 102, 149, 236
Teresa of Avila, 32, 185n, 237n
thearchy, 244
Theatine Order, 12n
Theophan the Recluse, 12n
Theophanis the Monk, 10n
theosis, xvi, 46
Thérèse of Lisieux, 31n
Thomas à Kempis, 16n, 57n

Thomas the Apostle, 158
thoughts, 13-14, 34, 40, 57-58, 61, 73, 91, 119, 122, 124, 175, 206, 208, 216
time, 229
Timothy, 223
Tolkien, J. R. R., 23n
Traherne, Thomas, 128n
transfiguration, 255
Trinity, xix, 59, 63n, 101, 103, 114, 145, 194n, 214, 223, 226n
tri-unity, 227
typology, 73
union, xviii-xix, 8, 52, 67n, 80, 104, 148, 179-80, 183, 185n, 186-87, 189, 200, 223, 237-39, 243-45, 247-48, 258
unity, 49, 52, 59, 100, 153-54, 190-92, 197-200, 213n, 214-15, 227, 233
universe, 19, 67-68, 99, 130, 147, 191, 194, 214, 217, 224, 229
Velimirovich, Nikolai, 226n
vigil, 45
vigilance, 92
Vincent of Lérins, 213n
virginity, 26, 77-78, 189, 192
virtues, 34, 60, 62, 75, 145, 150, 182, 199, 221, 241, 243-44
visions, 40, 113n, 163, 212
Vlachos, Hierotheos, 255n
voices, 224
void, 7, 126, 191, 247-48
Whichcote, Benjamin, 181n
Whitefield, George, 57n
Williams, Charles, 23n
wisdom, 9, 11, 15, 36, 60, 66, 74-76, 99, 102, 105, 113-14, 116, 122, 125, 129-30, 141, 152-53, 174, 183, 198-99, 203, 211-12, 214, 223, 226, 235, 249

(For a glossary of all key foreign words used in books published by World Wisdom, including metaphysical terms in English, consult: www.DictionaryofSpiritualTerms.org.
This on-line Dictionary of Spiritual Terms provides extensive definitions, examples and related terms in other languages.)